To Mum
    with love
From Anne

Christmas 1984.

D0542637

INDIRA GANDHI:
Her Road to Power

INDIRA GANDHI:
Her Road to Power

Nayantara Sahgal

with photographs

MACDONALD & CO
LONDON & SYDNEY

First published in Great Britain in 1983 by
Macdonald & Co (Publishers) Ltd
London & Sydney

Maxwell House
74 Worship Street
London EC2A 2EN

Partly published in a different form in India
as *Indira Gandhi's Emergence and Style*

ISBN 0 356 09166 X

To John Kenneth Galbraith in Gratitude

Contents

Indian Words

Bhai   Brother

CRP—Central Reserve Police ⎫
BSF—Border Security Force ⎬   The Union government's paramilitary forces

Harijan   "Child of God." Mahatma Gandhi's name for members of the untouchable community

Jai Hind   Victory to India, a popular slogan

Naxalites   A group of the extreme Left who believe in bringing about change through violent revolution

Lok Sabha   "House of the People" Lower House of Parliament

MLA   Member of the Legislative Assembly (the Lower House in a state)

Monsoon   Rainy season

Sarvodaya   Literally, the good of all, a service movement started by Gandhi's followers after his death

Rajya Sabha   "Council of States" Upper House of Parliament

Satyagraha   Literally, Truth Force, meaning civil disobedience in political terms

Shri.   Mrs.

Smt.   Mr.

Indian Personalities

Sheikh Abdullah   Chief minister of Kashmir.

Fakhruddin Ali Ahmed   Minister in Union cabinet, fifth president of India, 1974–77 (died in office).

Maulana Azad   Leading figure of the national movement for independence. Minister for Education in Union cabinet.

Bahuguna   Chief minister of Uttar Pradesh, minister in Union cabinet, broke with Mrs. Gandhi's party, along with Jagjivan Ram, to form Congress for Democracy, minister in Janata government.

D. K. Barooah   President of Mrs. Gandhi's Congress before and during the Emergency.

Y. B. Chavan   Minister in Union cabinet. After the Emergency, Chavan remained with the Congress, while Mrs. Gandhi and her supporters left it to form the Congress-Indira (Congress-I) party.

Morarji Desai   Fourth prime minister of India, 1977–79. Earlier minister in Union cabinet, and chief minister of Bombay state before its division into Maharashtra and Gujerat.

V. V. Giri   Fourth president of India, 1969–74.

Zakir Husain   Third president of India, 1967–69 (died in office).

Kamaraj   A leading politician of Tamilnad, influential in getting Mrs. Gandhi accepted by the Congress party as Prime Minister in 1966. Author of the Kamaraj Plan.

Mohan Kumaramangalam   Communist party (CPI) theoretician, Minister in Mrs. Gandhi's cabinet.

Rani Lakshmibai of Jhansi   heroine of the first Indian war of independence, 1857–58.

Sardar Patel   Leading figure of the national movement for independence, first home minister of India.

Rajendra Prasad   President of India for two terms, 1952–57, 1957–62.

Mujibur Rahman   First President of Bangladesh. Assassinated in August 1975.

C. Rajagopalachari   Congress leader, governor general of India, 1948–50, founder of Swatantra party, 1959.

Jagjivan Ram   Minister in Union cabinet since 1947. Broke with Mrs. Gandhi's party in 1977 to form Congress for Democracy, which merged with the Janata Party. Defence Minister in the Janata government.

Sanjiva Reddy   Sixth president of India, 1977–

Lal Bahadur Shastri   Second prime minister of India, 1964–66. Earlier, Minister in Union cabinet.

Charan Singh   Uttar Pradesh Congress leader, founder of Bharatiya Lok Dal (composed of seven national and regional parties), 1974, which merged into the Janata party, 1977. Home minister and later Finance minister in the Janata government. Broke away in July 1979 to form the Lok Dal party and become caretaker prime minister until general election of January 1980.

Kamalapathi Tripathi   Minister in Union cabinet. After the Emergency joined the Congress-I.

Atal Behari Vajpayee   Jan Sangh leader till its merger with Janata party, 1977. Minister for Foreign Affairs in Janata government. Now leader of newly formed Bharatiya Janata party.

Preface

This book originated with a paper I contributed on Indira Gandhi's political style to a conference on "Leadership in South Asia" at the School of Oriental and African Studies, University of London, in March 1974.

Mrs. Gandhi's style arises out of values fundamentally different from those of her two predecessors, Jawaharlal Nehru and Lal Bahadur Shastri. The essence of Indian politics in their time was the recognition that India needed the democratic process for the education, integration, and development of her large and diverse society. Variety alone teaches men and women anywhere to pick and choose, and judge for themselves. A people who had been politically, socially, economically, and psychologically deprived for centuries, above all needed the institutions and channels of open and diverse expression. Under Mrs. Gandhi, this climate, along with the political structures it involved, the debate and dissent it had encouraged, and the human give-and-take it had engendered, both within the ruling party and between the ruling party and the Opposition, began to be eroded. It became obvious after 1969 that Mrs. Gandhi, who saw herself as a humanist and a democrat, did not in any real sense partake of the democratic faith her father had held and served. The creation of a highly centralized governing apparatus and party machine under her personal command and the growth of a personality cult were accompanied by assaults on the institutional framework of democracy. The Emergency of 1975–1977 provided the setting for a one-party system, hugely enlarged executive powers, and a dynastic succession.

In 1975 I decided to expand my paper into a book, but the Emergency, declared in June that year, closed the doors to impartial knowledge, information, and inquiry. Many people whose opinions I would have sought were in prison. Some had gone underground to escape arrest. All known critics of the establishment were under vigilance or harassment. And there was censorship. I could not have written the major part of this book without the opportunity to work undisturbed, from June to December 1976, at the Radcliffe Institute, Cambridge, Massachusetts. My project was reported home by our diplomatic mission. The Indian embassy in Washington and the Indian consulate general in New York paid me an unintended compliment when they sent senior representatives to my colloquium at the Radcliffe Institute in November 1976 and to my talk to the International Affairs Department at Columbia University in December.

Mrs. Gandhi's return to power in January 1980 was an event not many, including herself, would have predicted after her decisive electoral defeat three years earlier. With this abrupt change in her fortunes, I took up the narrative in this book where I had left it in 1977. I found the factors responsible for her return as revealing of the condition of the Indian political system as of her own will to triumph. Her emotional spur was her assessment that only thus could she save herself and her son and desired heir, Sanjay, from the judicial processes the Janata government had started. The 1980 election became her vehicle particularly for Sanjay's salvation. Only a government she herself headed could render null and void the charges against him. That the hand of fate and not normal political developments removed Sanjay in its turn produced a near-paralysis in Mrs. Gandhi's functioning as prime minister.

I have been asked how I could be a critic of one so closely related to me, in a country where "family" commands unquestioning allegiance. A family in power is an even more formidable bastion, and in Indian culture the loyalty of those who belong to it is an effortless assumption. It would have been far simpler for me to succumb to this mystique and live on it, but I have rejected it utterly where it conflicted with my own observations and conclusions. Nor have I any worship to spare for "family" as such. My admiration for my uncle, Jawaharlal Nehru, had little to do with the fact that I happened to be of his flesh and blood. To my mind, he handled a titanic task with courage, grace, and the last ounce of effort wrung from each day's labor. He demonstrated that, in India, politics has to be the art of the *impossible,* requiring the dedication to sustain and fuel the "impossible" venture of an open society and government by consent in our conditions. Nehru's successes and failures were both manifest. Transcending both was the human being he was, searching, aspiring, heroic. He belonged to a much larger family than mine. Relationship with him had many meanings, and I shared this complex relationship with most of India.

When I started this book, it had a symbolic importance for me as a duty on behalf of the voices the Emergency had silenced in my country, as a duty also to the values of the free society that Nehru had devoted his life to building. Time has made issues relating to our democracy more relevant and more vulnerable. We have yet to consolidate the gains of the Nehru era, and to make the changes and adjustments that the securing and strengthening of democracy require.

I owed my opportunity at the Radcliffe Institute principally to Professor John Kenneth Galbraith. I have no words to thank him for his exceeding kindness, interest, and support. My gratitude extends to the hospitable family home of which I now feel a part.

I have been fortunate in my husband, E. N. Mangat Rai, without whom I could not have lived or written as I have done through difficult political times.

I am indebted to Philip Winsor, whose belief in this book has made its publication possible.

CHAPTER ONE

India's Third Prime Minister Is Chosen

Indira Gandhi was forty-six years old when her father, Jawaharlal Nehru, died on May 27, 1964. Though she was not a major political personality, she had shown signs of temperament and preference in political matters. Since independence she had been her father's companion and hostess at New Delhi and had accompanied him on official visits abroad. In 1955 she had been appointed to the Congress Working Committee, the party's executive, with charge of the women's and youth wings, and had become a member of its two subsidiaries, the Central Parliamentary Board and the Central Election Committee, soon afterward. These responsibilities placed her at the heart of election preparations for the second general election of 1957. Her emergence onto the scene of political and public endeavor took place during a period of marital strain and difficulty, and Nehru welcomed her increasing involvement in the party, both as the natural outcome of her background and as therapy for her troubled domestic life. The Congress Party's and his own championship of women's rights had been instrumental in creating a climate of pride in women's opportunities and achievements. It was a special satisfaction to him that his daughter, whose health and unhappy marriage had been a continuing anxiety to him, should now find a way to fulfil herself through national activity. He wrote to his sister, Vijaya Lakshmi Pandit, on March 12, 1957, from the family home at Anand Bhawan, Allahabad, where he had gone to cast his vote:

> When voting finished today, large numbers of our Congress workers turned up at Anand Bahawan, including many women. Indu has specially shaken up the women, and even Muslim women came out. Indu has indeed grown and matured very greatly during the last year, and

especially during these elections. She worked with effect all over India, but her special field was Allahabad City and District which she organized like a general preparing for battle. She is quite a heroine in Allahabad now and particularly with the women. Hardly eating and often carrying on with a handful of peanuts and a banana, she has been constantly on the move, returning at midnight, flushed, slightly gaunt but full of spirit and with flashing eyes.

In 1959, at the suggestion of its outgoing president, U.N. Dhebar, the Congress Party accepted her as his successor. Nehru did not think it was time for this distinction. His reservations were rooted deep in his respect for the process—personal, political, social, or economic—that lays sound foundations. Work was the crucible of human personality or political strength, and there were no shortcuts to excellence, a philosophy reflected in seventeen years of power that rejected the dramatic and the extreme and relied on the building of institutions. He was averse to hustle and haste. Part of a generation well and truly tried through the struggle for freedom and the years of nation-building afterward, he believed in time and trial. He was also concerned about his daughter's health and the inappropriateness of her holding the party's highest office while he was prime minister. These considerations had to be balanced against his conviction that he should not stand in her way, a point of view pressed by Govind Ballabh Pant, home minister and close colleague. He decided not to intervene.

> I gave a good deal of thought to this matter and I came to the conclusion that I should firmly keep apart from this business and try not to influence it in any way, except rather generally and broadly to say that it had disadvantages . . . normally speaking, it is not a good thing for my daughter to come in as Congress President when I am Prime Minister.[1]

Mrs. Gandhi accepted the office with tears in her eyes, and it was an emotional occasion for many present at the party meeting. Her father and grandfather were among the illustrious names in Congress annals who had held the distinction before her. Her elevation to the party's most prestigious post was its tribute to her family. After independence, the Congress president was almost invariably chosen on the basis of his previous experience in government. All party presidents between 1951 and 1969 were chief ministers. Mrs. Gandhi was the exception. Her earnestness was looked upon with favor and her inexperience with indulgence.

She occupied the office, normally a two-year term, for barely a year, though during this period she took two initiatives. She advised the division of Bombay state, convulsed at the time by agitations demanding its separation into Marathi and Gujarati-speaking states. Bombay was divided, bringing Maharashtra and Gujarat into being on May 1, 1960. She also urged the Union government's interference in Kerala, where the Communist government formed in 1957 was locked in a confrontation with the Roman Catholic and Nair communities over the issue of state control of schools and colleges. President's rule was established in Kerala, and fresh elections held in 1960, when an alliance of parties led by the Congress won a majority. There is a provision in the Indian Constitution that, if the president of India, on receipt of a report from the governor of a state, is satisfied that a situation has arisen in which government cannot be carried on in accordance with the Constitution, he can intervene and bring the state under president's, that is, the Union government's, rule. Governors of states are Union appointees and represent the president. Mrs. Gandhi believed that such a situation had arisen in Kerala and, when she was president of the Congress, advised the Union government to intervene and declare president's rule in Kerala. The outcome vindicated Mrs. Gandhi's advice as immediately beneficial to the Congress. It also demonstrated her approach to "action" as the surgical gesture to forestall possible developments. In contrast, Nehru's temperament made use of the tentative in decision-making as an area of positive value in arriving at action. The overthrow of Communist rule took note of the immediate situation, not of the meaning of the Communist phenomenon in Kerala. Chief Minister E.M.S. Namboodaripad later remarked on Nehru's reluctance to declare president's rule. Nehru had written to his sister, Mrs. Pandit, on March 12, 1957:

> In another three or four days' time we shall have ninety percent of the results, and this will give a clear picture of the States as well as of Parliament . . . Kerala is heading for a Communist majority. If so, there would presumably be a Communist government there. This will be the first occasion anywhere in the world when a Communist Party wins an election through democratic means. . . . They have toned down very much, and the programme they have issued is quite moderate. Nevertheless, this is an intriguing development.

Mrs. Gandhi was not, as her father knew, well enough to carry an arduous responsibility and had been under a strain for a long time. Writing to his sister in London from New Delhi, on January

11, 1955, Nehru had said, "Indira has been unwell for the last three weeks or so and mostly in bed. She has had rather a bad attack of anemia brought on partly by too much work and rushing about. Behind that, of course, is worry and unhappiness." She gave up the Congress presidentship and, without defining her dissatisfaction, made it known she was not being allowed to do as she wished in the party. She was operated on for a kidney stone on February 17, 1960.

In 1964 she was still comparatively unnoticed in her own right, and not seriously considered as a candidate for the succession to Nehru. She had had no training in a profession and no experience in government. Though her presence on the working committee indicated high status in the party, she had worked for the organization behind the scenes, and of choice remained in the background. A mother, occupied with caring for her two sons, she was devoted and imaginative about their upbringing, always torn between domestic and public responsibilities. She correctly described herself as a "private" person, so private indeed that no one knew her intimately. Her griefs were well-sheltered, her joys restrained. There was almost a pathos about her personality for those who tried to break through to it. It was a personality that would not step out. Inevitably involved in politics, she had hung back from the ultimate political trial—an election, declining at her father's death to stand for the by-election to the Lok Sabha (Lower House of Parliament) from his constituency, Phulpur, in Uttar Pradesh. It seemed right and proper, an act of rededication to the values he had represented, for a member of the family to contest Nehru's seat for the Congress in November 1964. Mrs. Gandhi's aunt, Vijaya Lakshmi Pandit, resigned as governor of Maharashtra to contest and retain the constituency for her party, though not before she had made certain that her niece did not want the seat.

A year later, on December 6, 1965, she had occasion to write to her niece, now minister for Information and Broadcasting in Lal Bahadur Shastri's cabinet:

> I have a feeling that you are not happy about my being in Phulpur. I am conscious of the fact that this seat should have been yours by right. It is yours today should you wish to have it. Nothing would give me greater pleasure now or in 1967 to retire from this particular constituency for you and work elsewhere. You have only to say so and it will be done and, believe me, done willingly. There are rumours that you do not wholly approve of my political views. I have never made

any declaration of where I stand because to me it seemed that adherence to Congress implied loyal acceptance of its basic policies and principles. I believe it is better in a country like our own to try and live according to one's beliefs rather than talk about them. This I try to do. I have during the sixteen years when I had the privilege to serve India abroad tried to explain and implement India's policies to the best of my ability and understanding. Since my return to public life here I have done what little I could to sustain the ideas and ideals which Bhai* gave to this country. It is true I have not joined any groups but this is because all groups today are founded on expediency and I do not approve of this.

I am a whole generation older than you are. I am at the end of my career and in the evening of my life. There is no desire in my mind to attempt to compete with the younger generation, least of all with you. Indeed this would be rather ridiculous.

I had hoped that my presence in the political field would give you strength and support. If the contrary is the case, then obviously there is something wrong and it must be remedied in the larger interest which both you and I have at heart.

    With love,
     Puphi

Mrs. Gandhi herself had been elected unopposed to the Rajya Sabha [Upper House of Parliament] after her cabinet appointment. Though she had taken part in election campaigns, she had never faced the electorate herself and did not do so until 1967, more than a year after she became prime minister, when the trial could no longer be postponed. She expressed a positive distaste for politics, replying to her aunt's letter on December 7, 1965:

> * I do not know who has been talking to you but there is absolutely no foundation in the remark that I am not happy at your being in Phulpur. . . . It may seem strange that a person in politics should be wholly without political ambition but I am afraid that I am that sort of a freak. . . . I did not want to come either to Parliament or to be in Government. However, there were certain compelling reasons at the time for my acceptance of this portfolio. Now there are so many crises one after another that every time seems to be the wrong time for getting out. . . .

She had been an observer, albeit close to the fount of power, during her father's lifetime. The party presidentship, like her earlier appointment to the Working Committee and its subsidiary bod-

* Brother—a reference to Nehru.

ies, had been bestowed on "Nehru's daughter"; these were not positions she had earned through the rough apprenticeship of state politics with their numerous considerations of region, faction, and caste. She had not had to work her way up through the vast amorphous organization, or show outstanding talent, in order to be singled out. And she had shown no desire to stand out as a political or public personality. Her predominant image was one of retreat and extreme reserve. The country knew her as her father's companion and the mother of two boys. If her father was grooming her for prime ministership, there was not enough evidence of it in events or in his own avowed aversion to undemocratic procedure to make his colleagues unduly suspicious or jealous of the possibility, though some believed, nevertheless, that her presidentship of the party indicated he was doing so. Above all, her own personality had given them no cause for alarm.

Later she recalled her role as her father's hostess:

> When I went to live with my father at Teen Murti House, the residence of the Prime Minister, it wasn't really a choice. My father asked me to come and to set up the house for him. There was nobody else to do it. So I set up the house, but I resisted every inch of the way about becoming a hostess. I was simply terrified of the so-called social duties. Although I met a large number of people, I wasn't good at "socializing" and small talk and that sort of thing. . . .[2]

She did not have the recognizable ingredients of public appeal or charisma. She was expected to play a greater role in national affairs, and her political involvement had grown to the gradual exclusion of her personal and private life, but front-rank leadership was not an idea easily connected with her. The imposing will and determination she later displayed in public life had as yet left their mark only on the family circle. At her father's death, grieved and undecided about her immediate future, she made no move to enter the leadership fray. Nor did the party's high command dwell on it as a possibility.

In order to avoid a contest for leadership that would present a picture of discord at Nehru's death, senior leaders headed by Kamaraj, Congress president, worked to bring about a unanimous choice. The principle of consensus, not new to Congress politics, was used this way and defined as such for the first time, and Lal Bahadur Shastri was chosen prime minister as the neutral and most generally acceptable candidate.

Morarji Desai, cut out by this procedure, saw the situation

differently. His standing in the party hierarchy was high and his ability proven during his chief ministership of Bombay state and his experience in Nehru's cabinet as commerce and later finance minister. With a right based on his record to lead the country, he wanted an open contest that would set a healthy precedent for the post-Nehru Congress, enabling the party to throw up its own choice rather than one arranged behind the scenes by those who controlled votes and patronage. A man of definite views and stern character, he did not have the pliability the bosses considered an important qualification for the job. He accepted their verdict as a matter of party discipline, and Shastri became the leader. The consensus was welcomed in India and abroad as an impressive exercise in mature political functioning, along with the fact that the parliamentary system had been upheld during this critical transition period and thus strengthened. It had, however, acted as a brake on the "natural" process of political selection.

Mrs. Gandhi, who had declared no personal stake in the succession, was a potent, if passive, presence on the scene. Even after the consensus, she remained, as daughter of the charismatic Nehru, a figure whom his party could not comfortably ignore in the emotional aftermath of his death. Shastri gave her the portfolio of Information and Broadcasting in his cabinet, but her relations with him were cool and distant, and she made no secret of her disdain for a man she considered a minor character whom chance had made a leader. Interviewed on November 11, 1965,[3] she said India had "swerved from the right path" after Nehru's death, and that socialism and nonalignment were being forgotten. She became a determined contestant for the succession when Shastri died suddenly at Tashkent in the Soviet Union on January 12, 1966, though she had described herself as "wholly without political ambition" and continued to see herself this way.

> When Mr. Shastri passed away, I really didn't think of myself at all. When he had come to ask me to become a Minister, I had thought it was just a huge joke and I had told him that, firstly, I was not in the mood for jokes immediately after the death of my father, and secondly, that this was a ridiculous proposition. . . . I must say I was worried at the thought of Mr. Morarji Desai becoming Prime Minister, because his policies were so diametrically opposed to what we stood for and I feared that India would immediately change direction.[4]

Nehru's daughter would be an important asset in the coming election of 1967, but her eligibility was linked chiefly to her party's insistence on uncontroversial leadership, in the void so soon again left by Shastri's death. Shastri's nineteen-month tenure had been dominated by two wars with Pakistan. There had scarcely been time to survey the post-Nehru scene and assess its priorities. And the party needed a period of reconstruction to rebuild its declining reputation. Indira Gandhi had what mattered greatly to the group of leaders who masterminded her rise—a reticence that made her apparently content to stay in the background of events. She had never been embroiled in controversy or ambition, and her subdued public manner insured respect for the principle of collective leadership. As between her and Morarji Desai, the other contestant, she looked colorless and manageable, the safer choice for a party whose political fortunes had suffered a severe setback with the Chinese attack in 1962 and needed to pull together. On her part Mrs. Gandhi knew she needed the party bosses, who did not favor her so much as oppose Desai. She tactfully refrained from canvassing for votes or formally declaring her candidacy and said she would abide by Congress President Kamaraj's wishes. Her reticence was noted and approved. After hearing from Kamaraj, she made her own moves to enlist support. There was less visible hurry and strain in New Delhi than there had been on Nehru's death. The Congress ruling clique felt that with its main crisis, the succession to Nehru, safely over, no other succession would present a critical problem. Desai's insistence this time on a vote was conceded, but the "open contest" proved, in effect, to be a trial of strength between him and the party bosses. There was little doubt that with the party machine behind Mrs. Gandhi, with the general election just a year away, and most M.P.s anxious for tickets and support, they would follow their chief ministers' orders to vote for her. The Congress Parliamentary Party elected its leader by secret ballot on January 19, 1966. Mrs. Gandhi, with the bosses and a coalition of chief ministers solidly behind her, won 355 votes to Desai's 169 and became prime minister on January 24. There were other reasons for her election. Desai belonged to the Old Guard. Mrs. Gandhi was young. Desai represented the Congress past, Mrs. Gandhi its future. A man of ascetic habits and implacable opinions, Desai had a "gray eminence" aura that could be forbidding. Mrs. Gandhi would be modern and flexible. Through her, Congress radicals believed, the party would be regenerated.

The selection of a parliamentary constituency for Mrs. Gandhi could no longer be postponed. She declined her aunt's offer to vacate Phulpur and refused an invitation from Shastri's constituency, Jumnapar, also near Allahabad, to represent it. She said she had offers from all over the country and would decide later. On August 28, 1966 Mrs. Pandit (my mother) wrote to me from Allahabad:

> I have filed my application for the Phulpur constituency after a talk with Indi* and her *written* consent ... [she] is still hesitating. Two safe but inconspicuous seats are being prepared, but it is the general desire which I share that she should stand from Allahabad City and face any challenge that is offered.

The Phulpur question remained open, though Mrs. Pandit's application had by now been approved and filed. She wrote to me from New Delhi on September 18:

> You must have seen from the papers that I offered Phulpur to the P.M. and she refused ... I did this because I knew she has wanted it and because inspired rumours were being circulated that "the people" want her there. . . . Before the meeting I spoke to Indi. She seemed pleased but said she would not permit me to make "this sacrifice." Or did I want something else? I said the offer was unconditional—there was no sacrifice. . . . When I announced my decision at the meeting, the very same people who had been turning around in circles carrying on a whispering campaign against me were a bit stunned and started saying I mustn't make such a "sacrifice.". . . In her speech Indi said I should keep Phulpur but added that "these things" were to be decided finally by Kamaraj. So we are held up until the end of October when the decision will be made.

Mrs. Gandhi was reluctant to stand from Allahabad or its environs. The Samyukta Socialist Party concentrated its full fire on this Congress stronghold, Nehru's birthplace and political base. "Dumb doll," Ram Manohar Lohia's mildly derisive description of Mrs. Gandhi, signified an irreverence that refused to concede special status to the Nehrus or to treat Allahabad as their fief. Lohia, who could rub shoulders in camaraderie with the crowd, also had an intellectual's appeal for the rebellious young. His language was incisive and brilliant, and Mrs. Gandhi, unsure and apt to seek refuge in her family's sacrifices for the national movement, was no match for it. She chose eventually to stand from Rae Bareli, the constituency of her late husband, Feroze Gandhi, and Mrs. Pandit kept the rural Phulpur seat. Congress credit was low, and each

* Indi, like Indu, is an abbreviation of Indira.

known and respected party member who could win an election was needed. Mrs. Pandit's political base was Uttar Pradesh, where she had twice been Minister for Health and Local Government (1937 and 1946) and twice been elected to the Lok Sabha after independence (1952 and 1964). This time the support extended to her by the party machine in Allahabad had noticeably cooled and dwindled. She wrote to me from Anand Bhawan on January 31, 1967:

> If I win this campaign it will really be something. I have to do everything on a shoestring—unpaid workers, very little transport facilities and no assistance, moral or otherwise, from the Congress elite.... Hardly any workers around Anand Bhawan—no noise or bustle—few flags and the rest of the trimmings. It will be fun to win, and I hope with a bigger majority.

The attitude of the "Congress elite" may be partly explained by this extract from the same letter:

> Broken roads and whirls of dust all through, but huge meetings at the end, and warm and genuine welcomes at every stop. There was only one difficult moment with a local bigwig who spoke about a ban on cow slaughter. I had decided to follow my father's line on this issue, so when the learned gentleman stopped for breath, I said very quietly, "Surely this painful subject is not a proper topic of discussion between two Brahmins." He begged my pardon and shut up immediately. Another difficult moment was when a dear old man got up and said he wanted to put a question on behalf of the village—why did I not seek election to the office of Prime Minister—the people of the constituency wanted me in that chair and so did many others all over India. I replied that my child was in that chair, and had all my attributes plus the advantage of being so much younger!

Mrs. Pandit's reference to "my child" was traditional. In India a brother or sister's child is regarded as one's own. In her case it was also indicative of her closeness to her brother. For the Indian public Mrs. Pandit's career in politics and diplomacy (at the United Nations, and as India's Ambassador to the USSR, the USA, and Britain) made her the senior and more mature Nehru presence in politics. Mrs. Gandhi reacted to her aunt with visible strain. Before the election campaign Mrs. Pandit had written from New Delhi: "I went yesterday evening by appointment to see Indi. We sat in stony silence for fifteen minutes after which I came home. Most frustrating. I don't know what to do to make a breakthrough. God knows I've tried and tried. It makes me sad."

Her victory in the campaign did not make matters easier, and the strain continued.

> Two days ago Indi asked me to see her in her office. I had asked permission to leave for Manila before the Presidential election* and she said it would be difficult to give me permission as there was going to be a grim struggle and every vote was needed. Could I get a day's postponement of the convocation etc. She then said she wanted to say something personal. Her eyes filled with tears and she was obviously distressed. She said she knew I was being wasted. She wanted to use my talents. She kept thinking what she could do for me. But she kept hearing things which shook her trust in me. I told her there was nothing I could do to prove my real affection for her and my desire that she should succeed in the task she had undertaken. Trust, I said, was something intangible. It was there or it was not. . . . I would have been satisfied if I could have been associated in a small way with either the Government or the Congress. What was mortifying to me was to be left out in the cold year after year when so many things required to be done intelligently and honestly. I said I had been thinking of resigning my seat as I was tired of being an extra vote for an organisation which had ceased to have any use for me. This last shook her and she said, "You can't resign—I wouldn't let you. We can't keep Phulpur without you." At this point I thought it best to leave and I asked her not to worry about me as I had infinite resources within myself.

Mrs. Pandit resigned her seat in the Lok Sabha in 1968.

Following the country's fourth general election in 1967, a little over a year after Mrs. Gandhi became Prime Minister, the question of leadership became a live issue again. Mrs. Gandhi's year in power had jolted the high command. She had devalued the rupee in June 1966 on the advice of her inner circle or "kitchen cabinet." Without the advance measures needed to cushion the economy against a drastic reduction of 57.5 percent in the value of the rupee, prices had risen, with consequent hardship to the consumer. Angry criticism assailed devaluation from all sections of opinion in Parliament. To the men who had put her in power, this showed a reckless disregard for the homework hard economic decisions require. It had also been an abrupt departure from the concept of joint cabinet responsibility for decision-making and an indication that either she did not understand parliamentary method or had

* The forthcoming election of the president of India. Mrs Gandhi had proposed Dr. Zakir Husain for the presidency and had achieved his nomination by her party against some opposition.

deliberately ignored it. Three days after devaluation, the party registered its disapproval of the action, though accepting it as a fait accompli. It marked a divide in Mrs. Gandhi's relations with Kamaraj. She now made it a point to distinguish between the party, as represented by its bosses, and the people, whom she identified with herself. Asked about her differences with Kamaraj in an interview with Kuldip Mayer before the 1967 election, she replied, "You see, here is a question of whom the party wants and whom the people want. My position among the people is uncontested." The publicly stated assumption of a privileged position distinct from, and even opposed to, her party made surprisingly little impression on a party wracked by election fever.

The election was a debacle for the Congress which lost power in five states, and in three others had a slender majority that did not last. In the Lok Sabha it was reduced to a small majority of about twenty-two, while in the states a new pattern emerged. Kerala and West Bengal formed Marxist (CPI-M)* led governments, while the Jan Sangh became the dominant party in the Hindi belt in the north. Some powerful Congressmen, including Kamaraj, lost their seats. Since 1963 there had been hard thinking and at least one concrete program (The Kamaraj Plan) to revitalize and strengthen the party at the grassroots. The election revealed how inadequate these had been. The last luster of the national movement had worn off the Congress. In these circumstances the party clung closer to "consensus" to avoid the friction of a new leadership contest, proposing Mrs. Gandhi remain prime minister and take Morarji Desai into her cabinet as deputy prime minister. There had been no deputy (number two in the cabinet) since Sardar Patel's death in 1950. Mrs. Gandhi, in a stronger bargaining position since Kamaraj had been defeated at the polls, agreed to Desai's inclusion as finance minister with the label of deputy, but not to "any duality of authority." Her authority, she said, would be "unfettered." In Nehru's time a rank had been assigned to each minister. She dispensed with this practice, instituting alphabetical order, so that cabinet positions provided no opening for conjecture about future power lineups.

* The Communist Party of India (Marxist), known as the CPI-M, broke away from the Communist Party of India (CPI) in July 1964 as a consequence of the worldwide split in the party. Contemptuous of the CPI, which it accused of being lured by power and office, the CPI-M rejected "the hoax of parliamentarianism" and believed it must "accomplish the people's democratic revolution through revolutionary people's war by uniting the fighting masses . . . on the basis of a worker-peasant alliance."

CHAPTER TWO

The Person

Mrs. Gandhi remained for the country at large a muted figure. A poor speaker and instinctively swift to prevent any encroachments on her position or prestige, she gave an impression of inhibition and wariness. Her first year in office, with the general consternation over devaluation, had made a weak start. Yet her remarks revealed her belief in herself as special to the Indian scene, in background, judgement, and above all in her Nehru birth. Her childhood or other personal references frequently figured in her speeches, containing the nuance that since her tender years she had borne a heavy burden in the struggle for freedom.

She appeared to be straining to convince through the medium of her family's role and reputation:

> Having lived in the midst of crisis from my earliest childhood, I am not overawed by present difficulties.[1]

> I have no doubt our difficulties will mount, almost 100% each day. But I go to difficulties head on. Since I was a child I have been able to proceed only in this way.[2]

> ... I have not eaten any cereals for a year except when I eat out. I just cannot when I know others are not getting enough.[3]

> You are all experts in your fields and I am not. ... but I am an expert at dealing with people. This is something, I think, I was either born with or I learnt from my very childhood ... I developed what may be called a "feel" of the people, and I find that this intuition helps me with the ordinary people. ...[4]

Politics rarely, if ever, produce modest, hesitant figures doubtful of their own capacities, and it is not surprising that Mrs. Gandhi

13

had a high opinion of herself. It was notable only because she sought at every opportunity to convey it to her audiences, and it contrasted with the lighter, more confident tread of speech and manner her father had had. The Indian public was not familiar with her as it had been with her father when he became prime minister. Nehru's life, his intellectual development, and even his private anguish were part and parcel of the events and literature of the national movement. Introspection and outburst were part of his public speaking. His ideas were on record in his writings. And those who could not read knew him, through personal encounter and public presence on the scene over many years, more intimately than most national figures are known among their people. He was in all his strength and weakness a thoroughly familiar quantity. Mrs. Gandhi was not. The heavy, brooding self-portrait she now revealed by stages seemed curiously at odds with what was generally known about the atmosphere of her home and the spirit inspiring it.

The extended family headed by Motilal Nehru included the children of his elder brothers and sisters, some of whom he had helped to educate and set on their feet in careers. Motilal was inordinately proud of his clan and made much of it. To him it was the most intelligent, attractive brood imaginable, and it, in turn, admired and revolved around him. A natural leader of men, his personal magnetism and the prestige he enjoyed in politics and the legal profession made his home the meeting place of some of the most brilliant, vital, and dedicated society of his time. His resounding laughter and flaring temper were both legendary, as was his generosity. His zest for life carried the family with élan through an almost revolutionary change in life-style, when he and his son joined Mahatma Gandhi. Incontestably a man of "family," in the great tradition of shelter and nurture, with the personality and instincts of a patriarch, Motilal lavished an extravagant affection and indulgence on the elder of his two daughters, his favorite Nanni or Nan, as she was known. But his most inviolable love was reserved for his only son. Jawaharlal, with his wife and daughter, were thus the focus of an entire clan's attention and concern in a way that princes and heirs apparent are.

Father and son entered with passion and humor into the freedom crusade. Jawaharlal's writings reflect the magic of the time, binding the household together in an incomparable adventure over and above the hardships involved. To some extent every member of Anand Bhawan, even visitors to it, were touched by the aspiration, the glow and romance of the national movement. In Mrs. Gandhi's recollections another picture emerges, somber, tense, aggrieved. Not surprisingly, as an only child, she turned the circumstances around her to exaggerate and dramatize her own importance in a busy, fully caught-up household and recalled her own role as one of drama. Her games, she told interviewers, had consisted of making fiery political speeches to her dolls and servants and triumphant encounters with the police. Whatever speeches she had made recently, she once said, she had been making since she was "twelve years old."[5] Home and childhood were associated for her with dark events and crisis: "So from September 1929 a part of the house was turned into a hospital. In the beginning doctors came only at dead of night and the women of the house, including myself, aged twelve, were the nurses.."[6] She told the Rajya Sabha: "As a small schoolgirl, at a time when Gandhiji undertook his historic fast in the Yeravda prison, I went to a Harijan colony to work there. This was one of my first activities in social work."[7] On the fiftieth anniversary of Jallianwala Bagh,* she said in a broadcast: "I was hardly more than a baby, but the impact of this tragedy on my elders could not but leave its mark on me."[8]

A more natural and charming glimpse of her emerges in this extract from her father's letter to his sister, Mrs. Pandit, written on November 23, 1926, from Montana, Switzerland, where his wife, Kamala Nehru, was being treated for tuberculosis. Indira was then nine years old:

> Indu came here for her birthday and spent three days with us.† Her English is becoming infected with her French and she talks of going jusqu' a the post office and it being presque ten o'clock! As for Hindustani, she tries to avoid talking in it. I insisted on talking to her in Hindi and I always write to her in Hindi.

As prime minister, Mrs. Gandhi told public meetings she had often faced bullets in her life, provoking a journalist to comment tartly: "If she did face bullets, it might have been in an unchronicled, unsung chapter of her much publicized life."[9] The publicity, however, depended almost entirely on her own statements, there being no other source for much of the material making its appear-

---

* A garden in Amristsar, Punjab, where an Indian crowd was massacred by order of a British Brigadier-General.
† Mrs. Gandhi was at a children's camp in the mountains at Chesnieres.

ance in written accounts about her. She frequently charged the Jan Sangh with trying to kill her, an accusation she had to withdraw when Jan Sangh M.P.s took it up in a stormy meeting of the Parliamentary Consultative Committee of the Home Ministry, and she admitted she had no evidence for such a statement. (The Jan Sangh was a political party which in 1977 became one of the five constituents of the Janata Party.)

Of her first and only imprisonment, from September 11, 1942 to May 13, 1943, in Naini Central Jail, Allahabad, she told an interviewer in 1969, "I was regarded as so dangerous that I wasn't even given normal prison facilities"—a recollection not supported by the evidence of the time. Mrs. Gandhi, aged nearly twenty-five, shared a barrack with her aunt, Mrs. Pandit, her cousin, Chandralekha Pandit, aged 18, and a number of women friends and acquaintances, all subject to the same rules and regulations. Mrs. Pandit writes in her preface to the prison diary[10] she kept: "The treatment given to me and to those who shared the barrack with me was, according to the prison standards, very lenient—the reader must not imagine that others were equally well treated." The diary starts on August 12, 1942, with Mrs. Pandit's own arrest, and ends with an entry dated June 11, 1943, just before her release. It covers Mrs. Gandhi's term of imprisonment and describes the daily lives of the inmates of the barrack. The following entries are illuminating:

> *August 19:* The barrack in which I live is a rectangular room intended to accommodate twelve or more convicts. There are gratings at short distances along each side, one of them being a door which is bolted and locked at night. One side of the barrack is raised four steps from the ground and serves as a latrine after lock-up. For day use a small bathroom and latrine have been added to the barrack. . . . The whole place is in a state of acute disrepair and the tiles on the roof are in need of renewal. I have only been supplied with a jail cot and a small rickety iron table. . . .

On August 22 Mrs. Pandit records that books and periodicals can come through the district magistrate. Chandralekha's arrest on August 30 and Indira's on September 11 are also recorded.

> *Sept. 13:* Indu, Lekha and I have been drawing up a plan. I am to cook the midday meal and they will arrange the supper. . . . The girls are planning to do a good lot of reading and Indu is going to help Lekha with her French.

Oct. 4: Yesterday the doctor informed me that Indira, Lekha and I had been placed in A class and that in future we would be entitled to 12 annas per day ration money. [An earlier entry records that Lekha has develped painful boils under her arm and Indira has a temperature.]

Oct. 6: Ranjit* has sent us some seeds and cuttings. The garden he started in his barrack last year is still flourishing and he brought me a bunch of lovely nasturtiums at our last interview. The soil of our yard is very stony, so the matron has offered to get us a few flower pots and boxes in which we can sow our seeds. The girls are excited.

Oct. 15: We were weighed today. Since arrival Lekha has lost 4 lbs. and I have lost 6. Indu is steady but that means nothing, as she is already below par and cannot afford to lose anything.

Oct. 22: The civil surgeon came to the see Indira today. He has been asked to see her and report on her health to Government.

Oct. 31: While we were having our tea this morning at about 8:30 A.M., the matron sent a note to say that Lekha and I would have an interview with Ranjit, and Indira with Feroze* at 9:30.

Nov. 2: The Superintendent told me at Parade this morning that all husbands and wives in the same jail would be permitted to interview each other once a fortnight for half an hour.

Nov. 7: Purnima† has given the whole barrack red glass bangles. We look quite gay.

Nov. 27: The girls have been busy "decorating" our corner of the barrack. Each part has a name. Indu calls hers Chimborazo. Lekha's bit is called Bien Venue because she now has the part formerly occupied by me and which gives a view of the main gate. I am obliged to call my abode Wall View because it's so obvious. In the centre we have an old blue rug . . . which I brought along with me in my bedding. We call the entire space the Blue Drawing Room and it's here we eat our meals and sit and read at night etc. Indu and Lekha are both gifted with imagination and the evenings are seldom dull. They are planning to save up rations and have a party in the Blue Drawing Room soon. The menu is discussed daily with great enthusiasm. They can't decide whether to write it in French or not. The jail cat named by Indu—Mehitabel—has had four kittens and Indu and Lekha are quite excited. . . . The girls have a habit of giving names to everything: the

* Mrs. Pandit's husband, Ranjit Sitaram Pandit, arrested and brought to Naini Central Jail on September 19, 1942.
* Mrs Gandhi's husband, Feroze Gandhi, arrested and brought to Naini Central Jail on the same day as herself, September 11, 1942.
† Fellow prisoner and old friend, Purnima Banerji.

lantern, table, bed, even the bottle of hair oil which has recently lost its top as the result of a fall. It is now referred to as Rupert the headless Earl. The lantern is Lucifer. After lock-up they read plays, each taking a part. I am the audience.

New Year's Day 1943: We were informed today that "the Government of India have permitted the members of the Congress Working Committee to correspond with members of their families, on personal and domestic matters only; any such letters addressed to Mrs. Pandit and Mrs. Indira Gandhi will be delivered, and they will be permitted to reply, subject to the same restrictions about subject matter."

The correspondence must soon have been established, for a letter to Mrs. Pandit from Jawaharlal Nehru, imprisoned in Ahmednagar Fort, is dated March 21, 1943: "My mind often travelled to you all and I was happy that you were together and could look after each other."

In two letters, dated April 9, 1943 and June 29, 1943 respectively, he wrote:

Both your letters were very welcome and to read them made me feel lighthearted and gay. Your account of life in Naini, of the energy and vitality shown by Indu and Chand, and of their continuous attempts to find humour in a depressing situation, soothed and pleased me greatly. I am worried, however, about your health . . . I have written to Betty* asking her to fix up with some fruiterer to send a parcel of fresh fruit weekly to Indu direct. Allahabad is very poor in fruit at this time of the year and both of you should have plenty of fruit.

I was glad to read about Indu in your letters—how she has recouped. I am pleased about this for it indicates that she has become essentially stronger and with greater powers of resistance. The experience of a hot weather in Naini after a dozen years of mountain climates and Switzerland and England was a very stiff one. Her coming through it, as she has done, is full of promise. It shows not only that she is better but that she knows how to keep well inspite of disadvantages and disabilities.

Mrs. Pandit's diary contains three more entries of interest:

May 11: On the 5th we were sent for to the office and informed that Indu and I would be released next morning and an externment order would be served on us requiring us to proceed to Almora and take up our residence at Khali . . . under the surveillance of the Deputy Com-

---

* Krishna Hutheesing, the younger of Nehru's two sisters, nicknamed Betty.

missioner of Almora. Obviously these terms could not be accepted by us and we refused.

May 13: Indu and I are being released this morning. I wonder if any order is to be served on us. If so we shall be back here before long.

May 27: Here I am back in Naini after an eventful week. . . . As we refused to comply with the externment order served on us, a police officer came to the house yesterday to enquire when I would be ready to return to jail. I said any time that suited him and he suggested 6 P.M., which I accepted. There was no warrant fortunately for Indu who is in no condition to return to Naini at present as she is down with fever and a very bad cold.

Far from being treated as dangerous and deprived of normal facilities, Nehru's daughter received specially courteous consideration. Yet this and the gaiety and vitality, with which she and her young cousin made a game of grim discomfort and dreary prison routine, did not appear to figure in her recollections.

Jawaharlal Nehru, a man bowed by many burdens as the years of the fight for freedom took their toll, remained curiously unbowed in spirit. In a conscious effort to share himself and to communicate with his child, particularly during his long absences in prison, he wrote his *Letters from a Father to His Daughter* and *Glimpses of World History*, books that did more than explain the scientific beginnings of the world, or the procession of men and events constituting its history. These pages held an approach to life compounded of buoyancy and optimism, a humorous tolerance toward life's foibles and even its trials. Indira saw life in another more solemn perspective, cast in an austere mould, shorn of lightness, as if lightness were a weakness, a trap to be avoided. Nor apparently could the written word take the place of flesh-and-blood human beings to turn to. Absent parents, though absent for well-understood and admired reasons, left a void that was never quite filled, though few parents could have given of themselves to an only child as Indira's did. Because of her mother's invalidism, her father was particularly involved with phases of her growth, with the sole responsibility for major and minor decisions concerning her, and even for periods with her daily routine, normally a mother's job, as during the long stay in Europe for his wife's treatment in 1926. He wrote to his sister in Allahabad from Geneva on May 6, 1926:

Indu has to be escorted to school and there being no servants or other helpful persons, I have to accompany her. . . .

I consulted the State enquiry department and with their advice fixed the Ecole Internationale here. This is a bilingual school and although most of the work is done in French, explanations are also given in English. I thought this would suit Indu to begin with and till she picks up a little French . . . she goes to school at eight and comes back at twelve for meals. At two she goes again and all the children are then taken out in a bus to a place in the country a few miles off, which belongs to the school. The afternoon lessons often take place in the open and consist largely of games. She comes back at four. This means that I have to go backwards and forwards between our pension and the school four times a day! The distance is not inconsiderable and I get quite a lot of exercise although we take the tram for part of the way. Fortunately there are two full holidays and one half holiday a week.

A week later he wrote:

Romain Rolland has sent me a nice letter. . . . He got to know from some teacher in Indu's school that a little Indian girl had joined the school. He guessed that the girl might be my daughter. He writes to say that Indu's French teacher is a great friend of his and is a highly cultured and affectionate lady who can be thoroughly trusted with children. This is very comforting as I was not at all sure that the school I had chosen was the right one.

Indu is progressing and developing in more ways than one. She now comes back from school all by herself and walks the whole distance of nearly a mile or takes the tram. Some change from the methods in vogue in Allahabad, where Khaliq* and the motor were not thought sufficient and Jessie-Ma† had to be constantly with her during school hours. . . .

Last Sunday I took Indu up a little mountain near Geneva called the Saleve. It is two hours' journey by tram and funicular. The view from the top is magnificent, one of the best in Switzerland. One can see the whole of the Mont Blanc chain and the Jura and the lake of Geneva and the valleys all around dotted with little villages and country houses. The whole country looked like an enormous and very well kept park. At some places the fields were so neat and green that one could almost imagine that rich carpets had been spread out in various shades of green. On top of the Saleve there were the remains of some snow. This was fresh enough and, to Indu's infinite joy, we made snowballs and threw them at each other. . . .

In a postscript he adds: "I enclose two recent snapshots of Indu.

---

* The family chauffeur.
† Indira's "ayah" (the woman who looked after her at home).

Compare them to the snapshots taken in India in February and you will notice how she is growing."

The parent-child relationship has its unanalyzed loves and hostilities, but, given the keen awareness Nehru had of his daughter, this relationship might have become a close mutual bond. That it did not partake of real human response and sharing, though it did of attachment, may have been because, though she spent most of her adult life in her father's house, there was a point beyond which Indira could not go in simple give-and-take. It seemed fraught for her with hazards. The intellectual and emotional labor her father expended on her did not bring the cherished child to flower. Somewhere within, her intensities locked, and the tight bud stayed closed. Her delicate health, a problem through childhood, continued into womanhood. Not disposed to study, and with no special aptitude, she was never driven to the kind of discipline that might have been expected of a sturdier child. She could not keep up with her studies at Oxford and did not get a degree, while her earlier schooling had been uneven because of her parents' jail terms or her mother's ill health. Indu, center of the larger family's loving concern, seldom lowered her guards. Her unresponsiveness troubled her father during her adolescence. She was fifteen when he wrote to his sister, Mrs. Pandit, from his barrack in Dehra Dun District Jail:

> During the last fourteen months or more I have written to Indu regularly and have hardly missed a fortnight. It has been a very one-sided correspondence as my letters have evoked practically no response. After about a couple of months of silence on her part a hasty letter would come with many apologies and excuses, and with no reference at all to my letters or the questions I had asked in them. I have sent books for her birthday and on other occasions. These are not acknowledged and I have no definite knowledge if they reached her. I gather that Kamala is treated in much the same way. Now it does not matter much if an odd letter comes or does not come. Nor does it matter fundamentally if a joy that I might have is denied to me or to Kamala. I can get used to that as to other things that I do not like. But I am naturally led to think why this should be so. It is not casual; it is persistent. And in spite of numerous efforts it continues. I know that Indu is fond of me and of Kamala. Yet she ignores us and others completely. Why is this so? Indu, I feel, is extraordinarily imaginative and self-centered or subjective. Indeed, I would say that, quite unconsciously, she has grown remarkably selfish. She lives in a world of dreams and vagaries and floats about on imaginary clouds, full prob-

ably of all manner of brave fancies. Now this is natural in a girl of her subjective nature and especially at her age. But there can be too much of it and I am afraid there is too much of it in her case ... I feel she requires a course of field or factory work to bring her down from the clouds.... She will have to come down, and if she does not do so early she will do so late, and then the process will be painful.

Getting through to Indu was a difficulty that surfaced vividly when she made her decision to marry, and later during the beleaguered course of her marriage. Feroze Gandhi, a Parsi, belonged to Allahabad, where his family owned a general store. As a student active in the national movement, he was no stranger to the Nehru household. In fact he was something of a protegé of Indira's parents. This connection was not altogether welcome to Feroze's family, who feared it might harm him. Nehru, with a characteristic regard for propriety and family feeling, went out of his way on at least one occasion to try to set their misgivings at rest. He wrote to his sister from Bhowali, Uttar Pradesh, on November 2, 1935:

And now rather a delicate matter and perhaps a troublesome job for you. It appears that Feroze Gandhi has got into hot water with his people because of his association with us, and especially his long stay at Bhowali. Even before this his political activities were greatly resented by his mother and the blame for them was cast on Kamala and me. It had almost been settled that he was to sail for Europe with his aunt, Miss Commissariat ... , but suddenly everything has fallen through and the poor boy is landed high and dry. Even ordinarily I would like to help him in this quandary, but now my responsibility is all the greater because we happen to be the cause of it.

Now my sympathy is entirely with the poor mother. I can perfectly understand and appreciate her distress and anger at us. Very probably I would have felt much the same if I had been treated in this way by my son. I think also that we have been remiss in almost ignoring the mother. But circumstances somewhat controlled the situation and what with Kamala's illness and my absence in jail, we did little ...

... It is difficult to understand other people's family quarrels and even more difficult to interfere in them. Still something has to be done to save the boy from endless trouble (he is so downcast that he talks foolishly of entering some wretched ashram!)—and to put ourselves right with his family ...

... I repeat that I thoroughly sympathise with the family and even quite understand their anger. We cannot presume to interfere and to tell them what to do with the boy, but I do want to tone down that anger and to remove any obstructions in the way of a reconciliation. After that a mother's love will do the trick.

So I would like you to pay a visit to the mother and sister . . . and to soothe them and apologise to them on my and Kamala's behalf and to tell them that we are extremely sorry that we should have unwittingly come in between them and their boy. That is the very last thing we would like to do. We have grown fond of the boy because he is a brave lad and has the makings of a man in him. He has our good wishes in every way and we hope that he will train himself and educate himself in accordance with his own wishes and those of his family for any work that he chooses. It is not for us to interfere. . . .

This is rather a ticklish job but yet there should be no difficulty about it as really the chief trouble is a phantom of the imagination. But phantoms are often troublesome. . . .

Nehru's reaction to Indira's decision to marry Feroze, made while she was still in her teens, rose chiefly from his regret that she had too early closed her mind and feelings to the wide world of opportunity around her. His suggestion that she should think the matter over at home before taking a final decision resulted in a scarring experience for him. Indira, at Oxford at the time, wanted to remain in England with Feroze for her vacation and told her father she would not speak to him unless he agreed, an ultimatum he did not take seriously. She kept her promise. A fortnight's silence on the voyage to Bombay continued unbroken on the train journey to Allahabad. On their arrival home, Nehru—gentle and affectionate in his family relationships—was too shaken to endure the ordeal further. He asked his secretary to book Indira's passage back to England. Her marriage took place in Allahabad in March 1942. Although her father's advice, and later Mahatma Gandhi's, to think again about her choice, had not prevailed, the marriage had their blessing. For Indira, it was a promise to Feroze fulfilled and her own personality asserted, in circumstances where another woman might have yielded to family opinion.

Indira's choice of Feroze was influenced by her mother's fondness for the young man who had nursed her devotedly at Bhowali during a phase of her illness. Indira's own shyness and stiff uncommunicativeness, mistaken in her youth for hauteur, had never made friendship or close companionship easy. Feroze represented the known, comfortable, and familiar. The relationship inevitably foundered in the role she later chose of being at her father's side at the nation's political center. It compelled them to live substantially apart and subjected the marriage to strains and stresses from which it never recovered. Her father's house in Delhi remained Indira's priority, a setting into which Feroze, with a career and personality of his own, could not conveniently be absorbed. A journalist who became a member of Parliament with a reputation for unearthing facts and figures, Feroze was responsible for instituting the inquiry leading to the resignation of Finance Minister T. T. Krishnamachari in 1958. He reacted bitterly and outspokenly to the unofficial separation, and it came to have untidy political and personal overtones. Those who watched this tragedy unfold, above all her father, felt their failure to work out a solution, either in complete separation or in compromise, would affect Indira in many and manifold ways and shut a door forever to the possibilities of normal living.

Feroze was in many ways self-educated, with a gift for the mechanical as well as a knowledge of classical music and fine china. He was an extrovert, generous with his help and money, popular with colleagues and subordinates. His sense of humor enlivened the Central Hall of Parliament. He was short and square in build, fair-skinned, with a face that reddened with laughter, and people warmed to him easily. Parliament came to have a healthy regard for his grasp and use of facts. He had green fingers, and after the death of Ranjit Pandit in January 1944, Feroze took over the supervision of Anand Bhawan's gardens. The prime minister's house, where Feroze's wife and sons lived, remained his domestic base, but his business was conducted from the parliamentary accommodation he rented, and no slur of political advantage attached to him. One aspect of the growing chasm between him and wife was to give Indira an aura of self-sacrifice and nobility of choice, qualities people had associated with her invalid mother. These must indeed have been poignantly present in her private conflict. Apparently she saw no way out, either in final break or in final healing, for it remained with her unresolved, except for a brief reunion the summer before his death, until Feroze died in September 1960.

The shadows in Indira were in part a reflection of the mismatching of her parents. Their marriage, arranged by Motilal Nehru and Kamala's aunt, was a grievous mistake for these two profoundly dissimilar people. Kamala's problems of adaptation, from her orthodox, barely educated background to the liberal, emancipated, Westernized environment of the Nehrus, built up into symptoms of illness, while the bruises of the relationship drove Nehru deeply into himself and strengthened his emotional and intellectual links with his sister. Since marriages in which the wife was not her husband's equal in education or opportunity were the rule rather than the exception, the flaw in this one must have resulted from more intractable problems of personality. Ten years older than his wife, Nehru tried and failed to overcome the gulf between them. The national movement, claiming them both, performed this task to some extent but could never complete it, for Kamala died of tuberculosis after a long illness in February 1936. During his last vigil over her failing health, there seemed in him a foreshadowing of the event to come. Released from prison in September 1935 to join her at Badenweiler (Germany), he was shocked at the deterioration in her condition and moved into the sanitarium with her, leaving Indira and her cousin, Vidya Nehru, invited from Oxford to spend the Christmas vacation with them, at their pension. Trying to finish his autobiography, keep an eye on Indira and Vidya, and watch over his wife, his only outlet for solace and companionship lay in writing every few days to his sister, with news intended for the whole anxious family at Allahabad, yet reaching out especially to Nan.

> Badenweiler
> 31-12-35

Nan darling—Was it yesterday I wrote or the day before? I am getting mixed up. I have sent you a fair number of letters during the last four months or less, to make up, to some extent, for the long silences of previous months and years.

I write to you again so soon because I feel like doing so. The old year is passing as I write—it is almost the stroke of midnight—and the desire to write to you on this coming of the new year became strong within me. To send you all my love.

The bells are ringing and the sound rolls up the valley in waves which seem to envelop me. There is also gun firing going on somewhere. The New Year has come. What will it be, I wonder? I have just been out on my balcony and I saw in the distance the twinkling lights on the far side of the Rhine, in France.

There was something oppressive in the air, or was it my imagination? The firing suddenly made me think of war and suffering and disaster.

But whatever terrors the New Year may hold in its womb, why should we worry about them in anticipation? It is enough that a new year is born, and somehow a feeling of growth comes with it, and a shedding away of the past year's burdens and sorrows.

All my love to mother and you and Ranjit, and Chand and Tara and little Rita. Give my greetings to Upadhyaya also, and Hari, and all others whom Anand Bhawan shelters.*
Your loving brother
Jawahar

One terror was soon realized. Kamala died in February 1936. Nehru's dedication of his autobiography—published soon after her death "To Kamala Who Is No More"—was his deep mourning of a discovery cut short. His later writing movingly described her wasting illness and his admiration for the burning patriotism that had become so strong a bond between them.

On the publication of her mother's biography[11] in May 1973, Mrs. Gandhi said in an interview with its author that her mother had had the greater influence on her. In her teens she had felt her mother was being wronged by her father's family and had fought for her. "I saw her being hurt and I was determined not to be hurt." With a chronically ailing mother, it may have been hard, too, for a child to forgive those in robust health around her, to feel part of an active household radiating energy and accomplishment. The effect for Indira was to range her parents' families, even her parents at times, on opposite sides, with a gap in understanding, sympathy, and culture between them. The distinction between the two "sides" persisted in her mind. The Nehru name was a talisman she needed, and she had been deeply attached to her father. But her trust and instincts reposed in the simpler uncritical background of her mother's relations and her own preference was for them. Toward the Nehru relatives, those who had shared the family home and background at Anand Bhawan, her feelings were mixed and not often given full human play. The idea gained currency that she particularly resented the beautiful vivacious elder aunt who occupied a special place in her father's affections.

Undeniably, the bond created problems for the less confident Kamala Nehru. Mrs. Pandit recalled much later:

the tensions the family lived through when Bhai* insisted that he and I were going home by that route in his car. It seemed natural then. Now it seems fantastically wrong that eight months after his wedding Bhai should do this. Again, I was reminded of our early morning rides

---

* Chand (Chandralehka), Tara (Nayantara), and Rita are the daughters of Mrs. Pandit. Upadhyaya is Nehru's secretary. Hari is Nehru's valet.
* Brother.

together in Allahabad—all this in 1917–18—breakfast together because the family had sometimes finished when we got home, and there was a complete sense of contentment in just being together. Perhaps Bhabi† had a valid point in disliking me—not for anything I had done but for the obvious oneness that existed between Bhai and myself. Ranjit, shrewd and perceptive, got the picture in a minute but he was himself deeply absorbed in Bhai and loved him in an unquestioning manner, so no problem ever arose. Isn't it strange suddenly coming back to me like this? It was the growing demands of the national movement that brought a balance into Bhai's life. I was too little anyway and thought only with my heart and not with the intellect (of which there was not much!)[12]

Yet simple formulas seldom tell the whole story of family relationships, where the immediate and personal often becomes blurred and mellowed by the larger cushioning of common living and common interests. Motilal Nehru's family was closely and loyally knit. If Indira resented her aunt, there was not much evidence of it during her childhood. Indira did not write frequently, but she kept in touch with her aunt, and, in the abundant correspondence between Nehru and his sister, her occasional paragraphs and postscripts are warm and spontaneous.

On June 23, 1935 she adds to her father's letter from London: "Darling Puphi—Just a very hurried line to send you my love. Just now the telephone takes all my time. I daren't budge from it. It is glorious seeing Papu again. He looks well but thin. . . . There goes the phone! Love Indu." And a postscript on her father's letter, two days later from Sir Stafford Cripps's home, Goodfellows, at Lechlade, Glocestershire: "You would have loved this very charming house and still lovelier garden. Lots of love, Indu."

The family had its tensions, but perhaps because they were acknowledged and discussed, they did not affect the normal current of family life. From jail Nehru wrote to his sister:

Little things sometimes touch and ruffle our tempers and disturb the cooperation that should exist. We lead an abnormal life—in and out of gaol—and those who are out have the more difficult time for they have to shoulder many a burden when their heart is not in it. And so sometimes tempers get frayed and a spirit of non-cooperation steals in and that of course is not only unbecoming but it makes matters worse. Almost unconsciously we allow ourselves to become victims of trivial circumstances and the harmony that should be life—even

† Brother's wife.

though it be tragic—becomes marred and we develop the hard look that is neither beautiful nor helpful. That is a true sign of age! If we presume to dabble in big things, we have to carry the shadow of bigness even in our little undertakings. We cannot control life, the joy and the sorrow of it, the achievement or otherwise, but one thing we ought to be able to control, and that is our attitude to it. We can, I believe, make a work of art of our lives, a song or a beautiful melody, even though that song may clutch at the throat and bring tears to the eyes. No one can deny us that artistry of living if we are ourselves capable of it. If we are capable; it is a big if! Not to reject life but to accept it in all its fullness, and yet to go through it finely and with light steps and refusing to allow it to besmirch us. That is a worthwhile ideal, a difficult undertaking, and the very few who may have the good fortune to approach it can never regret the choice. Success, if it comes, comes worthily, with no tinsel or vulgarity; failure itself approaches with noble and tragic mien.

But . . . I was thinking of an occasional lack of harmony, a touch of non-cooperation that I had sensed in our household. That is a matter of sorrow for me and I write to you because you are very dear to me. There are very few people who really count in my life and you are one of them, and you have brought great comfort to me in moments of trial. I should like you therefore to remove any discordant notes that might have unwittingly crept in. It is futile to consider how they came, whose fault or carelessness permitted them. It is everybody's fault. We have all to face nervous strains which are more difficult to bear often enough than actual physical pain. We must be tolerant of each other's failings and help to lighten each other's load.[13]

On Ranjit Pandit's death in January 1944, not long after his relase from jail, it was Indira and Feroze who gave their aunt the support she needed, with Nehru still in jail. During the years of Nehru's prime ministership, the family tie was manifest in shared concern for matters affecting all their children. Any early resentment on Indira's part might have found its ordinary level in private life. The palpable difference, the cool, empty distance Indira established between herself and her aunt, came with her own entry into the cabinet.

Spontaneity was not, in general, her style. Daring was. In 1962 Mrs. Gandhi had gone to Jabalpur in Madhya Pradesh to investigate Hindu-Muslim riots, though she was not in the government at the time. She could show a refreshing disregard for her own safety. During the Chinese attack that year, she had flown to Tezpur, headquarters of the sector commander, to meet soldiers and officers. She had gone to the front line at Haji Pir in Kashmir during the

Indo-Pakistan war of 1965, inspiring the comment that she was the only man in the cabinet. Two years later, during an election meeting in Bhubaneshwar, Orissa, she faced stone-throwers coolly, not losing her nerve when a stone struck her, cutting her lip and displacing a bone in her nose.

Mrs. Pandit's resignation of her Lok Sabha seat in 1968 closed a domestic chapter. Nehru's presence had been home for his two sisters, eleven and seventeen years younger than he, and for their children. When he became prime minister, his house in New Delhi continued the hospitable tradition of Anand Bhawan, providing a sense of warmth and embrace for the larger family. Perhaps few men at the center of power and helm of affairs for so many years have had his talent for enduring relationships or his intimate concern for private problems. Deeply affectionate and considerate, he had friends, not just followers, and a grace in dealing with people that did much to soften controversy and make political combat a stimulating and civilized affar. His most virulent critics in politics and the press respected him. One of the most sensitive tributes to him *The Gentle Colossus*, was written by Hiren Mukerjee of the Communist Party of India.

Mrs. Pandit had been passionately devoted to her brother, and they had shared an uncommon closeness. She was strongly traditional in her belief that her brother's daughter was her own and that the family must be united after Nehru's death, when Mrs. Gandhi, in her new exacting position, needed support. Nehru's death and her own entry into the cabinet, however, gave Mrs. Gandhi the opportunity to dissolve the relationships that had surrounded her father. If she had indeed considered her elder aunt an obstacle to her mother's happiness in the Nehru family, this had not affected the stuff of the relationship in her father's lifetime, when close family bonds had been maintained. Yet now she was more comfortable once her aunt retired from politics and moved out of the capital to Dehra Dun. The family tie was not encouraged. In 1970 when Anand Bhawan was converted by Mrs. Gandhi into a memorial, Mrs. Pandit was refused permission to stay at the house overnight, as Mrs. Gandhi was doing, for the ceremony next day. Mrs. Pandit attended the ceremony as a guest. Bequeathing Anand Bhawan to his daughter in his will Nehru had written:

> In the course of a life which has had its share of trial and difficulty, the love and tender care for me of both my sisters, Vijaya Lakshmi Pandit and Krishna Hutheesing, has been of the greatest solace to me.

I can give nothing to balance this but my own love and affection which they have in full measure. . . . This house, Anand Bhawan, has become for us and others a symbol of much that we value in life. It is far more than a structure of brick and concrete, more than a private possession. It is connected intimately with our national struggle for freedom, and within its walls great events have happened and great decisions have been reached. . . . [It] should always be open to my sisters, their children, as well as my brother-in-law, Raja Hutheesing, and they should be made to feel that it continues to be their home where they are welcome. They can stay there whenever they like and for as long as they like. I should like them to pay periodic visits to the house and to keep fresh and strong the bonds that tie them to their old home.

On the occasion of Anand Bhawan's conversion by Mrs. Gandhi to a memorial, I was asked to recall my memories of my home for the *Hindustan Times*.[14] This extract conveys my own feeling for the house and the atmosphere it provided for the children and adults it sheltered:

I felt a special kinship with the house. It was as old as I was. It had been built when my grandfather gave his palatial residence to the Congress Party. . . . Our love and admiration for mamu* was inextricably entwined with the soil and stones of Anand Bhawan. Both seemed enveloped in a radiance of purpose, both wide open to the world, nothing in either limited to the purely personal. Nor was there anything grim or glum about either. Even the people who came and went, villagers, town workers, university students, the little known as well as the galaxy of leaders, had a buoyancy and gaiety of spirit. There was a lot of laughter in the house. Never was history made with the joy of living so amply woven into it. . . . Even a child felt it, sitting on the verandah after dinner, the floor still warm from a day of sun, looking up at the stars.

"I'll never let it down," I promised the stars, "I'll carry it everywhere as long as I live."

And "it" was all that Anand Bhawan stood for. Without "it" I would have had a country but no passionate identification with it. "It," I discovered, made searing demands on integrity as one grew up, exacted the best of oneself in truth and endeavour, but somehow also provided the courage to give it. And to renew myself at great moments—my marriage, the birth of a child—I had to go back to Anand Bhawan. . . .

What stands out in recent memory is the journey to Allahabad with Mamu's ashes in 1964. We were weary and heavy-eyed after a long night of vigil in the train, our ears filled with the tempestuous mourn-

* Maternal uncle.

ing voices that had besieged the train all night. In Allahabad there was silence. Our slow motorcade took us through soundless streets where people lined the route stock still, just watching. And then we were at Anand Bhawan, servants, friends, relatives—all those for whom Anand Bhawan had also been home—gathered on the front steps. I went upstairs away from them all to the library where Munshi Kanhaiyalal† had lovingly laid out a panorama of old newspaper and magazine clippings and pictures. Here was Mamu at all ages, unbelievably beautiful in youth, later time-scarred as he identified himself more and more closely with the sufferings of his people and through them with suffering everywhere. Here was Mamu as I had first become aware of him—a Galahad in search of the Grail—Mamu of the impassioned speeches at Allahabad University—carrying his ardour to every corner of the country. . . . He had lived in the light, submitting with equal grace to its gentle glow and its harsh glare. It became clear all over again as the chimes of the University clock tower brought me back to the present, that we must not retreat into shadows of any kind, personal or national. We belonged where he had led us, in the light, and this house had embodied it through the years, passing it in some measure to everyone who had ever come in contact with it.

I hope that aura will remain as Anand Bhawan enters a new phase, and is put to a new use. I hope the people who come and go there will sense something of that past, remember a time when in the words of the hymn "glory shone around." I wish I had been invited there when it was given to the Nehru Memorial Trust, to stand in the garden for one last look round. But perhaps it does not matter. I had said my own farewell when Mamu died—and the atmosphere of Anand Bhawan is one I will carry to the end of my days.

Mrs. Pandit belonged to a generation whose traditional values are not easily discarded. She said, in a poignant recollection of her brother that the *Statesman* quoted in its "On record" column on February 1, 1970, "My tie with Mrs. Indira Gandhi is, as far as I am concerned, of abiding value." Birthdays provided an opportunity to restablish the bonds that had been abruptly severed. A typical reply from Mrs. Gandhi to such an attempt at communication reads:

New Delhi
November 19, 1971

Dear Puphi,
Thank you for your card of birthday greetings.
I find birthday celebrations increasingly wearisome, although tour-

† Munshi Kanhaiyalal was the Nehru family's clerk cum general supervisor in charge of household affairs.

ing cyclone-affected areas can hardly be considered a more cheerful way of celebrating a birthday!

With good wishes,
Indu

Mrs. Pandit's gestures were not reciprocated, and she was not invited to Sanjay Gandhi's wedding in 1974. On February 14, 1977, Mrs. Pandit came out of retirement to campaign for the newly formed Congress for Democracy and the Janata Party in the approaching national election to Parliament against "the authoritarian trend that has grown to vast proportions." Her strongly worded statement included the sentence: "I cannot live at peace with myself if, by my silence, I seem to agree with the destruction of all I have been taught to hold dear." She made it clear, however, that she bore her niece no personal animus and would do nothing to hurt her personally. In reply to a question at her news conference, she said she would not visit Rae Bareli, Mrs. Gandhi's constituency, during the campaign, "because I do not want people of ill-will to exploit my stand," and "there are some decent values and family relationships which I cherish." Mrs. Gandhi made neither reference nor response to this development, though a group in her party reacted vehemently against it, issuing a public statement against Mrs. Pandit. After Mrs. Gandhi's electoral defeat, it was Mrs. Pandit who called on her.

The breach came near being healed when Mrs. Pandit arrived from Dehra Dun to be with her niece on the day of Sanjay's death, June 23, 1980.

Indu's dignity and calm are amazing and I am full of admiration for her courage. . . . I can only say that all the various religious disciplines she has been undergoing for the last year have helped her. She gets up at 3 A.M. for *puja* [prayer] and again worships in the evening. . . . (She) met me with affection and took me inside—presently brought out the baby Varun [Sanjay's son] and put him in my arms. Later Maneka [Sanjay's widow] was brought to me. Seeing the fat smiling baby moved me and I began to cry, whereupon Indu came up and said, "Now, now Puphi, you know we don't cry." She has shown care and concern for my comfort and been very affectionate. . . . Only the red-rimmed eyes give any indication of tears shed in private. With all this she has fasted for two days. . . . She is back at her desk today. (27th).[15]

CHAPTER THREE

Emergence—1967–1969

Just before the 1967 election the Soviet journal *New Times* commented that the prestige and influence of the Congress Party had notably declined and India had lost its socialistic zeal after Nehru (a sentiment expressed by Mrs. Gandhi earlier). After Shastri, the journal said, the conservatives in the party had kept the radicals out of government, while a "prominent right winger," Morarji Desai, had been installed. This analysis ignored the fact that Nehru's choice of men in the composition of his cabinets was not bound by the conventional Left-Right division. It had been based on the complexities of the parliamentary and federal system and on his vision of India as one of the world's most complex societies, capable of generating great strength through its political and cultural heterogeneity, once it was planted firmly in freedom. Morarji Desai and Lal Bahadur Shastri had both held portfolios in Nehru's cabinets. The view that India had lost it socialistic zeal after Nehru is, however, significant, because it became the platform for events to come, featuring a more facile outlook and a more impetuous breed of politician than had been able to surface in Nehru's time.

Nehru's own opinion and assessment of Shastri, a man he liked and trusted, are on record. In a letter dated November 27, 1956 to his sister Vijaya Lakshmi Pandit, who was then high commissioner for India in Britain, Nehru wrote:

> Over and above all this came Lal Bahadur's resignation which I decided to accept, though very reluctantly. He resigned because of the terrible Railway disaster recently which was the second of its kind in two months. Of course it was not Lal Bahadur's fault. But taking everything into consideration and more especially Lal Bahadur's extreme unhappiness, I decided to accept this resignation. It is odd and pleas-

ing to me to find how much this resignation has affected people. There has been a cry of regret and almost of sorrow from all kinds of quarters all over the country. It shows how popular Lal Bahadur is. He has gone up in people's estimation by this resignation. So far as I am concerned, he will not be out of Government for very long. That is, if things function as expected, he will come back into Government after the general election.

A later letter written at midnight on June 6/7, 1961 to his sister in London confirms this opinion over the years:

A little while ago Lal Bahadur came to see me. He came direct from Palam where he had arrived from Assam via Calcutta. We sent him from Durgapur to Assam because of the language trouble there. He has dealt with this matter with great tact and ability and come as near to a possible settlement as we could have hoped for. Of course, there are extremists who will create trouble and I am by no means sure of the settlement yet. Anyhow, Lal Bahadur has done a first class piece of work. It pleases me to see how he has grown with additional responsibilities. This is not my opinion only, but the general impression.

Mrs. Gandhi, who did not share her father's opinion of Shastri, later wrote:

For the general elections of 1957, I campaigned all over the country. Lal Bahadur Shastri, who was then Railway Minister, was put in charge of the elections and this is really why he resigned. There was a railway accident and everybody thought that he had resigned his ministership merely because of the accident. It may have had something to do with it, but one reason was the elections.[1]

Nehru's satisfaction in the accomplishments of younger colleagues and the responsibilities he gave to men and women whose political reputations were made as a result of their exercise, produced an array of experience in the Congress, providing it with the material of leadership. His consistent refusal to name a successor showed confidence in the men who would come after him. He valued Shastri's roots in the soil and the quiet conciliatory manner distinguishing him as a successful negotiator on thorny issues. Gravely ill in 1964 from a stroke he had suffered at Bhubaneshwar, he chose Shastri to take over his work, a factor that weighed with the party leaders who made him prime minister on Nehru's death.

The Soviet analysis with its black-white political divisions was not yet reflected in Mrs. Gandhi's utterances. Asked by a journalist what the significance of her election as the country's leader was, she replied, "Perhaps it ensures some kind of continuity—continuity of policy, and also perhaps continuity of personality."[2] The reply showed she believed she had stepped into her father's shoes as the imaginative rallying point for all Indians. Yet Nehru had been, of desire and discipline, a man of his party, shaped and molded by his service of it and profoundly conscious of his debt to it. Mrs. Gandhi already saw herself as something more, a party-plus image not yet attributable to her own leadership or record, and taken for granted as a birth right. Asked if she represented the Left, there was more than a touch of impatience in her reply, "I am a representative of all India which includes all shades of opinion."[3]

The press and the public automatically identified her with her father, until marked differences of political style and behavior became obvious and finally erupted into the open in 1969. The overt likenesses were there, and she cultivated them. She had adopted his mannerism of flinging back garlands she received to delighted observers, especially children, and of delving into a crowd to find out for herself what was happening. Her speech from the Red Fort on August 15, 1967, an annual event, was patterned on Nehru's own. Mrs. Gandhi, who made an awkward impression as a public speaker on formal occasions before discerning audiences, when her delivery of a written speech was flat, came into her own before a crowd, where she was fluent and emphatic. On this occasion she congratulated the people on their courage and fortitude in facing drought. Warning them of difficulties ahead, she said India was in "midstream," where the water is deepest and current strongest, a rural analogy of the kind her father often used, easily understood by countryfolk used to crossing monsoon-swollen streams. She gave them "a simple definition of socialism": "Poverty should be eradicated; disparities between the rich and poor should be reduced; the backward people, be they Harijans or the hill people, should have equal distribution of national resources." And she ended with a Nehrulike flourish: "Through your veins runs the blood of heroes and great men. Let diffidence give way to confidence; let despair give way to hope. . . ." In conclusion, she asked, as her father had always done at public meetings since independence, that the crowd shout "*Jai Hind*" ("Long live India," Or "Victory to India") after her.

Her father had presided over a very different political picture from the one she now faced. Other programs and ideas, besides those presented by the Congress, were beginning to influence Indian voters. Four general elections had built an expanding and more selective political consciousness. There were choices, and the voter made use of them. The chief feature of the 1967 election was the gain of the Jan Sangh in the north, and the two Communist parties in West Bengal and the south.

Two kinds of violence had made their appearance: the Hindu-Muslim riot, of which Indians thought they had seen the last after the shock of Mahatma Gandhi's assassination, and the activities of the Naxalites. So named because of their seizure of the tribal village of Naxalbari in north Bengal (an uprising put down by the Marxist government of the state), Naxalism spread and formed cells in other states, often in universities, with a powerful attraction for sections of the educated young.

This picture showed no single ideological trend, leaving the Congress, though it had lost its privileged status, with a vital central role to play in the country, once it adjusted to post-election realities. Yet with the death of the towering figure to whom its factions— always forthright in inner-party debate—had given their allegiance, its dissident voices spoke louder. The long argument over the respective importance of its organizational and governmental wings began again. And with its loss of power in five states, the Congress now entered a phase of hard bargaining with other political parties in state assemblies. Coalitions were made and unmade by a parade of floor-crossers and defectors, as unprincipled on the part of the Congress as other parties. These gave a caustic new term to Indian politics—"*Aya Ram Gaya Ram*" ("Easy come, easy go"; with reference to defections and floor-crossings). President's rule was imposed on states where government broke down, followed by fresh elections with no firmer majorities.

Though she was still "Nehru's daughter" to the country, Mrs. Gandhi's style showed differences from his, some of them fundamental in outlook and value. In her first broadcast as prime minister, on January 26, 1966, she had spoken of "the disconcerting gap between intention and action." "To bridge this gap we should boldly adopt whatever far-reaching changes in administration may be found necessary." She repeated the theme during the year and developed it in her convocation address to Roorkee University on November 18, 1967:

> I have no doubt that our present administrative system uses the expert inadequately and indifferently. It gives undue weight to the generalist

and persists with criteria of competence developed in times when the range of Government decision was very limited and was unrelated to the demands of economic management and growth. . . . The officer mentality is also responsible for holding up progress.

Administrative reform had been the subject of expert advice and investigations since independence. With the government engaged in an enormous expansion of its activity and its bureaucracy, some of the ground it covered was experimental, directives not uniformly backed by political will, and the resulting performance uneven. This situation was to worsen, not improve, under Mrs. Gandhi who saw a "committed" civil service as essential to remedy. "Commitment" struck at the concept of the neutral civil servant, trained to advise about the risks and practicality of schemes. It left the government (many of whose members, later handpicked by her, were inexperienced in practical matters concerning administration) free to embark on poorly assessed ventures on the platform of "ideology." The civil service found itself the scapegoat for the whims and often the failures of policy. But it was the beginning of the inner structure of personal loyalty to Mrs. Gandhi that was to be the trademark of all her functioning.

"We have to ensure," said Mrs Gandhi at a meeting of the revived National Integration Council in June 1968, "that our educational processes, the books we read, the radio we hear, the films we see, do not distort the Indian mind but lead it to integration and solidarity." Her remarks were not then construed as a call for reins on the mass media, but they were the first sign that the media must be more pointedly directed by government, the first sign, too, of a policy, contrary to the principle and practice so far, that expression must be free and it was the leadership's duty to safeguard that freedom until it became part of the people's natural expectation. India had inherited a government-controlled broadcasting system from the British regime. Mrs. Gandhi, who had been minister for Information and Broadcasting in Shastri's cabinet, was the first prime minister to show a recognition of its importance as an instrument of power. In April 1971 she took charge of the portfolio herself.

Though she had at first welcomed opposition governments in the states as part of the democratic process, she later said in reply to a questionnaire from *Asia Magazine* (Hong Kong): "Fanatic and parochial forces are much in evidence. Some of them have been fomented by parties or individuals. I am deeply conscious of the danger they pose to our democracy." She found it hard to accept as "Indian" any view that did not accord with her own. ". . . our intellectuals, our industrialists and businessmen do not yet feel proud of being Indians," she told an interviewer from the Spanish magazine *Revista de Occidente*,[3] voicing her suspicion of a section of her own people for foreign readers. These attitudes, perhaps because they were so unlike her father's, paradoxically went unnoticed. Nehru had regarded an ineffective and even obstructive opposition as integral to democratic growth and had, both as philosophy and deep personal impulse, included the various elements of society as partners in progress.

Mrs. Gandhi's position within the Congress and her standing with the Old Guard, were by no means secure or friendly, and she was clearly unable to cope with what she felt was an animus directed personally at her.

> . . . every time we had a meeting of the Executive of the Parliamentary Party, there would be tension and some people would deliberately try to—I won't say insult, although it was pretty near—but needle me on any small point and make it as unpleasant as possible.[4]

Nehru had dominated the Congress, but his innate civility and courtesy had gone far in keeping diverse teams of colleagues together and had given him the personal regard of those who crossed swords with him over policy. Mrs. Gandhi's determined advocacy of herself did not endear her to men who had given their lives to the struggle for freedom, been repeatedly imprisoned, and since independence had occupied important positions, some in her father's cabinets. When in 1967 she considered taking the Congress presidentship herself after Kamaraj (as her father had done for a time), the suggestion was not approved by her party, and Nijalingappa became president. At the annual session of the Congress in Hyderabad in January 1968, six of the seven elected seats on the Working Committee went to Old Guard candidates, and only one to Mrs. Gandhi's choice. These circumstances, where she had the symbols but not the actuality of power, frustrating to pride and authority at home, may have led her from the start to establish wide personal contacts abroad. She went on her first foreign tour as prime minister in March 1966, less than two months after taking office, visiting London, Paris, Moscow, and Washington. In September 1968 she toured Latin America and the Caribbean (the first Indian prime minister to visit these areas) and visited the USA, Britain, and West Germany.

In sharp contrast with her father, too, she was ill at ease with the press. Nehru, whose relations with it were confident and cordial, met the capital's press corps once a month. Mrs. Gandhi held her third news conference in three years on January 1, 1969. The national press was generally indulgent toward her. Men who had covered her father's speeches, activities, and policies for decades and had praised or condemned him with equal fervour were apt to tread more softly with her in her inexperience and to be generous in their judgements. Her inhibitions were often puzzling to them. Frank Moraes, a leading editor, recalled, "Nehru talked a great deal in an interview. You started him off, and off he went. She is not forthcoming. She's rather like a convent schoolgirl, tongue-tied. Nehru didn't care what the newspapers said about him. With her, if there's an article, editorial or cartoon she doesn't like, one of her entourage lets her disapproval be known." Her disapproval was generally ignored by the editors and proprietors of leading newspapers, who had a healthy disrespect for authority, but it became noticeable enough after 1969 to be raised in Parliament, when Opposition M.P.s objected to governmental pressure to silence dissent.

At Mrs. Gandhi's news conference on January 1, 1969, Trevor Drieberg, Ceylon-born member of Delhi's press corps, noted more poise and confidence than she had shown since becoming prime minister. Her two flashes of temper were "whether natural or carefully stage-managed, very effective. There was more than a touch of the old Nehru fire about them. The P.M. still lives very much under the shadow of her illustrious father, as her references to him in the course of her replies showed."[5]

A critic, Rajinder Puri, later put the same view somewhat differently:

> Indira, in fact, does not have a style which she may call her own. And because the style is phony, the words ring false, with a jarring clatter against the manner she perhaps seeks to emulate, that of her father. Her every gesture, every mannerism, seems to be modelled on that of the late Jawaharlal Nehru. The hurried, almost running walk, the rambling informality, the stimulated anger with an uncomprehending public, it is all there, a trifle parodied, a little grotesque, as it evokes nostalgic memories of the original. . . .[6]

The standard people remembered was her father's, and whether the comparison was made by supporter or critic, in kind or harsh terms, it found her lacking. Yet the comparison persisted, no one yet recognizing her as being differently constituted and inspired. Her belief in her own superior knowledge and judgement dating from her tender years displayed itself once again when, on August 23, 1968, she spoke in the Rajya Sabha on the situation in Czechoslovakia. Members had objected to the government's mildly stated stand on Soviet interference, and her minister for petroleum and chemicals, Asoka Mehta, had resigned on the issue. Mrs. Gandhi said:

> I have said in the other House and I would like to repeat here, that perhaps there is nobody in this House who has had such close contacts with Czechoslovakia for so many years as I have had personally, not as a member of the Government, but ever since I was a small girl. I have known the people of the country very well, and I have known large sections of the people in the universities and in other spheres of activity.

Yet it took another year until, in the struggle for power that split the Congress and startled the country, her typical assertiveness finally burst through to the public, and people put her in a class by herself, no longer in her father's shade or mold.

CHAPTER FOUR

The Congress Breaks— 1969

On January 1, 1969, Mrs. Gandhi ended her news conference[1] with the reprimand, "I hope it will be a year of better reporting." It had not begun to her liking. A journalist had asked: "What are your views about the activities of the Young Turks who attack the Ministers and sometimes even the whole government, and who, at the same time, swear their loyalty to you?" Mrs. Gandhi replied: "I think this is for you to judge." When he persisted, she said: "We have always given considerable latitude to our party. This is not something that is happening for the first time."

Journalist: "I would like to know when it happened except when you came to power. It did not happen when Shastriji was here, much less when your father was in office."

Prime Minister to the company: "I am sorry, he is not well-informed. It happened many times when my father was in office."

Journalist: "Could you give me one instance?"

Prime Minister: "This is not a cross-examination. I resent the tone of the question. I am not going to be spoken to like that."

This crisp rejoinder, put down to the Nehru temperament, was however different in kind from the brief flares enlivening Nehru's speeches and conferences. Mrs. Gandhi did not feel the need to explain or argue. Questions she did not like could simply be cut short by a reminder of who she was. And here she showed a flash of irritation at the unfavorable contrast drawn, by implication, between her and her father. The above exchange is interesting, too, for its light on the vocal emergent radicals in the party known as the Young Turks, whose broadsides against members of the government were attracting notice as being unusually outspoken criticism for public consumption. Mrs. Gandhi's protection of this growing personal following, hostile to men in her own government, was a noticeable enough departure from the past to be taken up at a news conference.

In mid-February 1969, midterm elections in five states showed a continuing downhill slide for the Congress. Mrs. Gandhi's own equanimity at this time, a particularly bleak time for her party, may have resulted directly from this political picture. Important members of the Old Guard had been defeated in the last general election, while her own following was developing into a vigorous and distinct camp. The balance of power in the Congress was changing with the tilt in her favor.

The newspapers commented on the decline of the Congress with gloom, speculating about the new crop of fortune hunters, the unprincipled defections encouraged by all parties, and the danger to democracy in these circumstances. On March 19, 1969, the *Indian Express* commented editorially on the uneasy relationships between the Congress Party and the government and even within the cabinet:

> . . . if the Congress breaks up, it will be calamitous for the country. . . . Mrs. Gandhi is at times prone to ruffle her colleagues by her speech. More often she is apt to startle them by her studied silence. . . . This habit of mind and approach does not make for happy individual relations, or for the smooth conduct of public affairs. . . . Collective Cabinet responsibility is the cornerstone of our Constitution. Lapses from the principle account for much of the misunderstandings and controversies generated in recent weeks. . . . A close understanding between the Congress Party President and the Prime Minister is overdue.

A highly unusual situation had arisen out of Mrs. Gandhi's "habit of mind and approach." Effective consultation and discussion with her cabinet and party were nearly at a standstill. This editorial appeal for "collective Cabinet responsibility" did not, however, take into account the personality of the leader who, confident now of a party following, saw no reason for cooperation with men she needed much less than before.

That the Congress was not one happy family had been evident for some time. Trevor Drieberg wrote of the Congress session at Faridabad in April: "The time has come when Young Turk and Old Gandhian can no longer hang together—even if the alternative is hanging separately."[2] But the division between young and old, radical and Gandhian, Left and Right was by no means so plain or simple. Between the Young Turks, now grouped behind Mrs. Gandhi for radical changes in the country, and the Old Guard, whom they accused of holding the national scene static, there was a general body of convinced moderates who preferred to proceed with caution and usually carried the day. There was now, in addition, the need for stocktaking. Congress, held in thrall by Nehru's charisma during his life time, now seemed about to reexamine some of the sacred texts of policy in the light of the country's new priorities and the electorate's verdict. Shastri had introduced some personal preferences in policy—small-scale projects and the completion of large ones, rather than new investments in the public sector and attention to neighbors rather than the global involvement India had pursued in Nehru's time. This post-Nehru development, cut short with Shastri's death, was viewed with grave suspicion by Congress radicals, who now projected the issue before the party as socialism or its sabotage. There were obvious fallacies in a lineup so categorical, within a party whose historic position had been centrist by choice. In their bitterest ideological battles, Congressmen had found scope for cooperation. Defeat had been graciously conceded, and the victor had shown magnanimity. Periodically, the party had shed its fringes, both radical and conservative. In 1947 the Congress Socialist Party had left its parent body to become the independent Socialist Party because the Congress program did not go far enough in radicalism. In 1959 C. Rajagopalachari had broken away, to found the conservative Swatantra Party. Reacting strongly against the cooperative farming resolution adopted by the Nagpur Congress (the annual convention of the party held in Nagpur) in January that year, he had flatly rejected the idea of cooperative cultivation, "except in countries where private personal property is absent and forced labour is commandeered under Communist regimes."[3]

A determined fighter for greater economic definition against the communal and conservative elements in the Congress, Nehru had been at pains to keep its frictions within bounds and prevent a schism. Both national integration and development demanded a strong unifying focus. His own domination of the party had been accepted because, apart from the shared adventure of the national movement and the enduring human ties it had created, the party saw him as a national inspiration, indispensable to its own success and significance. Nehru's unique position within it remained tempered by inner-party criticism, by his recognition of state leadership, by his view of Congress strength as basically a local strength, and by the reliance others placed on his code of ethics and conduct. In the impasse now developing between Mrs. Gandhi and the Congress, no comparable cushioning existed, either of an unassailable personal and political position to her credit or of give-and-take, to shield the party from the shocks it was about to receive. Distant thunder, heralding a storm, hung in the air at the Faridabad session.

President Zakir Husain died a few days after the session, and the choice of his successor precipitated a showdown between Mrs. Gandhi and the Congress president. Zakir Husain had been Mrs. Gandhi's personal choice for the country's president. His death removed a reliable political lever from her side. The president could, on the prime minister's advice, dissolve Parliament and order a new election. Her opponents in her party believed this had been Mrs. Gandhi's main hold on Congress M.P.s, who did not want to face another election so soon after the recent debacle. The situation could go against her with a new, unsympathetic president if enough Congress M.P.s expressed a lack of confidence in their leader and asked the president to assure himself of the extent of her support. The choice of the country's president became crucial for both Congress factions, whose poor opinion of each other had for some time been ill-concealed. The nature of the clash that followed lifted it out of political or party confines and gave the country its first glimpse of an intractable character.

Mrs. Gandhi, in consultation with colleagues, considered several names—V. V. Giri, Jagjivan Ram, Swaran Singh, and Sanjiva Reddy—and agreed to Reddy. Soon afterward she became convinced Reddy was not "her" man, that the party bosses would use him to test her strength in Parliament and remove her from the prime ministership. She had every reason to believe this might happen. Her performance as prime minister had not impressed senior leaders, and her aloof imperiousness had been resented. Her removal, in the same orderly way as she had been elevated, was entirely possible. Her opponents would maneuver in the manner of professional politicians through the usual politicians channels, as they had done in the past, to gain acceptance for a candidate of their choice. This was a fight she could not be sure of winning. Her technique would have to be different. It started with a campaign of rumor to establish Reddy as the bosses' choice, not hers, though individuals in her camp urged her to declare her open support for V. V. Giri, vice-president.

Mrs. Gandhi then sent a note on economic policy to precede her arrival in Bangalore, where the Congress Parliamentary Board was meeting to elect its candidate for the country's president. She described it as "a few stray thoughts" on the need to "re-state our economic policy and set the direction in which we have to move to achieve our goal."

The note was indicative of the lack of cohesion in recent Congress functioning. The "stray thoughts" broadly repeated the Working Committee resolution of May 1967, known as the Ten-Point Programme. Among these were nationalization of general insurance, removal of monopolies, curbs on property, state control over exports and food grains, "social control" of banks, and the abolition of princely privileges. The Working Committee meeting had been poorly attended, with no detailed study beforehand of the items on its agenda. The thorough preparation characterizing policy discussions in the past was absent, as was a proper consideration of each item. The program, superficially discussed, was adopted. During its ratification by the All India Congress Committee, the abolition of princely privileges was extended to purses, and social control of banks was changed to nationalization. Almost immediately controversy over the Ten Points began. Mrs. Gandhi's cabinet did not agree to them all. In October 1967 her cabinet reverted to social control of banks, to be operated by a national credit council run by the Reserve Bank, to give more aid to agriculture, small industry, and exports. Lacking the vivid gesture of outright nationalization, Morarji Desai argued it was capable of achieving more solid benefits.

The "stray thoughts" sent to Bangalore would, therefore, have been better argued exhaustively, even battled for decisively within the policy-making forum of the party, rather than, as followed, taken as theater to the streets. Mrs. Gandhi's purpose was to make it clear the initative for party programs was to be hers, at governmental level, and was not to rest with the organization. Theater, too, was intended as publicity to illustrate this parting of the ways and establish her undisputed authority over the organization. Bank nationalization, one of the "stray thoughts," was soon to symbolize the new era of radicalism.

The party, still unclear about the Ten Points, accepted Mrs. Gandhi's note in the interests of peace, and it was commended to the Union and state governments, a victory to Mrs. Gandhi, but the Congress Parliamentary Board elected Sanjiva Reddy as its official candidate with five votes against two (Mrs. Gandhi and Fakhruddin Ali Ahmed) for Jagjivan Ram. Mrs. Gandhi told the press next day that the board's decision was a "calculated attempt" to humiliate her and to challenge her authority as prime minister. She thus gave public notice that she would fight any attempt to undermine her position. Her father, twice overruled by the board when it chose Dr. Rajendra Prasad for the presidency in 1952 and again in 1957, had both times accepted its decision.

Mrs. Gandhi's answer to being ignored was to retaliate with a dose of the same medicine. A week later she made the surprise announcement of the nationalization of fourteen leading banks, by-passing the party to make a direct impact on the public. The manner of the measure, by ordinance—though Parliament was to open in two days—was as sensational as the measure itself. Before taking this step, she relieved Morarji Desai of the Finance portfolio, though she offered him another berth. Desai chose to resign, and Mrs. Gandhi took over Finance herself. This lightning strike at independence from her party sent a tremor of excitement through the country. With its apparent disdain for party forum and for due processes of law, the prime minister's action removed some invisible restraint and decorum from public and political behavior. Politics flared overnight into the streets. Rallies were arranged daily outside Mrs. Gandhi's residence, to congratulate her on bank nationalization and acclaim her leadership. The use of money and transport to bring workers to meetings, along with government's control of radio, had always given the ruling party an edge over others. But this was the first time street demonstrations had been staged by a prime minister. Their size and regularity and the expertise now in evidence had the gloss of preparation and planning, and of the Communist genius for efficient organization. Also recognizable Communist technique was Mrs. Gandhi's vocabulary of class war and the cry that all who were not with her were against her.

Mrs. Gandhi and her camp did not anticipate the breakup of the Congress, nor did they desire it. But, as the crisis proceeded, it became evident that unity was not a concern either, unless the party put her in sole command. That she would settle for nothing less and saw the battle through to rupture seemed to indicate her plans were not of an order acceptable to the party's broad centrist approach and that a sharp turn in its affairs was intended. To bring this about, the Old Guard had to be discredited, so that the new leadership could emerge without the taint of the old. At the same time homage to Mahatma Gandhi and Nehru—essential for a hold on the masses—had to be maintained. Both these objectives were brilliantly accomplished in a series of moves resembling a coup, leaving Mrs. Gandhi's opponents confounded and confused. The rallies at her residence blazoned bank nationalization as a people's measure, pushed through against vested interests in the Congress. They marked the beginning of populist politics and a leadership cult. With its dynastic, emotional flavor, the cult highlighted the theme of Mrs. Gandhi's uniqueness among her contemporaries and her special claim to patriotism by virtue of her Nehru blood. A souvenir, *Re-birth of the Congress*, published in December, featured an extract from a book by Mrs. Gandhi's late aunt, Krishna Hutheesing: "In her veins flows the blood of her father and grandfather . . . like the Ganga she belongs to India and India is the one passion of her life."

This sentiment was more poetic than accurate. Though she belonged imaginatively to India, Mrs. Gandhi was probably less a product of the Indian environment than any contemporary in Congress circles. She had, intermittently with her Indian schooling, attended schools in Switzerland and England. Her father had never considered an Indian university for her. His own education had been British, and his plans for his daughter reflected this preference. Nehru had written to Mrs. Pandit from Badenweiler on November 15, 1935, when Indira was four days short of her eighteenth birthday:

The problem of Indu's further education is not an easy one to solve. Practically all the countries, excepting England, France and Switzerland are barred for some reason or other. . . . After a great deal of thought I came to the conclusion that she might go to Oxford in October 1936 and after completing her three years there, proceed to Paris for a year or so, subject to political developments on the continent. . . . The examination for October 1936 takes place in December 1935, that is, next month. Indu cannot appear for it so soon. The next examination is early in 1937 for October 1937, which means that Indu has to wait for two years before she joins Oxford. That is rather a long time. A year would have been the right period and would have suited her, for she is not quite grown up enough, intellectually or otherwise, for the university. . . . For the present I propose to send Indu, probably next week, to Mlle. Hemmelin at Bex. . . . From October 1936 onward for about a year she might be in Paris attending lectures at the Sorbonne, and if so decided, taking the Somerville entrance and scholarship exam early in 1937. . . .

V. V. Giri declared his candidature for the presidency when Mrs. Gandhi failed to get Jagjivan Ram accepted by the Parliamentary Board. She had filed Reddy's nomination papers and, as prime minister, still ostensibly supported her party's candidate, but the campaign had become a prestige issue for her, and it was an open secret that she did not intend to abide by her commitment.

This explosive change from the political style of her two predecessors lit up Mrs. Gandhi's individual approach in a way that none of her statements and emphases had done till now. The dynamic for political action had earlier issued from the national movement, from the multilayered following of Mahatma Gandhi constituting a great social force, and its continuance by Nehru into the independence era. The earlier phase had been distinguished by the discipline of nonviolence. After independence the Indian scene remained unusual in Asia because of the restrained, educated tone the leadership employed in seeking the cooperation of a vast, unlettered electorate for the understanding and solution of long-term problems. This atmosphere began to be rapidly dissipated. In search of support, Mrs. Gandhi had found the CPI, anxious for political respectability and power, eager to cooperate. The skillful use of economic conditions and the vivid vocabulary of class war as political weapons yielded rapid initial dividends. The campaign of street arousal introduced a throbbing undercurrent of exaggeration, excess, and violence, waiting like electricity to be switched on.

The national newspapers expressed their downright dismay at these developments, seeing them as a virulent struggle for power carried too far for the country's good, and deplored the inflaming of uninformed sentiment by dramatic methods and catchy slogans. When the Supreme Court issued an interim stay order on bank nationalization, this, together with the reservations of the national press, gave Mrs. Gandhi cause to say "the people" were with her, while "vested interests" were not.

Meanwhile the quarrel over the presidential candidate raged furious. Till this election, it had been a routine affair decided by mutual consultation between parties so that the highest office in the land—one above politics—should not become a matter for political bargaining. Mrs. Gandhi accused Nijalingappa of "collusion" with the Right parties, Jan Sangh and Swatantra, over the choice of the presidential candidate. It had been accepted practice to solicit the votes of other parties for one's own candidate, and the Jan Sangh and Swatantra had agreed to support Reddy, though the two Communist parties had declared for Giri. In the new political atmosphere, the arrangement acquired the ring of betrayal and Nijalingappa the label of "reactionary" in a precision attack directed against his political integrity. The threatening mood of the party's radicals prompted him to ask Mrs. Gandhi to issue a whip to Congress M.P.s to vote for Reddy. On August 15, five days before the election, Mrs. Gandhi called instead for a "vote of conscience," saying, "I feel that the issues go beyond the presidential poll." That morning her speech at the Red Fort had referred to the "tremendous and spontaneous reception" bank nationalization had received. "Today we have taken a new turn and a new dawn has set in. . . . I want to assure the rich and the capitalists that the step we have taken is not directed against them."

Mrs. Gandhi's personal and public image—indeed her political future—were heavily dependent on the election result, and it is interesting to speculate on the turn of events had Giri been defeated. He won by a narrow margin in the second count, with 420,077 votes in his favor and 405, 527 against him. This was the signal for a fresh turnout of rallies and street celebrations outside the prime minister's house. Nijalingappa called the "personality cult a mischievous and dangerous trend in democracy," but with his candidate's defeat he and his supporters had suffered an irreparable loss of face. When the Working Committee met in New Delhi on August 25, Y. B. Chavan, minister for Home Affairs, attempted to hold the party together by means of a "unity resolution" separating the scope and tasks of its parliamentary and organizational wings. However, Mrs. Gandhi did not attend the meeting, and her supporters held an angry demonstration at Congress headquarters at 7 Jantar Mantar Road while the meeting was in progress, in defiance of the prohibitory orders then in force. The demonstration, organized by Shashi Bhushan, M.P., consisted of more than the M.P.s who officially constituted it. Rajinder Puri, journalist, gives the following account:

When I approached the spot there was a great commotion going on. The demonstrators, a few hundred of them, stood in the middle of the road in front of the Congress Party office building, waiting to leap into their orgy of screams and abuse, of kicking, shoving and spitting, as each member of the Working Committee drove up to attend its meeting, Mrs. Gandhi and all her supporters having boycotted it. Most of the journalists were inside the gates on the lawn, while she stood outside it watching the spectacle. Movie cameramen from the Government Films Division and the TV men from the Ministry of Information and Broadcasting stood in strategic positions with their cameras posed to record for posterity and cinemas throughout the country the historic scenes of mass upsurge being enacted there on that otherwise quiet, mild autumn day in Delhi. . . . They were all in at last, only C. B. Gupta coming in without any mishap as his car drove into the gateway through the milling demonstrators, C. B. himself smartly rapping a cane on the knuckles of those who had the temerity to push their hands through the window of the car. . . . Poor Nijalingappa walked all the way through the yelling screeching demonstrators, barefoot, with footwear in hand, and his glasses slipping all over his face. . . . There were two aspects of it which were particularly ugly. These were for the most part old men, incapable of violence, who were being threatened in such cowardly fashion. . . . The police prevented any real violence from taking place, it is true, but they did not prevent the demonstrators from offering real provocation for a violent retaliation, which naturally could never come from Nijalingappa and company. . . . The more disturbing aspect, however, was the fact that in the capital of India this ugly demonstration with fascist overtones was not only allowed to take place but actually encouraged by the government. . . .[4]

The "unity resolution" was accepted by the party, but the war between its factions, now out in the open, continued. Mrs. Gandhi launched a signature drive for an early session of the AICC (All India Congress Committee) to elect a new president, though Nijalingappa's term was not over. Nijalingappa called this a violation of party discipline and asked her to explain her conduct. But the legalities and proprieties now looked anemic next to Mrs. Gandhi's bank nationalization coup and the election of V. V. Giri. She received the presidential seal of approval for her conduct when Mrs. Giri, receiving her joyfully after her husband's victory, welcomed Mrs. Gandhi as "my darling daughter." On November 8 Mrs. Gandhi released a Letter to Congressmen:"

What we witness today is not a mere clash of personalities, and certainly not a fight for power. It is not as simple as a conflict between the parliamentary and organisational wings. It is a conflict between two outlooks and attitudes in regard to the objectives of the Congress and the methods in which Congress itself should function.

The letter established her personal links with the Congress past and her special claim to the Mahatma Gandhi-Nehru inheritance:

> The Congress was moulded by Mahatma Gandhi and my father to be the prime instrument of social change. . . . In his last years my father was greatly concerned that there were people inside the Congress who were offering resistance to change. My own experience even before the fourth general election was that the forces of status quo, with close links with powerful economic interests, were ranged against me.

On November 12 Nijalingappa expelled her from the Congress, and the break was complete when two parallel AICC sessions were held in Delhi on November 22. In December rival Congress sessions were held at Ahmedabad (Nijalingappa) and Bombay (Mrs. Gandhi). The *Hindustan Times* noted that "there was little specific to differentiate them." K. Rangachari, economic analyst, writing in the *Statesman* on January 5, 1970, agreed that "the economic manifestoes of the two Congress factions have much in common as they both take the 10-point programme of the undivided Party as their starting point. In the context of the controversy raised over the sincerity of their pursuit of socialism, neither wished to yield to the other in its desire to appear more radical. . . ."

Rangachari detailed the economic steps the undivided Congress had taken toward socialism, comparing them with the measures taken or proposed by Mrs. Gandhi's Congress at Bombay. The first social measure taken in independent India had been the nationalization of the Imperial Bank of India, which gave the state

> a commanding height in the banking system, which along with the Reserve Bank's control of monetary policy, gave all the power it required to make the banking system subserve the needs of planning and industrial development. The takeover of fourteen more banks last year has merely extended the public sector's share in banking from one-third to four-fifths . . . achieved at the cost of creating misgivings in many quarters about future policy, and jettisoning the principles of the mixed economy . . . the nationalisation of life insurance in 1956 . . . transferred large public funds to Government; the proposed nationalisation of general insurance [by Mrs. Gandhi's Congress] is unlikely to provide anything equally substantial either in terms of resources or of opportunities of improving public welfare, since general

insurance does not touch the life of the ordinary citizen in the way life insurance did.

The right of property had earlier been modified:

> The exemption of 64 State laws on land reform from the scope of the fundamental rights, the exclusion of the courts' jurisdiction on questions of adequacy of compensation, sanction for interference with the rights of joint stock companies, and for modification of mining leases, and the wide definition given to the term "estate", together constituted a major assault on property rights. It is significant that on the present occasion the radicals could only think of abolishing the fundamental right to property altogether.

He listed the tax measures already taken toward the socialist orientation of economic policy: estate duty (1953), capital gains (1956), taxes on wealth, expenditure, gifts, company dividends, and bonus shares. In 1960 Morarji Desai had introduced the corporation tax as a separate entity and the super profits tax. Desai was responsible, too, for the gold control order, initiated when he was finance minister in Nehru's cabinet, "as a measure of social reform to discourage the craze for gold ornaments."

> And the outstanding contribution to the socialist ideology was, of course, the massive investments in the public sector under three Five Year Plans which gave the State a dominant position.... State undertakings in industry alone have claimed more than Rs. 3,000 crores; to this has to be added large outlays on irrigation, power, shipping, air and railway transport. The commanding heights are now all in the public sector. The State Trading Corporation occupies an important position, in both the import and export trade.... Her [Mrs. Gandhi's] theory of obstruction cannot therefore stand scrutiny.

I myself assessed the Congress split in 1969 and the main current thereafter as a publicized "radicalism," which masked the entrenchment of personal rule:

> During the months since the Working Committee last met as one body on August 25, the government has put on a performance worthy of the best gangster tradition in politics. With the throwing aside of its own party's constitution . . . with the summoning of mass rallies . . . and with the full use of all its powers in its intraparty warfare, it has launched a new unprincipled era in Indian politics. . . . The word "leader" has assumed menacing proportion. Apparently it no longer

requires answerability to a party. . . . It denotes personal rule with all the dangers inherent therein. . . ."[5]

. . . what the Indian people have achieved in two decades of toil and aspiration may soon be blotted out in the interests neither of socialism nor revolution, but merely of brazen power.[6]

The Congress split and the way it was brought about transformed the political atmosphere. Nehru and Shastri, inheriting the Gandhian approach to politics, with its marriage of ends and means, had personally practised and upheld a meticulous standard of political behavior. Mrs. Gandhi's role in the presidential election had been one of manipulation and intrigue, and her strategy to gain control of her party had displayed a militancy foreign to Congress tradition. She represented something ruthless and new. She had astonished people with her flair for cold assessment, shrewd timing, and the telling theatrical gesture; above all, with her capacity for a fight to the finish, even to bringing the eighty-four-year-old party of liberation to rupture. She had made use of realpolitik, suiting the action to the moment's need, undeterred by any backlog of sentiment or ethics. Her own emergence from an image of extreme withdrawal and reserve was now complete.

The effect on her party was immediate. A swing to the winning side began, with the majority deserting the sinking ship of the Old Congress. Morality was not, in any case, the order of the day. Jagjivan Ram, one of Mrs. Gandhi's crucial supporters during the split, had not, it now appeared, filed tax returns for ten years. Questioned about this at a meeting of the Press Club in New Delhi, Mrs. Gandhi remarked that he was a busy man and had probably forgotten. Jagjivan Ram, who controlled the Untouchable vote, was an important ally. He was obliged in the glare of publicity to pay his taxes but, at a time when stringent laws for default existed, not penalized for the delay. His forgetfulness provided excellent material for the cartoonists and more acid comment on the political scene.

The shine had rubbed off most politicians for a country that was tired of their calls for sacrifice from their own safe and comfortable berths. Mrs. Gandhi evoked considerable public admiration for having outmaneuvered them all, the exponent of a tough new breed. She later described herself in much the same terms: "My father was a saint who strayed into politics. I am a tough politician." The public hoped that her toughness, along with fresh blood in the organization, might provide the momentum the country needed. She had sympathy in abundance for her fight against boss-ism and the enthusiasm of many who hoped for the "new dawn" she had spoken of at the Red Fort. As a child she had imagined herself a Joan of Arc, leading her people into battle. To this, her public relations office now added the more relevant Indian image of Rani Lakshmibai of Jhansi, who had so valiantly led her army against the British during the Revolt of 1857. She was no longer the mere leader of a party; she was now projected as the agent of a historic process, women of destiny, champion of the poor, in touch with the people's urges and aspirations, and uniquely qualified to lead them. She was now in command over a thoroughly roused public, to whom she had promised a new era in socialism in the language of incitement and emotion. The outward resemblance to her father was over, and this showed most clearly on the public platform. Nehru's speeches had had a quality of intimacy with the crowd. A huge assembly became for him a person and a "speech" a conversation. He was given to displaying his doubts, to self-searching, to taking the people he addressed into his confidence. It is likely that the unsophisticated, who formed the bulk of his audiences, came to listen to a chat, albeit about grave and solemn affairs of state. The political air one breathes affects the talk in streets, market places, and drawing rooms. The talk had flowed over a scene extraordinarily lacking in political tension. Mrs. Gandhi's pent-up intensity, finding release on the public platform, charged the atmosphere with peculiar tension.

Her successful disregard of the proprieties had paved the way for her to begin to exercise a degree of open authoritarianism. On December 13, 1969, the Union government issued a directive to State Governors at their annual conference in Delhi, telling them they had "unfettered freedom" to use their ultimate weapon: pres-ident's rule. The dictatorial use of powers by governors became the subject of Opposition protest in the Lok Sabha. The directive con-trasted with Nehru's to governors in 1949 and 1952, reminding them they were constitutional heads and that a governor "should not and cannot override or interfere with the decisions of his cabinet who are responsible to the State legislature."

A month earlier Mrs. Gandhi's younger son, Sanjay, had ap-plied, along with seventeen other applicants, for a licence to man-ufacture an indigenous small car. The following November he be-came the sole recipient of a licence and undertook to produce

50,000 cars a year, roughly equivalent to the whole annual production of cars in India in a good year. His principal backer was K. K. Birla. The Birla family's best political investment had been Mahatma Gandhi, and it had continued close to the Congress leadership after independence.

CHAPTER FIVE

The New Congress Reveals Its Style—1970

When Parliament opened on November 17, 1969, the government, represented by Mrs. Gandhi's New Congress, found itself in a minority, with sixty M.P.s of the undivided Congress now sitting in the Opposition. But it had a working majority with the support of regional parties and some independents. Its vital support came from the CPI, whose style and slant began to be felt in some of the ministries. In spite of her reduced numbers, Mrs. Gandhi was in a buoyant mood. The Congress split had secured for her an independent identity, status, and following. She told the Indian Science Congress on January 4, 1970: "The last few months have been exciting ones. Swift and dramatic events have taken place. As a result, you will find everywhere a sense of quivering urgency, an atmosphere of heightened expectations and a demand for quick results." She delivered a uniform message at mass meetings through the year: the need for reducing disparities, and for ceilings on property and land. The country faced danger, she said, from those who wanted to block socialist policies. She would implement these undaunted by the canards spread against her.

She did not specify the "canards" except on one occasion after the Emergency of 1975, when she told a delegation from Nehru Youth Centers of "baseless canards" spread by the Opposition that she smoked and drank. Her opponents, referred to in her letter to Congressmen on November 8, 1969 as "the forces of the status quo, with close links with powerful economic interests," could not by definition include the Socialist Party and the CPI-M, committed since their inception to radical change. It did not apply to the Old Congress, till yesterday her own party, dominated till the end of his life by her father, and responsible for the vistas of change since independence. With all its scope for elasticity and interpretation, it was avowedly a socialist party and would not have survived as a credible entity but for this. The terminology she employed did not apply even to the Jan Sangh, whose interest in the status quo was based on religion and culture rather than economics, and whose "links with powerful economic interests" were negligible, nearly nonexistent, compared with those of the undivided Congress, and later so publicly identified with Mrs. Gandhi's party. Her forceful, insistent, and repetitious language, when analyzed, seemed puzzlingly remote from actual data. What did Mrs. Gandhi mean? What she meant was further complicated by the pervasive personal element in her statements. Her letter to Congressmen said there was an opposition to her personally, bent on keeping her out of power. Earlier she had construed the vote of the Congress Parliamentary Board for Reddy (rather than Jagjivan Ram) as an insult and a "plot" against her, not the prosaic procedural exercise it was, of outvoting the leader as leaders are regularly outvoted and replaced by their parties. The dislike and distrust her former colleagues had of her— dull, inadequate material for drama—was converted by her intensely imaginative faculty into the grander stuff of hate and fear of a more-than-leader, a national symbol. Her own utterances invented the beleaguered heroine, fighting the shadowy forces of evil, one whose victory or defeat would be the victory or defeat of socialism in India.

Did Mrs. Gandhi's colleagues mean the same thing she meant? The confusion arising at times out of official statements blurred issues and debates. A haze descended on argument and was, it seemed, deliberately held there. The New Congress had broken with the old so that it would be free to move decisively Leftward, but Left was most of the modern Indian horizon, from the Mahatma's socialism to that inspired by Marx. Where in the spectrum did the New Congress lie, and what did it want? What was needed, at this time of absolute break with the old party, was clear explanation, and this was lacking. Cries against the "rich," the "big," and the "monopolists" rose with a great stir and beating of wings, like flocks of birds into the air and vanished. No one quietly nailed problems to the ground. "Commitment" was demanded of the civil service, the judiciary and the press. Yet it meant not an educated sensitivity to what was best for the common welfare, but government control, an idea so repugnant to these institutions of free India that it had stormy repercussions. On February 9 Mrs. Gandhi was obliged to say: "Recently my remarks that we needed government servants with commitment have been, perhaps deliberately, misinterpreted to mean that I want civil servants to support me and my political ideology. On the contrary, I do not want politically convenient or servile civil servants." Yet Mohan Kumaramangalam, distinguished CPI theoretician, now in Mrs. Gandhi's Congress and credited with having an increasing influence on her policies, said plainly that the government needed "civil servants who thought like us."[1] Kumaramangalam, who entered the cabinet as Minister for Steel and Mines in April 1971 and was probably its chief spokesman after Mrs. Gandhi, gave "commitment" its final seal of authority on May 2, 1973 in the Lok Sabha, when he defended the supersession of three judges of the Supreme Court—Justices Shelat, Hegde, and Grover—and the appointment of a junior judge, A. N. Ray, as chief justice. In naming a chief justice, he said, "the government is entitled to look into his philosophy and outlook and decide that we must have a forward-looking and not a backward-looking man." It was clear what a Communist meant when he said this, and in government pronouncements only its CPI spokesmen spoke in understandable language and with recognizable intent. This particular step, designed to bring the Supreme Court in line with the government, proved crucial in later events for Mrs. Gandhi's political survival. A. N. Ray, chosen for his acceptability to the CPI coterie in Mrs. Gandhi's camp, was a good example of the "commitment" required of the judiciary. Had the principle of selection of a chief justice, on the basis of quality rather than seniority, been explained and suitably canvased, it is probable that it would have won many adherents and been hailed as a reform in the judicial system. Ray's appointment had no such high purpose to recommend it.

In 1970, at the beginning of the controversy, events had not yet forced definition, and confusion reigned supreme. Mrs. Gandhi told the Rajya Sabha in early March 1970 that she believed in democracy and an independent judiciary. What she meant was again in question when the governor of West Bengal, S. S. Dhavan, speaking to the Bar Association and Bar Library Club of the Calcutta High Court, held up the Soviet legal and political system as an example to his audience. Mrs. Gandhi's own actions clouded her meaning in what was becoming a simmering confrontation with the Supreme Court. On February 10, 1970, the Court had struck down as invalid the Act of 1969 nationalizing fourteen banks. Mrs. Gandhi overcame this by a presidential ordinance on February 14 renationalizing the banks with retrospective effect from July 19, 1969. This was the first of several presidential ordinances used to enact business outside the parliamentary process, with Parliament in due course endorsing the measure taken. Government by ordinance, used at first to push through measures she could not get accepted by Parliament for want of a majority and her otherwise free use of presidential powers, became a marked feature of her style and demonstrated how valuable a cooperative president was to her concept of government. In September 1970 a presidential order was used to derecognize the princes when the government bill to abolish privy purses and privileges failed by one vote to get a two-thirds majority in the Rajya Sabha, though the Lok Sabha adopted it. On October 1 President's Rule was imposed with undue haste on Uttar Pradesh, and the proclamation suspending the state legislature signed on Russian soil, the president being on a visit to the Soviet Union at the time. An obvious and unseemly political maneuver, it had to be revoked after sixteen days of controversy, when Charan Singh, BKD (Bharatiya Kranti Dal) leader, whose coalition had fallen apart with the sudden desertion of its New Congress members, formed a majority government without them.

The privy purse issue, and the vote concerning it in the Lok Sabha, provided a contrast with the receding values of the Nehru era. The abolition of privy purses had been raised at the AICC in 1963. Nehru had opposed abolition on the ground that the figure of Rs 50 million was automatically going down, each successor inheriting a reduced purse. Another more fundamental consideration ruled his approach: the Government of India had a covenant with the princes, and a government must keep its word. Writing to his sister, India's high commissioner in London, on April 3, 1955 on the subject of foreign investment and the government of India's attitude toward it, he had expressed much the same sentiment:

> It never pays to destroy one's credit in the foreign market, and we have no intention of doing anything which might have that effect. Also, all major investments by foreigners are usually by contract with the Government of India. For the Government to break its own contract would be bad. Governments do not do this kind of thing. Therefore there is really no question of apprehension on the part of foreign investors in India. I have made this clear already in parliament and

elsewhere. This evening I spoke at length at a huge public meeting in Delhi and again made this clear. I shall refer to it when the Bill comes up before Parliament again.

The bill to abolish privy purses got the required two-thirds majority in the Lok Sabha by a narrow margin of eight votes. Opposition members discovered six were invalid, as five voters had recorded their vote twice "by mistake," and one vote had been recorded for a member not present in the House. The Speaker agreed to hold an inquiry, but declared himself satisfied that the majority had not been affected. An episode which for its impropriety would have had repercussions of shock under Nehru and Shastri, and would have been cleared to the satisfaction of the Opposition in order to restore faith in parliamentary procedure, was glossed over. The Speaker's reputation for impartiality suffered as did the standards expected till then of Parliament.

In March 1970 Mrs. Gandhi told the Rajya Sabha: "At any moment if any privately owned industry is operating against the national interest or is impeding social progress, we should not hesitate to take it over." But since "national interest" and "social progress" had not been reduced to directives, it was not predictable what direction government's economic policy might at any moment take, and in what context industry should plan to operate.

In contrast with this (perhaps deliberate) lack of philosophy, a specific direction was taken by the government during the year in matters concerning information and culture. On February 20, 1970, diplomatic missions were required to close culture centers other than those located at their headquarters. This followed the discovery of an unauthorized Russian building under construction in Trivandrum, but the effect of the order was to shut down five offices of the United States Information Service and two French centers. The Soviet embassy gave the running of its Trivandrum center to the Indian government, on whom it could rely for patronage to its programs. By the end of 1970, although foreign culture centers had been closed, there were 115 embassy journals in circulation. The government's Publications Division annual *India 1971–72* listed forty-seven, the highest number, produced by the USSR, and seventeen, the second highest, by the USA.

On August 23 the BBC was ordered to close its office in India for showing Louis Malle's film on India, with its reported concentration on the grimmer sights of Calcutta. Later the import of American movies was stopped, on the ground that there was no reciprocity in the film trade between the two countries. Film selection and imports were to be channeled through the State Trading Corporation. Later (1973) the STC was authorized to take over the import of textbooks, and it was suggested the control might be extended to general books to prevent "pornographic" and "politically offensive" books from entering the country.

The free circulation of information and ideas had been a cardinal principle of India's leadership. Mrs. Gandhi's incursions, actual and projected, into the fields of knowledge, information, and culture were evidence of another value system altogether. She was heavily dependent at this time on Communist support and had former CPI members as ministers and advisers. This may have accounted for the categorical line she took and her monotonous espousal of the obstructionist theory, calculated by sheer repetition to gain credence, especially among the uneducated population. There was a Communist stamp also to her violent aversion to the "uncommitted" intellectual, the Opposition, and the press. Yet she had herself earlier advocated greater government control of the media. During the presidential election, radio and television had effectively projected V. V. Giri as the candidate with her blessing, and herself as the symbol of a mass upsurge against vested interests. It is reasonable to assume that her mind and its direction were her own. She displayed an awareness of the vital levels of power once again when on June 26, 1970, in a major cabinet reshuffle, she took the Home portfolio herself. This gave her control of the intelligence network and the police, and supervision of the Election Commission. The Research and Analysis Wing (RAW), as the intelligence network was named, operated, in part, under Mrs. Gandhi's direct command, though in name it was made accountable to the cabinet secretariat. RAW did not remain an anonymous, behind-the-scenes agency, but became an actor on the political stage, with the press commenting on its activities, including the bugging of telephones of government's political opponents, censorship of their mail, and the impressive growth within a few years of its five-crore (50 million) rupee budget to 100 crores (1,000 million). RAW was also reported to provide Mrs. Gandhi with dossiers on Union and state ministers and officers of the rank equivalent to brigadier and above of the armed forces. Commenting on its methods, Jyotirmoy Basu

(CPI-M) told a meeting of the Home Ministry's Consultative Committee in Parliament:

> On April 20, 1972, while speaking during the demands for grants for the Ministry of Home Affairs, I said that the Research and Analysis Wing formulates, operates and executes through fascist methods; with it came subsidiary bureaus and other sister organisations. The function is to keep Left forces out of power, destroy democratic methods and oppose by all possible means the persons and political parties which are against the ruling coterie headed by Mrs. Gandhi. . . . My information is that seven unprinted, unmarked crates arrived in Bombay dockyard a few months ago which were not even touched by the customs or port authorities under instructions from the top. The same day these boxes disappeared for Delhi. The Research and Analysis Wing is being organized purely on the lines of the Hitlerite forces, and its sole job is to destroy democracy in the country, and a White Paper on this organisation is absolutely essential.

Jyotirmoy Basu's warning against a sinister and unaccounted growth of extraconstitutional power in Mrs. Gandhi's hands was soon backed by other parties. Mrs. Gandhi's personal interest in surveillance extended to finance. Intelligence relating to revenue, though formally under the Finance Ministry, took its orders from the prime minister's secretariat, operating both from South Block, New Delhi, and her house at 1 Safdarjang Road.

The aura of personal fealty to Mrs. Gandhi surrounding RAW came from its head, R. N. Kao, one of the Kashmiri Brahmins in her confidence. (Other Kashmiri Brahmins in the administration were: P. N. Haksar, Principal Private Secretary to the Prime Minister; T. N. Kaul, Foreign Secretary, later Indian Ambassador to the United States; P. N. Dhar, Economic Adviser to the Prime Minister's Secretariat, later her Principal Private Secretary; D. P. Dhar, Indian Ambassador to the USSR, later chief of the Planning Commission; B. K. Nehru, Ambassador to the United States, High Commissioner to Britain.) Here, as elsewhere, she provided a marked contrast with her father's relaxed tread and his approach to the tasks of governing. The Kashmiri Brahmin clique implied a strong, almost tribal suspicion of the "outsider," a prejudice that found its ultimate expression in her later unabashed promotion of her son, Sanjay.

In July 1970 the Opposition brought a no-confidence motion in Parliament, charging Mrs. Gandhi with rigging the state election in Kerala. She replied: "It is obvious that the entire motion is designed as a personal attack on me, on the supposed concentration of power in my hands. . . . I have been compared, not for the first time, to Hitler, Stalin and Mussolini. I think the people will laugh at the preposterousness of these comparisons." Her persistent reduction of all criticism to "a personal attack on me" had the effect of slamming a door, much as tears or an emotional outburst put an end to argument. Mrs. Gandhi's public speeches through the year had a strong defensive flavor, the lonely furrow ploughed against mighty and dangerous forces.

The forces visibly at work in the country were not, however, vested interests obstructing socialism so much as those demanding speedier and more radical change (e.g., the Naxalite movement) by violence, though communal violence had also taken its toll at Bhiwandi, Jalgaon, and other parts of Maharashtra. It was to the theme of obstruction by reactionary and communal forces that Mrs. Gandhi returned in her broadcast of December 27 announcing a midterm election. She was insecure in Parliament with her reduced majority and her dependence on other parties, besides being up against a far from docile Opposition. Her reliance on extraparliamentary devices showed her path had not proceeded smoothly. In February the Supreme Court had struck down bank nationalization. In April the government bill to end the special privileges of the Indian Civil Service (ICS) had not secured a two-thirds majority in Parliament. And on December 15 a special bench of the Supreme Court had ruled the presidential order on the princes as ultra vires of the Constitution. She would go to the polls to get a fresh mandate for her policies. For their implementation some amendments to the Constitution would be necessary: ". . . I want to be clear . . . we are not in favour of removing all the fundamental rights nor are we even against the right to property, but we do believe in having a certain ceiling on property, whether urban or rural."[2]

At her news conference on December 29 a journalist asked, "Your broadcast speech on television and radio [on the 27th] the Opposition claimed was a political speech and wanted equal time. Do you forsee in this election campaign that All India Radio will be open to the Opposition to make political speeches?" The prime minister replied, "Well, mine was not a political speech at all. I was exceedingly careful not to say anything that could be counted as party propaganda. As far as the other question is concerned, it has been debated, and we just could not get agreement on the subject."

The proposal of the Chanda Committee to make All India Radio

(AIR) an autonomous corporation on the lines of the BBC had been rejected by the government on October 21, 1970. The Opposition was to complain of government's unfair and unprincipled use of the media at its disposal. After the election Mrs. Gandhi brushed this aside in the Lok Sabha (April 2, 1971): "The complaint of some members about the functioning of All India radio and TV, that they were used by the government for party ends, need not be taken seriously." Two years later, the minister for information and broadcasting, I. K. Gujral, announced the prime minister's "firm and irrevocable" rejection of the Chanda Committee recommendations and said AIR would be run "in the manner that served the country best."

At her news conference, the prime minister was questioned about the contradiction of her party's electoral pact with a communal party, the Muslim League, in Kerala. She agreed the Muslim League was a communal organization, but said the way to meet it was to try and solve some of the genuine grievances of the minorities. She closed her conference by wishing the correspondents a happy New Year, "and, I hope, a less jaundiced view of the Indian situation."

This period marked the end of a convention that a caretaker government functioned once an election was announced. Patronage was freely distributed by Mrs. Gandhi's government, and licences "worth millions of rupees" were issued to industry. Kuldip Nayar adds in *India After Nehru* (1975): "One conscientious objector in the Prime Minister's Secretariat was Haksar, who at least stopped the distribution of brochures containing Mrs. Gandhi's speech which she broadcast on the day of the Lok Sabha dissolution."

CHAPTER SIX

The Midterm Election

India prepared for its first midterm general election in a tense and fevered atmosphere dominated by Mrs. Gandhi rather than issues. Her party fielded a large number of unknown candidates, "lamp posts" to the press, with the appeal that a vote for the candidate was a vote for Mrs. Gandhi. The prime minister's picture and personal message accompanied their posters. A loose alliance formed to oppose her, the "grand alliance" to the press, was not able to unite under a common program. The men in it were uncomfortable in each other's political company and agreed only in their shared alarm at Mrs. Gandhi's style and in their determination to remove her. Their slogan *Indira Hatao* ("Remove Indira") contrasted miserably with hers, *Garibi Hatao* ("Remove Poverty").

Most voters wanted a stable government and felt the New Congress with enough majority would not be at the mercy of extremists, even those in its own party. The constitutional amendments Mrs. Gandhi had said would be necessary caused no concern. She had repeatedly said she was a democrat. Her statements had always carried the assurance of a democratic framework and civic freedoms, whatever constitutional changes were made. The legacy of Nehru, of the democratic norms and conventions he had established and scrupulously served, was such that few anticipated any threat to democracy as India had till now understood the word and system, least of all from Nehru's daughter. It was felt there had been pressures on her during her quarrel with her own party and her year of reliance on other parties. Once free of these she would show good judgement and balance. The Gandhi-Nehru-Shastri era, for all its mass participation, had also been an age of the educated in politics. Gandhi had welded the educated with the mass, convinced

65

that progress to freedom required a true identity of interests between the different sections of society, a tradition carried on after independence. Gandhi's war had been against India's most ancient injustice—caste. Philosophically this was the reverse of class war. The challenge was projected not as rich against poor, but as civilized men against the injustices of their society. The Indian intelligentsia had, by and large, played a responsible role in independent India, in its contribution to the wide-ranging development Nehru had termed "adventure." The welding had survived principally because Indian leadership had nurtured it. It was not yet obvious that it was being taken systematically apart.

The question arises: Was Mrs. Gandhi trying, within the framework of existing democratic institutions, to blaze a new trail toward an egalitarian society against the combined weight of an outdated bureaucracy and legal system inherited from colonial times? Or were her intentions of a different kind? Was she using the credentials of her father and Mahatma Gandhi to play on the feelings and understanding of the masses, and to take in the process a calculated turn toward an authoritarian order? A singleminded woman, with a categorical sense of good and bad, for and against, not given to self-examination, forgiveness or compromise, if she saw any contradiction in her role, she may have believed herself capable of resolving it. For, above all, she believed she knew without the shadow of a doubt what needed to be done. Mission and opportunity met in her in a blaze of purpose. She had once listed the four most important influences on her character and thinking as Motilal and Jawaharlal Nehru, Mahatma Gandhi, and Rabindranath Tagore. Her genuine yearning towards the vision, humanity, and universality of these men may have found fulfilment in another career. The road to power distorted and finally destroyed it.

The election raises some points worth considering, inextricably connected with Mrs. Gandhi's highly personal style in politics. In 1969, before the Congress split, donations to political parties had been banned. The ban had worked since, without much secrecy, to the advantage of the ruling party. Industry knew it must invest in a winner. This alone seemed to assure permission to carry on business in a system of complex controls and lengthy delays, now surmounted by threat of takeover, and the credo that to oppose government was to be a reactionary and an enemy of the people. Ajit Bhattacharjea wrote in the *Illustrated Weekly of India* on July

15, 1973:

> Money had been collected for election and other party purposes be-
> fore, but never on the scale and in the manner it was for Lok Sabha
> elections in 1971 and the State assembly elections a year later. Crores
> are known to have been extracted from the business community, but
> there is no account of these transactions. The entire sum was paid in
> black money; no legal accounts were kept. . . . So a premium was
> placed on massive dishonesty and corruption and the parallel black
> money economy—with all its degrading social and economic effects—
> was legitimised.

There was a procedural change in the conduct of this election.
Up to now each ballot box had been separately counted at the end
of polling. This time ballot boxes from several polling stations were
mixed, resulting in a lapse of time, sometimes of days, before counting could begin. The reason given was that no one should know
how a particular area had voted. This innovation had been considered and rejected by the Election Commission in its report on the
fourth general election. The change in procedure, which involved
a change in rules, should have been placed before Parliament for
scrutiny. It was, however, introduced after Parliament had been
dissolved and the notification for the election had been made.

The change applied to parliamentary constituencies, not state
assembly constituencies. It did not affect the three states of West
Bengal, Orissa, and Tamil Nadu, where assembly elections were
held simultaneously with the general election, a fact of some significance later.

Mrs. Gandhi's victory had been expected, though no one, including her own party's best forecasters, had predicted a two-thirds
majority. The Opposition parties had been expected to win in areas
where they existed in strength and enjoyed a good reputation on
the basis of their past performance. Their almost total rout, an ab-
normally clean sweep, even in these areas, had an unreality, particularly when they were defeated by unknown New Congress candidates who themselves had expected to make a scant or mediocre
showing. The Opposition held that deviation from established election procedure gave scope for mischief on a vast scale, particularly
as this deviation, unobtrusively introduced, coincided with an election where a leader's political reputation and future were linked
to an unusual degree with the outcome.

The prime minister, who as home minister had intelligence, the police, and the Election Commission under her supervision, told the Lok Sabha after the election on April 2, 1971, "The complaints against the Election Commission have already been dealt with by my colleague, the Minister of Law and Justice." The Jan Sangh leader, A. B. Vajpayee, retorted, "Not satisfactorily." But, in the aftermath of Mrs. Gandhi's victory and the awe created by the pendulum swing of power, criticism died away and questions remained unanswered.

The only nationally known Opposition leader to take rigging charges to court was Balraj Madhok of the Jan Sangh, defeated in his South Delhi constituency, who claimed evidence of a plan to ensure a New Congress coup. The following extracts from his book *Murder of Democracy*[1] have some significance in view of the dictatorship Mrs. Gandhi launched with ease in 1975:

> The first information about the projected fraud on the Indian electorate accidentally reached a Delhi school teacher when he was . . . enrolling new voters in the Karol Bagh area of Delhi. When he approached an officer of the Government of India who lived in that area but whose name did not appear on the electoral rolls . . . [the officer] casually remarked, "You may enrol me and I will vote for your party but you are not going to win. This time chemicals will be employed and all your candidates will be defeated." . . . Nobody, including the officers of Delhi State Jan Sangh, took serious note of the information. . . . A few days before the polling a letter reached the Jan Sangh office at Lucknow. It said that the writer of the letter was staying in a dak bungalow in the Rae Bareilly constituency from where Mrs. Gandhi was contesting. He overheard some Congress high-ups staying in the adjacent room talking about the certainty of Mrs. Gandhi's victory because of the use of a certain percentage of chemicalized ballot papers which would be pre-stamped in her favour. He thought it his duty to convey the information to the major opposition party in the State and so he wrote that letter. . . .
>
> On March 2, three days before the polling was to begin in New Delhi, a chit [colloquial for note] came on the stage of a public meeting organised by the Jan Sangh in Karol Bagh which was to be addressed by A. B. Vajpayee. The chit said: "I am a senior officer of the Election Commission. I want to warn you that some serious mischief is being done in regard to ballot papers. Be on guard." . . . On March 3, a young man met Vidyarthi [Jan Sangh candidate from Karol Bagh] in his office and gave him detailed information about the modus operandi of the contemplated fraud on the electorate. He told Vidyarthi that a certain percentage of ballot papers will be chemically treated and an invisible

RIGHT: Kamala Nehru with baby Indira, 1918.

BELOW LEFT: Motilal Nehru, grandfather of Indira Gandhi.

BELOW RIGHT: *Left to right:* Kamala, Nehru's sister Krishna, Nehru, his sister Vijaya Lakshmi. The child is Indira.

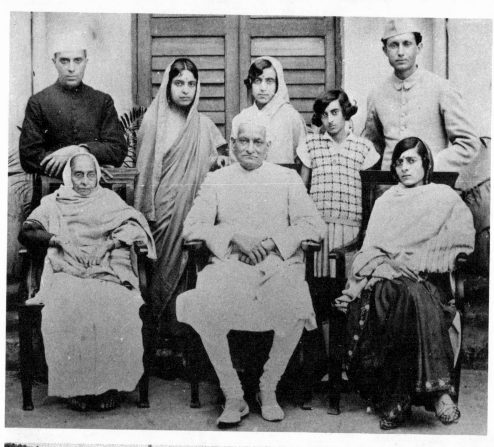

LEFT: The family. *Back row, left to right:* Jawaharlal Nehru, Vijaya Lakshmi Pandit, Krishna, Indira, Ranjit Pandit (husband of Vijaya Lakshmi). *Front row, left to right:* Mrs. Motilal Nehru, Motilal Nehru, Kamala. Approximately 1927–28.

BELOW LEFT: The Nehru family home, "Anand Bhawan," Allahabad. *Courtesy Press Information Bureau, Government of India, New Delhi.*

RIGHT: Nehru with Indira on the table and Lekha, Mrs. Pandit's eldest daughter, on his lap. 1928.

BELOW: Nehru addressing the first meeting at Red Fort after Independence, 1947. *Courtesy Press Information Bureau, Government of India.*

ABOVE: Nehru with Nayantara Sahgal, the author, on his birthday, November 14, 1947, New Delhi. *P. N. Sharma.*

BELOW: Jawaharlal Nehru at Buddhist Temple in Ladakh.

RIGHT: Nehru, Nayantara
Sahgal behind his shoulder,
Mrs. Pandit.

BELOW LEFT: Indira Gandhi,
mid 1950's.

BELOW RIGHT: Rajiv Gandhi,
approximately 1948.

TOP LEFT: Nehru with Indira Gandhi and her sons, Rajiv and Sanjay, placing flowers on the Samadhi of Mahatma Gandhi on August 15, 1956, the Indian Independence Day.

BOTTOM LEFT: Sanjay Gandhi, Mrs. Pandit, Bakshi Ghulam Mohammed (Chief Minister of Jammu and Kashmir), Rajiv Gandhi, Nehru, and Indira, in Kashmir, July 11, 1962.

ABOVE: Rajiv and Sanjay Gandhi carrying the urn containing their grandfather's ashes, May, 1964.

RIGHT: Mrs. Pandit congratulating her niece on her election as Prime Minister, 1966. *P. N. Sharma.*

LEFT: Wedding picture of Rajiv and Sonia Gandhi, 1968.

BELOW: The author as a member of the Indian delegation to the United Nations, accepting the Anti-Apartheid Award to Jawaharlal Nehru, October 11, 1978.

stamp will be affixed on the cow-and-calf symbol of the Indira Congress. Stamps put by the voters in polling booths on such ballots will disappear because of that chemical, and the invisible stamp on the cow-and-calf symbol will become visible after some days. . . .

It is difficult to believe how responsible people who got this information dismissed it as fantastic and took no step either to inform the public about it or even to tell their senior colleagues, some of whom also happened to be candidates in the election, about it. . . .

The first concrete evidence of rigging . . . came to light at the time of counting. A number of opposition candidates and their counting agents in Delhi, Bombay and elsewhere noted that stamp marks on the cow-and-calf symbol [of Mrs. Gandhi's party] on a large number of ballot papers appeared to be uniform, fresher and brighter than the stamps on other symbols. It was also noted that the colour of such ballot papers was somewhat different from other ballots. The matter was brought to the notice of returning officers by a number of people including Madhu Mehta, General Secretary of the Swatantra Party, who was present at the counting of votes in one of the Lok Sabha constituencies of Bombay. But the returning officers expressed their inability to take legal cognizance of these observations. . . .

The first definite information about the fraud . . . came on the night of March 11, when a senior officer of an important department of Government burst into tears before two other officials and told them the whole story to unburden the load on his conscience.

This was followed by a spate of unsigned letters giving details of the fraud to important leaders of the Opposition, including Nijalingappa . . . Charan Singh and the writer. The details given in some of these letters coming from authoritative sources were startling.

As the information started pouring in, the first thing the writer thought of was to apprise the President of India of all the facts, with the request to act in the interest of the Constitution which he was under oath to uphold . . . urging him to order a judicial probe into the conduct of the elections and appoint a commission of scientists to make chemical examination of ballot papers. . . .

Madhok received an acknowledgement of his letter to the president, but no reply. On March 30, 1971, he sought the chief election commissioner's permission to inspect the ballot papers of his own South Delhi constituency. Permission was refused. On April 24 Madhok filed an election petition in the Delhi High Court, setting forth his case for an inspection of ballot papers in his constituency. The trial judge, Justice Andley, ordered an inspection. The New Congress candidate appealed against inspection to the Supreme Court. Madhok notes that Supreme Court judge, Daftary, who categorically opposed any kind of inspection, and particularly a chemical inspection of ballot papers, was not long afterward nominated to the Rajya Sabha. Two Supreme Court judges, Hegde and Khanna, however, ordered a sample inspection of a few hundred ballot papers before any general inspection was ordered. In the course of their judgement they observed:

> The march of science has shown in recent years that what was thought to be impossible just a few years back has become an easy possibility now. What we would have thought as wild imagination some years back is now proved to be reality. Hence we are unable to reject the allegations of the election petitioner without scrutiny. We shall accept nothing and reject nothing except on satisfactory proof.

In compliance with the Supreme Court judgement, Justice Andley of the Delhi High Court made a sample inspection of 800 ballot papers cast in favor of the New Congress candidate and 550 cast in favor of the Jan Sangh candidate (Madhok), taken at random out of bags containing them. Madhok writes:

> At the very first sight of the two sets of ballot papers, they revealed some difference in colour. While all but five ballot papers cast in the writer's favour were found to be white, almost all the ballot papers cast in favour of the ruling Congress were found to be "off white" in the language of the court . . . [The trial judge] also asked the writer to keep his scientist and formula ready for chemical examination and reserved his order for November 12. . . . But the judgement could not be delivered on November 12 as the court was closed that day because of the sudden death of a judge of the Supreme Court. Prime Minister Indira Gandhi who had been abroad also returned to New Delhi on the same date.

Madhok records his astonishment that the judgement when it came was a complete reversal of the trial judge's stated position. The judge rejected the request for chemical inspection of ballot papers. He also struck the issue off the election petition.

Unwilling to let the matter rest, Madhok took his case to the Supreme Court with the plea that the suspect ballots be chemically examined. He argued the case himself on August 9, 1972, saying the ballots were the only evidence of a calculated coup, which if the evidence were borne out, would reveal the extent the ruling clique had gone to ensure a sizable victory. If tests could be undertaken in cases of forged documents or currency notes, the ballots, on which a country's fate depended, should be tested. The Supreme Court now refused the plea.

The voting pattern did indeed reveal that, in the states where assembly elections had been held at the same time and where, in accordance with past election procedure, there was no time lag between polling and counting, the Opposition had done well. In Tamil Nadu, where the Congress did not contest, the DMK swept the assembly poll. In West Bengal the CPI-M did better than the New Congress,* and in Orissa the Swatantra Party made a good showing. Losing candidates lost with fairly narrow margins in these states. As against this, in other states Congress candidates won by uniformly high margins of about 100,000 votes.

Madhok did not get his party's support in his charges and was expelled from it on differences of ideology after the election. He was considered a die-hard and the Jan Sangh was anxious to relax its conservative image to combat the "Indira wave." A fierce critic of Nehru, whose policies the Jan Sangh had adamantly opposed, Madhok makes observations in his book about Nehru and Mrs Gandhi that are interesting for their contrast:

> Pandit Nehru's greatest contribution for which his memory will be cherished by every democrat was that he gave respect to democratic institutions and kept the structure of democracy alive when he was in a position to destroy them if he so wanted . . . by showing due respect to fundamental rights, particularly to freedom of thought and expression, and by preserving the independence of the judiciary and sanctity and fairness of elections. . . .

Of the midterm election and Mrs Gandhi he concludes:

> The allegation was not about any electoral malpractice but about rigging of the election on a large scale. . . . The plan to rig the elections must have been a closely guarded secret, and no non-Communist colleague of Mrs. Gandhi, including her Party president and Defence Minster, Jagjivan Ram, was privy to it.

Madhok's account is painstaking and pedestrian, and carries no breath of the sensational. The handling of his charge makes strange reading, with its inexplicable reversal of the stand taken both by the High Court and the Supreme Court after a sample inspection of ballots had been ordered and carried out, the results

* In the West Bengal state asembly election in 1971 the New Congress won 105 seats (29.8 per cent votes) and the CPI-M won 111 seats (33.8 per cent votes).

found revealing enough to merit a chemical examination, and that examination ordered. If the whole issue was a crank's fixation, thorough scrutiny wouuld have shown it up for what it was. Instead, the legal process was suddenly halted and reversed. A tradition of investigative reporting might have served India well at this time, but if any newspaper thought it worthwhile to pursue this line of enquiry, it did not do so in the glitter of Mrs. Gandhi's victory and her well-known intolerance of opposing opinion. Madhok's charge, moreover, had the ring of fantasy about it. Though two Supreme Court judges were on record as saying that not even the most fanciful possibility could be lightly dismissed in this age of sophisticated technology, most people did so dismiss it. Four general elections had already taken place since 1952, and the public believed in the fairness of elections. Even those politicians who, according to Madhok's account, received information about a "conspiracy" beforehand, did not imagine so brazen a scheme could be perpetrated, though they were opponents of the regime. It is perhaps a strain on the imagination to suggest that a familiar process is going to be subverted under one's gaze while the sun shines. The average person, who has come and gone in freedom, spoken, written, and voted as he pleased, does not recognize the alien chord struck on just such an ordinary day.

If one were to give credence to the possibility of a coup through a certain number of spurious ballots, the election of 1971 could become a link in the chain starting with Mrs. Gandhi's charge of the Home Ministry, and the unorthodox manner of change in election procedure. One question would still remain: Why was a "coup" necessary, if indeed it took place? The New Congress was, in the general assessment, more than likely to win. The element of chance hung only on its majority. Yet Mrs. Gandhi needed a two-thirds majority to control Parliament and to carry through her amendments to the Constitution. Anything less would have put a continued brake on her functioning. She had gambled for high stakes when she broke with her party on the question of unfettered command, a meaningless gamble if lack of majority at the polls were to render her ineffective once again. That the stakes in the power game became higher, until in June 1975 she wiped all element of chance off the scene, imprisoning her opponents within and outside her party, seems to suggest that the 1971 election might have been a stage in a process.

The character of this election may also explain the subservience of Parliament in accepting and consolidating the dictatorship after June 1975. If many M.P.s—"lamp posts"—were her creatures rather than known and accepted personalities in their constituencies, they would have a vital interest in prolonging their tenure and displaying the perfect obedience that would keep them in the leader's favor.

CHAPTER SEVEN

"The New Dawn"

The *National Herald* commented on the election result on March 12, 1971: "It is a mandate for carrying on the socialist processes to the climax of a social revolution with vigour and speed. . . . It is not a mere mandate, it is a strong wind of change that has swept the country. . . ." The *Patriot* called it "a forceful assertion of popular opinion in favour of radical change that . . . will provide equality of opportunity for all and enable equitable sharing of the fruit of economic development."

These comments represented the general enthusiasm that marks the beginning of a political era promising great new momentum. If the methods by which Mrs. Gandhi had routed the Old Guard of the Congress had created a thrill of apprehension in neutral observers, if the controversy over "commitment" and the rousing vocabulary of class war during the past eighteen months had raised a wild wind of speculation about the government's intentions and direction, there was now an expectation of concrete programs and efficient administration. Mrs. Gandhi's landslide victory gave her an uncluttered opportunity with virtually no Opposition in Parliament to hinder it. The New Congress had won 350 out of 518 seats in the Lok Sabha. What remained of the opposition consisted chiefly of the CPI-M, followed closely by the CPI, and in Tamil Nadu, the DMK. Such pressure as could now be exerted on the government in Parliament would come from the Left. A Leftward trend began to be noticeable in the Right wing parties, too, in whom the "Indira wave" had produced some rethinking. Since its founding in 1952, the Jan Sangh had been linked in sympathy with the Hindu Mahasabha, which it had substantially replaced, but it had moved steadily away from orthodoxy after 1957 in wooing a wider electorate. The midterm election accelerated this trend toward a moderate, liberal approach. The Swantantra Party, later further reduced by a split, debated at its 1973 convention the need to shed some of its antipathy toward socialism and not condemn it outright. Region-based parties of varying hue had to take note of the "wind of change." A clamor for "socio-economic" innovation and drive filled the air.

Not all was enthusiasm for Mrs. Gandhi's victory. The *Statesman* treated it with frank foreboding:

> What distinguished the present poll from any other is the degree in which it has been dominated, as a matter of deliberate calculation, by a cult which subordinates all considerations of principle, party programmes and manifestos to the image of a single leader. That it has yielded dividends is not too surprising. The simplistic message of Mrs. Gandhi as the guardian of the underprivileged and as the only genuine advocate of socialism was an incomparably more efficient gatherer of votes than anything the Opposition was able to produce. The latter suffered from the initial disadvantage of being burdened by a heavily intellectualized and argumentative thesis, unsupported by the charisma of an all-India personality. Whether such charisma exploited with ruthless determination is in the long run compatible with a healthy democratic system is something on which some thought is clearly overdue ... Congress-R candidates from whom little was expected have blossomed into successful competitors under the general benediction of a leader with a masterly grip on the techniques of the emotional appeal ... the line between an election and a referendum can no longer be seen. ...

From this point of view, the nature of the election and the events preceding it boded ill for the future. Moral example, expected of those who lead, had been flamboyantly deserted by Mrs. Gandhi during the Congress crisis. The performance had been exciting and inflaming, creating a leader-image bound by no rules or restraints. The election was proof that the performance had succeeded. A roused and restless student population, trade unions, taxi and transport operators—these and other elements, potential fuel for the fires of a growing lawlessness—had now to be persuaded into channels of work. Yet the election triumph had released a fresh militancy in the ruling party. In New Delhi a crowd led by its office-bearers marched on the disputed Congress headquarters at Jantar Mantar

Road and took forcible possession while the police remained spectators on the scene. The Supreme Court had earlier decreed that ownership was for the courts to decide, and until such time the headquarters remained by law with the Old Congress. A Congress election majority was no novelty. There had been no effective challenge to the government in Nehru's time. But the framework for challenge had been strong. In the present political environment, its main pillars had been under attack. The fundamental rights, an independent judiciary, the freedom of the press, clearly did not carry the same meaning for Mrs. Gandhi they had had for her father.

The government began its fulfilment of election pledges by a presidential ordinance nationalizing general insurance on May 13, 1971. Its program in Parliament centered on amendments to the Constitution. These went through during the year, amid cheers and applause in both Houses. The 24th Amendment (August 1971) gave Parliament the sovereign right to alter the Constitution, including the fundamental rights. The 25th Amendment (December 1971) provided that compensation for nationalized properties would no longer be based on market value. The word "compensation" was replaced by "amount," to be fixed by Parliament and not challengeable in a court of law. The Articles of the Constitution, giving the citizen the right to acquire, hold, and dispose of property, and to protect it against arbitrary seizure, were no longer valid. The 26th Amendment (December 1971) ended the privy purse and extinguished all rights, liabilities, and obligations in respect of the princes.

In the pursuit of social justice, the government of India had earlier set limits on the right to property with the first constitutional amendment in 1951. The right to property could not be invoked at all against specified acts passed by state governments relating to land reform, while the government could interfere in a specified area of property rights, where these conflicted with the general public interest. Compensation for nationalized property could not be challenged in a court of law, but it was based on market value. The 1971 amendment avoided a definition of government's powers altogether, making government subject to no principle and no responsibility regarding its incursions into property rights and the compensation payable in cases of takeover. A meticulously defined procedure was thus abrogated. The word "amount" in place of "compensation" made compensation a matter of government's whim. Nationalization, in these circumstances, amounted to confiscation and expropriation, as the takeover of general insurance companies and coal companies soon afterward demonstrated:

> Some companies found that the amounts they received were less than the value of their government securities and the amounts of their currency notes and bank balances after providing for all liabilities. . . . One insurance company was paid Rs. 10,000 for acquisition of its *net* assets worth more then Rs. 2,300,000. . . . All assets of nationalised coal companies are taken over by government but none of their liabilities. . . .[1]

It was this lack of definition and responsibility, with no limits placed on government's powers, that sent a spasm of doubt and fear through the public. The amendments, including government's power to axe the fundamental rights—free speech, press, occupation, worship, and assembly—reflected a wide-ranging unaccountability that was the chief feature of the new era. Instead of concrete proposals for change, even considered changes within the political system, it was the checks and balances within the system that were being demolished, leaving it unprotected against the dictatorial designs of this or any future government. Mrs. Gandhi's grandfather, Motilal Nehru, had, during the struggle for freedom, defended the inviolability of fundamental rights. Thirteen out of nineteen fundamental rights listed in the (Motilal) Nehru Report had been included in the Indian Constitution in 1950. With reference to the future Constitution of free India, Motilal Nehru had said in the Central Assembly in 1928: "It is obvious that our first care should be to have our fundamental rights guaranteed in a manner which will not permit their withdrawal under any circumstances." The statement, quoted by an Opposition M.P. during the Lok Sabha debate on the 24th Amendment, represented a philosophy closer to the moderate opposition than to New Congress thinking. The government spoke another language. Mohan Kumaramangalam, piloting the bill along with the law minister, H. R. Gokhale, said it would "clear the road blocks" to progress "erected by the Supreme Court" (by an earlier judgement). Supreme Court judges, he said, had "an inbuilt conservatism born out of the class from which they come. . . . Judges in our country come from the class of men with property." K. D. Malaviya, New Congress M.P., defined democratic socialism as state control of all sources of production and distribution. The prime minister presented no argument. She merely condemned the scare created about the bill as another of the unending attempts by vested interests to divide the people and mislead the minorities.

The notable fact about the amendments and the debate accompanying them was their Communist inspiration. The effect was of an unexpected transplant, set up on the body-politic without the groundwork, and certainly without the political system, to ensure its acceptance and success. The transplant had, as it were, sprung up noiselessly overnight, and now ruled the political daylight, yet Mrs. Gandhi firmly denied Communist influence or direction. With no clarification available from her, only guesses could try to explain this anomaly. With her election majority she no longer needed CPI support. The CPI's presence at the power feast indicated a larger political bargain, a friendly price paid in return for hemispheric considerations, a pointer to the assiduously cultivated and steadily growing Soviet alliance. There was, too, Mrs. Gandhi's own Leftist posture, which had been her reason for the Congress split, but this appeared, as time went on, vague, romantic and adolescent, without the hard supporting structure of thought or program.

While thought was not her strength or style, Mrs. Gandhi's thorough grasp of the nuts and bolts of politics was. Philosophy, i.e., a clear statement of what she stood for, drifted cloudlike, irridescent and insubstantial above her hardheaded businesslike strategy in the control room. In his admiring *Profile of Courage*, Trevor Drieberg says of the post-election period: "[Mrs. Gandhi is] on a political pinnacle, holds absolute power. . . . She speaks direct to the people today, over the heads of her own partymen, who need her much more than she needs them." The "pinnacle" was insured by the control she established over the bowels of the Congress machine, indispensable to effective, centralized power. The apparatus for choosing candidates for the State Legislative Assembly (SLA) elections due in early 1972 was replaced by groups appointed by the Working Committee. The prime minister herself decided which of the state ministers would get party tickets. Four veteran chief ministers, Mohanlal Sukhadia of Rajasthan, Brahmananda Reddy of Andhra Pradesh, M. M. Chaudhury of Assam, and S. C. Shukla of Madhya Pradesh, each powerfully backed in his state, were replaced by her nominees, respectively Barkatullah, P. V. Narsimha Rao, S. C. Sinha, and P. C. Sethi. Political lightweights in their states, and dependent on her favor, their chief qualification was their allegiance to her. Drieberg writes:

> This set the stage of things to come. When Congress candidates were chosen for seats in the State legislatures, the heads of six more Chief Ministers rolled. In drawing up lists of candidates, only three Congress Chief Ministers, in addition to the four whom Mrs. Gandhi had chosen in the months preceding the [Assembly] elections survived. . . .

Posts for the party's state units were similarly operated by Mrs. Gandhi. The Congress constitution empowered state units to name and elect their own office bearers. Nominations and election had been the responsibility of a returning officer chosen by the state Congress. Returning officers were now selected or approved by Mrs. Gandhi and lists decided by her. Elections were a foregone conclusion. Office bearers thus "elected" could be as easily unseated without reference to the state units they represented. Pradesh Congress Committees, District Congress Committees, and lower down party units upon which rested the party's local base and strength were shorn of their rights under its constitution, and could be appointed or superceded at Mrs. Gandhi's pleasure.

An atmosphere of fealty, feudal in texture, descended on the Congress. Her colleagues and associates, with few exceptions, had no political bases of their own and were dependent on her for their positions. Nehru had been surrounded by an aura of deference, even reverence, but his ministers had been personalities in their own right, some of them powerful and impressive men. The contrast extended to the secretariat. Nehru, often impatient and short-tempered, tended, all the same, to support his civil servants, and they were sure of the ground beneath their feet. The government's intentions and objectives were known. Mrs. Gandhi's lack of a defined philosophy left those working with her in uncertainty. There was no clear-cut framework within whose rhythm and logic they could take decisions without getting clearance from her, no orchestration of men and ideas to produce teamwork. There was an ad hocism, a compartmentalization of subjects, and long delays in making senior appointments that often lay vacant for months. And with Mrs. Gandhi's instinctive antagonism to criticism, known or suspected, only a show of loyalty guaranteed a career.

Lining the outer atmosphere of radical rhetoric, the tightening of the nuts and bolts of power continued. During the summer of 1971, the government made its first move toward control of the press when Mrs. Gandhi's own Ministry of Information and Broadcasting prepared a draft scheme to "diffuse" ownership of newspapers with a circulation of more than 15,000. This climaxed Mrs. Gandhi's bias, faithfully reflected in her minister of state's (Nandini Sathpathy) pronouncements about the "monopoly" press. The draft scheme proposed that 95 percent of a newspaper's shares would be offered to journalists and other employees, and 5 percent to existing shareholders. But each shareholder would exercise only half a vote per share, their combined voting rights amounting to 50 percent. The remaining 50 percent of voting rights on the management would go to a government appointee. The management would thus bear the final imprint of government authority and decisions.

I expressed my views on the scheme:

> The worker will get a seat on the management but his voice will scarcely be heard. . . . What is only too plain is that if this proposal goes into effect it will systematically shatter not the bogy of "monopoly," but the reality of one of the healthiest, most stable institutions of our society.

The most anguished cry against the scheme appeared in a three-column editorial in the *Hindustan Times* headed "Freedom is in Peril, Defend it with all your Might." B. G. Verghese, calling it "a monstrous perversion that will destroy the freedom of the press," wrote:

> It amounts to a scheme of backdoor nationalisation and projects an extraordinary concept of workers' management that entails a unique separation of responsibility from control. It is astonishing that such an unworkable and destructive piece of legislation should be contemplated by a democratic government. . . . The whole exercise is a frightening warning that wild men enjoy wide rein within the administration . . . the Bill proposed by the government would . . . strike a deadly blow against the most vital aspect of the freedom of the press, namely the right of dissent and the duty to defy uninformed opinion brought out on the streets as a demonstration of "the will of the people. . . ." The highest duty of a free Press is not to follow the mob but to lead it and educate it. . . . We would appeal to the Government, and to the Prime Minister in particular, to repudiate the vicious and undemocratic principles underlying this unworkable and incomplete draft scheme . . . which constitutes a diabolic attack not merely on the Press but on the citizen by seeking virtually to extinguish . . . the fundamental right to "freedom of speech and expression."

Verghese's appeal "to the Prime Minister in particular" was part of a genuine public belief that Mrs. Gandhi herself was not directly associated with, or responsible for, authoritarian proposals or measures. The newspaper "diffusion" scheme was drafted by the secretary to the Information and Broadcasting Ministry, R. C. Dutt, and the stinging backlash of criticism against it was absorbed by him and by the minister of state. Nandini Sathpathy, whose opinions on newspaper control had been forthright, had also been made responsible for answers about the control of film imports. Mrs. Gandhi herself preserved a democratic image, remaining untouched at the center of controversy, and could be appealed to whenever democracy appeared to be in danger—an oasis of moderation in the extreme views and proposals around her. During the midterm election, she had portrayed the fighting radical, yet along with this she conveyed the image of a leader, centrist by instinct, and driven only by necessity to compromise with extremists. She maintained both images, which seemed to obscure the fact that each actual step she took embodied the extremist view. The "diffusion" scheme struck at a 100-year-old tradition of intellectual vitality and individualism in Indian journalism, which had given the community respected and influential citizens. Its spirit of independence had flowered in opposition to British rule. Men like Verghese found themselves up against something new—a threat to freedom of expression from the Indian rulers of India. The reaction to it was strong. The scheme was adversely compared with Nehru's attitude toward the press. "I have no doubt that even if the Government dislikes the liberties taken by the press and considers them dangerous, it is wrong to interfere with the freedom of the press."

Nehru, inaugurating *Shankar's Weekly* (of political satire and cartoons), had told Shankar, "Don't spare me." Durga Das, head of India News Feature and Alliance, a leading syndicate, remarked: "Mrs. Gandhi does not accept the basic philosophy of a newspaper, that it has to convey the people's problems, not the Government view, that a columnist must carry the voice of dissent to the corridors of power. It is the best safety valve a Government has. Her father understood that." A letter from Nehru to his sister, Mrs. Pandit, in London, dated November 7, 1959, vividly conveys his response to press criticism during a time of tension between India and China:

> We are having a curious time here in India. People are worked up to a high pitch of excitement over the Chinese border issue. The principal newspapers here, which are opposed to our internal policies, have taken advantage of this to attack all our policies, internal and external, and to make me a target of attack. They dislike me for our internal

policies and for trying to go too fast toward what they call socialism. . . .
So you will observe that I am having a fairly interesting time!

Commentators pointed out the total circulation of 755 dailies,
variously owned, did not exceed 7 million, and government already
exercised control through newsprint allocation and the supply and
import of printing machinery. Mrs. Gandhi was, therefore, perhaps
disproportionately sensitive to the power of the press and the damage the "big" newspapers could do if they disagreed with her.

The measure was shelved as opinion against it rose to a crescendo, and government's understanding of fundamental rights remained unexplained. A religious trust in the south took the issue,
relating to its property, to the Supreme Court. In October 1972 the
fundamental rights became the subject of a debate before a thirteen-
member bench of the Supreme Court.

Mrs. Gandhi's hold on party members, including senior ministers, and her ability to ease them out of long-occupied berths came
from her use of the Intelligence apparatus at her command. The
deeper currents she manipulated in men and money came to light
by accident through the Nagarwala affair.[2]

On May 24, 1971 Ved Prakash Malhotra, chief cashier of the
State Bank of India, received a phone call instructing him to deliver
Rs 6 million in cash to a man who would identify himself as
Bangladesh ka Babu ("man from Bangladesh") on a road in New
Delhi. The call, Malhotra later told the police, came from the prime
minister. Taking a taxi, he delivered the money as instructed and
hurried to the prime minister's house to report the completion of
his mission. The prime minister's principal secretary, P. N. Haksar,
who met him, denied absolutely that Mrs. Gandhi had made the
call and advised the astonished Malhotra to go to the police immediately. The money was recovered on the same day. Captain
Nagarwala, the man who had taken delivery of it from Malhotra,
seemed to have left an open, easy trail for the police to find and
arrest him. He confessed he had wanted the money for support to
Bangladesh and had impersonated the prime minister's voice to
obtain it.

Nagarwala's case was conducted in a highly unorthodox manner and with record speed. In three days, three different magistrates
dealt with it. On the third day, May 27, he was sentenced to four
years' imprisonment and a fine of Rs 4,000. The police did not
produce as evidence in court the tape they said they had taken of

Nagarwala's impersonation, and Nagarwala's account of it was very different from Malhotra's earlier account. Malhotra was not examined in court.

On the day of Nagarwala's arrest, Opposition M.P.s demanded an answer in Parliament to the question: Had the prime minister spoken to Malhotra on the telephone? A member, drawing attention to her sudden exit from the House, was sternly reprimanded by the Speaker and told to "desist from making any allegations." The uproar raised by New Congress benches prevented a discussion.

Malhotra, arrested after Nagarwala had been convicted, clung to his story. He wept, insisting he had only obeyed the prime minister's instructions. Nagarwala, docile and cooperative enough until his conviction, seemed to have second thoughts in jail, showing signs of disillusion and despair. He appealed for retrial, saying his trial had been rushed through contrary to all principles of justice, and asked that Malhotra's story be fully investigated first. This request was refused, though a retrial was ordered. In November Nagarwala tried to get an interview with D. F. Karaka, editor of the Bombay weekly, *Current*, and a fellow Parsi. Karaka, too ill to travel to Delhi, sent a representative, but Nagarwala would speak to no one else. In February he was removed to hospital, reportedly complaining of a pain in the chest. He died on March 2, 1972. In the army before independence, Rustam Sohrab Nagarwala is believed to have been employed as an intelligence officer in RAW at this time.

The case was closed. The money was returned to the bank. Malhotra was dismissed. He later appeared on the Delhi scene as owner of a transport operation and fully supported the official version of the story. The prime minister's role in the affair remained a mystery. Had she spoken to Malhotra on the telephone? Could Malhotra carry Rs 6 million out of the bank on receipt of a phone call unless there were some precedent for it?

The public had other questions: Was Nagarwala made a scapegoat when Haksar (unaware of the arrangement) inadvertently exposed it by sending Malhotra to the police? What use was made of funds such as these, so casually removable from the valuts of a bank? Had Nagarwala died a natural death? Had D. K. Kashyap's death been accidental? Kashyap, assistant superintendent of police, the officer most closely connected with the investigation, had died in a car collision on the Grand Trunk Road near Mathura on November 20, 1971.

The code phrase in the Nagarwala affair had been *"Bangladesh ka Babu,"* and events across the East Bengal border were, along with her consolidation of control over the Congress party machine, Mrs. Gandhi's chief preoccupation in 1971. The Opposition closed its ranks solidly behind her when, on March 31, she moved a resolution in both Houses of Parliament expressing ". . . deep anguish and grave concern at the recent developments in East Bengal." High tension and suspicion had developed between East and West Pakistan, resulting in widespread and ruthless suppression of public opinion and dissent. This led to a popular movement in the East Bengal for independence and secession from Pakistan. Sympathy for the stream of refugees becoming a flood of millions was mixed with alarm at the severe strain they were imposing on India's resources, and the danger to stability in West Bengal, always a vulnerable region. If for a time Mrs. Gandhi seemed robbed of initiative, her announcement of the Indo-Soviet Treaty of Friendship and Cooperation, signed in New Delhi on August 9, put a stop to all such conjecture. In keeping with her government's style, which did not include open discussion or parliamentary debate about issues affecting the country, the treaty was presented as an accomplished fact. Consummate showmanship marked its announcement at a rally at India Gate, New Delhi's most spectacular vantage point and scene of Republic Day parades. At another time its full implications would have provoked more thought. In essence a security-based alliance, it represented a complete reversal in foreign policy, while its other clauses would intimately and diversely affect internal affairs. But, in the tension and anxiety caused by events in East Bengal, it spelled relief for India, for the first time since independence provided with a powerful ally in case of war. Coming upon the official indifference of most governments to the tragedy of genocide across the border (there were notable exceptions, whose support, however, did not count in the international power game), the partisan pro-Pakistan policy of America, and the grave danger to which India felt exposed, the treaty came at the psychological moment when it would find an enthusiastic welcome. Very few were concerned in this context with analyzing the extent to which it brought India's defence, economy, and culture under Soviet influence and pressure for the next fifteen years. Those who attempted analysis were denounced as unpatriotic.

Mrs. Gandhi was able to go abroad at the end of September, cushioned by the treaty, to try to rouse heads of governments to the calamity on the subcontinent. The prime minister abroad exhibited a normality and balance she lacked at home, though she carried her annoyance at Indian critics with her and displayed it on occasion. Speaking to the Society for Foreign Policy and International Relations in Austria, she said, "In our fifth general election last March, 152 million people went to cast their votes, in spite of the fact that . . . there was great deal of mischievous and false propaganda about our policies and programmes." In the Soviet Union, she said, "There are some, in India and abroad, who are trying to misinterpret its [the treaty's] meaning and purpose." At President Nixon's banquet for her, she spoke of "the people" as distinct, by implication, from those who opposed her: "So the campaign became not a campaign of a political party, but a campaign of the people . . . people came to the fore and said. 'If this is a candidate belonging to Mrs. Gandhi's party, we will make him win'."

The efficient conduct of the Indo-Pakistan war of 1971 was both balm and stimulant to a nation humiliated by the Chinese in 1962 and, in the hope of peace, persuaded into an indeterminate conclusion with Pakistan in the war of 1965. Mrs. Gandhi's handling of this period of crisis and danger, during the tense months preceding the war, and the war itself, illustrated that, when reality had to be faced, when it could not be obscured by rhetoric or enveloped by the slide and slither of innuendo, she could come to grips with it. In the process and through the war, Mrs. Gandhi attained the recognizable leadership that continued to elude her in her inability to come to grips with daily realities on the home front. The unilateral ceasefire she declared immediately on Pakistan's collapse in East Bengal was an act of statesmanship. Her broadcast announcing the war's end was quiet and calm and had the added grace of restraint in victory, a restraint she had not been able to exercise after her election victory at home. The two fronts, external and internal, continued divided. Precise, if ruthless and insensitive action, marked Mrs. Gandhi's style in her incorporation of Sikkim into the Indian Union. A pattern of cordial relations began to be efficiently established with neighbors. Wounds with Pakistan began to be healed and ties resumed. China and India reopened full diplomatic relations. Yet, at home, a state of "war," narrow unyielding, and locked in inconsistencies, went on. Neither concession nor discussion had any part in Mrs. Gandhi's politics at home.

A news conference on December 31, 1971 warmly congratulated Mrs. Gandhi on her leadership through the Bangladesh crisis and directed its questions at the war's aftermath, the future with Pakistan, and the safety of Mujibur Rahman. The dazzle of a victory, this time a military one, once again left its deeper implications unexplored. India's role in bringing it about had meant an involvement far beyond any yet undertaken in foreign affairs. The Indian army, along with Bangladesh, had taken the Pakistani surrender. The massive Soviet support that had made this possible meant the end of nonalignment and brought India into the politics of competitive power. The long-term effects on Bangladesh did not take long to appear.

The direction now taken by foreign policy was partly the result of America's policies in Asia and more recently its stand on Bangladesh. But it coincided, too, with Mrs. Gandhi's leap to individual recognition in 1969 and her consolidation of her position thereafter.

The CPI, until it became Mrs. Gandhi's ally in 1969, had enjoyed little credit or credibility in Indian politics. Founded in 1925, in 1933 it had 100 members. Banned by the British Government, it struggled for survival during the Stalin years, when revolution outside the Soviet Union found little besides moral support. Between it and the peasant-worker masses stood the figure of Mahatma Gandhi, a 100 percent Indian obstruction, clasping India to him through religion, tradition, and continuity, recognizing no class distinctions, and piloting a movement for freedom that did not tolerate violence. The CPI lost further ground with World War II, when an "imperialist" war became, with the Soviet entry into it, a "people's" war and enlisted the CPI's full cooperation. The mood and tide in India were fiercely nationalist, and Congress leaders were put in jail for refusing to participate in the Allied war effort unless India's freedom was granted. After independence, Nehru's position in the ruling party and the country could not be upset by conspiracy or manipulation. He invited the cooperation of all "socialists" but he did not need political allies. Mrs. Gandhi did. The Soviet Union's interest in the CPI-New Congress alliance was not one of ideology. Mrs. Gandhi's struggle for power in her party was backed by the Soviet Union for more important considerations. There were giant global considerations in the balance. With the birth of a new country, Bangladesh—blessed by India and the Soviet Union—and with the enfeebling of Pakistan, a bloc encompassing the land mass from the Soviet Union to the Indian Ocean could become a reality. In Mrs. Gandhi, there was an Indian leader of the style and temperament required, herself unburdened by ideology or conscience, to play with great flair the game of power.

At Mrs. Gandhi's news conference, no reference was made to the new law, Maintenance of Internal Security Act (MISA), passed in June 1971, giving the government "deterrent powers against antisocial elements" and providing for arbitrary arrest and imprisonment without trial for six months. The Emergency (against external danger), declared when the war broke out in December, remained in force, although by mid 1972 the Simla agreement had been signed, and relations between India and Pakistan had never been more cordial or promising.

The CPI leadership in government showed its customary energy when it invited "intellectuals"—actors, writers, singers, dancers, painters, and academics—to a meeting arranged by the Education Ministry in the capital to discuss ways and means of strengthening "national solidarity." Mohan Kumaramangalam, and not the education minister, was in the chair. The procedure and terms employed differentiated it from similar gatherings in the past, when plenty of time was allowed for a ventilation of opinion. Kumaramangalam called upon the assembled company to elect a "presidium" of five, and these were named and elected with obviously rehearsed speed. The head of the presidium, the distinguished communist writer, Sajjad Zaheer, took the chair. Selected members of the audience were called upon to speak, leaving no time for discussion. The "manifesto," to be drafted by the presidium during the coffee break and discussed after coffee, had, the invitees discovered, already been drafted. Copies of it lay in front of Kumaramangalam. A few writers heatedly objected to being hustled, but the manifesto was duly adopted.

In January 1972, Mrs. Gandhi used the opportunity provided by Mujibur Rahman's halt in Delhi (from London en route to Dacca) to address a mass rally jointly with him. In her Letter to the Voter, appearing as an advertisement in national newspapers on March 10, 1972, she reminded people of the Bangladesh victory and the return of the refugees to their own country, and urged voters to return her party to the state assemblies in overwhelming strength in the coming elections. The Congress, backed by a mood of national excitement and euphoria, had an impressive success. The Congress-CPI electoral pact in Bihar, West Bengal, and Punjab had its most spectacular result in Bengal,* where the CPI-M was reduced from 111 to 14 seats. The Congress-CPI landslide was preceded by an eventful history.

* Bengal is used from now on, rather than West Bengal, as with the end of the 1971 war with Pakistan, East Bengal became Bangladesh.

President's Rule, imposed on Bengal on March 19, 1970, had ended a year later, with the 1971 election in that state giving the CPI-M 111 seats in a house of 280 and the position of single largest party in the assembly. The governor, S. S. Dhavan, however, was directed to favor the formation of a "Democratic Front" six-party coalition, supported by the New Congress. During the next two months, the Democratic Front was reduced by defections, while the CPI-M improved its position by two more seats in constituencies that had held late polls. The coalition announced its inability to continue without a fresh mandate, and President's Rule was imposed on the state once again.

An organized police terror then subjected the CPI-M rank and file to arrests and killings. The revival of the Preventive Detention Act by ordinance in May 1971 and the enactment of MISA in June facilitated this campaign, described by a Bengali film director as the Second Great Calcutta Killing—the first having been the country's most ferocious communal orgy in 1946. In the course of it, the CPI-M was lamed and the Naxalite movement broken, its members hunted and jailed or killed. A bloodied CPI-M contested the assembly election in 1972. In July 1973 the death of the activist Charu Mazumdar in a "police encounter" completed the rout of the extreme Left outside the CPI-M and crippled its impact. According to an Amnesty International report[3] published in 1974, the Bengal government held 20 to 30,000 political prisoners, apart from 17,800 "under-trial detainees." Among the methods of torture it listed were: (*i*) severe beating, sometimes resulting in fractured limbs, (*ii*) hanging prisoners upside down with pins inserted into their nails and other sensitive organs of the body, including genitals, (*iii*) electric shock, (*iv*) burning with cigarettes, (*v*) denial of medical aid to tortured prisoners. Justice Sarma Sankar, heading a commission to investigate the deaths of five Naxalites in Howrah Jail, concluded that "firing inside Howrah Jail in 1975 violated the jail code, the penal code and the human code."

There was irony in this formidable bloodletting to end the established hold of the CPI-M in Bengal and make way for a Congress* victory at the polls. Its chief beneficiary was the CPI, Mrs. Gandhi's ally, whose avowed goal was a political system identical to that desired by the CPI-M. It bolstered an alliance based on a degree of opportunism that was beginning to repel sensitive sec-

---

* Congress is used from now on rather than the New Congress.

tions of both the CPI and the Congress. Communist critics would have preferred the dignity of an ideologically reliable partnership with the CPI-M or a neutral role between it and the Congress. Congress critics found Communist philosophy and methods altogether alien and unpalatable. Mrs. Gandhi's indifference to political principle, so graphically illustrated by her partnership with the CPI, had already been seen in her electoral pact with the Muslim League in Kerala and later in Congress collaboration with the Shiv Sena, a militant mafia-type organization in Maharashtra. In her pursuit of immediate political advantage, the Congress was smearing its respected stand on basic issues and, through the widespread use of police terror, forfeiting its claim to just and decent political functioning. Scrupulous sentiment within her own party surveyed this debris of a high moral and political stand with apprehension and dismay.

The campaign against the CPI-M represented Mrs. Gandhi's violent answer to political violence. It also effectively crippled the legitimate functioning of this particular adversary. In 1974 a campaign as thorough was mounted against a nonviolent movement in defence of parliamentary democracy that threatened Congress rule in Bihar, and ultimately in India.

CHAPTER EIGHT

Reaping the Whirlwind

Victory in Bangladesh and the return of the refugees gave the country a psychological lift unequaled since independence. Mrs. Gandhi's prestige and popularity were at their height. To the mandate she had received in the 1971 election was now added the resounding success of the Congress in the 1972 State Legislative Assembly elections, reflecting the country's hope that stable majorities in the states would provide the base for economic improvement. With an immense fund of goodwill and no political challenge to impede her, Mrs. Gandhi could begin her program for the removal of poverty. Urban and rural unrest, the growing militancy of organized labor, the general impatience of the electorate, all demanded it. Yet this proved to be a period of total political involvement for Mrs. Gandhi, to the neglect of economic affairs, though her party kept up a high temperature of vocal demand for "radical" change, along with a denigration of those said to be obstructing it. This may have been useful strategy where, in the nature of things, lightning changes cannot take place, while it also furnished a smokescreen for measures that had profoundly altered the body politic under the guise of "constitutional" change.

India's political system, a marriage between the British liberal constitutional tradition and Mahatma Gandhi's humanitarian ideals, was also a deliberate choice at independence. It rested on the belief that a country so large and diverse could most humanely preserve its unity, as well as its legitimate diversity, within a parliamentry and federal system. While Mrs. Gandhi functioned within the system she had inherited, an obsessive concern with her own importance led her progressively to tamper with the brakes and balances it provided and to block the vents that might in time and in the natural course of events give the system a chance to replace her. She did not openly challenge it. She simply maintained the continuous contradiction of publicly professing concern for parliamentary institutions, while undoing their inner scaffolding, a style that had significantly altered the Indian landscape.

She had used Parliament to endorse ordinances promulgated when she encountered resistance to a measure. An assembly in which Nehru's meticulous regard for democratic principle and procedure had produced a high level of debate had descended to the bulk and intimidation of sheer numbers, blunted to, or contemptuous of an opposing opinion. Nehru had run government on big majorities, but much of the modification or acceptance of policy had come from an exchange of views within the party as well as criticism outside it. Mrs. Gandhi treated the Opposition as illegitimate, and this inevitably affected fresh air and freedom within her own party. The strict conformity demanded as patriotic paralyzed expression and ideas. The civil service was similarly affected. Administrative reform, accented by her as a vital need, had in actual working become an arbitrary exercise, with administrators dependent on government favor, instead of an overhaul of administrative procedures themselves.

The atmosphere for magnanimity and cooperation, now that her own political strength was secure, was vitiated by a cultivated arrogance. Congress M.P.s were told not to foregather with Opposition M.P.s in the central lobby of Parliament, traditionally a meeting place for politicians and journalists, where political crosscurrents met in a relaxed exchange of views and humor. The directive was condemned as absurd by A. B. Vajpayee (Jan Sangh), Hiren Mukerjee (CPI), and Madhu Limaye (Socialist Party), but the absurdity had a somber touch. The ruling party behaved not only as dominant but permanent, and the prime minister seemed temperamentally unable to adjust to the very concept of Parliament. In an article published in August 1973, Hiren Mukerjee wrote:

> Unlike her father, who rejoiced in Parliament, Mrs. Indira Gandhi, though Leader of the Lok Sabha, apart from being Prime Minister, has an allergy to it. One may understand a certain personal reticence, for Parliament today is a peculiar and sometimes repellant kettle of fish, very different from what it was till ten years ago; but it is representative of our people's soured mood and the Prime Minister must come to terms and make friends with it. She prefers, however, to let hordes of people interview her, and listen rather than talk, keeping away even

when most needed in Parliament sessions. One wonders if she prefers the Presidential form of government, but meanwhile the business of the country suffers. Her massive majority and the fact of the Opposition being miscellaneous and very differently motivated, has enabled a gloss to be placed even over what can be called a political enormity, namely, the phenomenon of unprecedentedly heartless treatment of political prisoners, large numbers of whom have been beaten up and killed, inside and outside of jails, without anything like a judicial process, without conformity with routine regulations regarding post mortem and other investigations.

Her style had affected the balance between the states and the central government. With many, and eventually all, of Congress chief ministers her nominees—not the choice of the party's state units—the Center's* detailed interference became the norm in state affairs. While this enormously strengthened Mrs. Gandhi's own grip on her party's state units and made reward and punishment in the form of granting or withholding loans and assistance from the Center to state governments her own prerogative, the damage to the federal structure soon showed. State politics revealed an instability resembling the period of unsteady coalitions after the 1967 election, with bargaining and defections confined now to factions of the Congress. A jungle of intrigue and intraparty feuding sprouted, unlike the factional differences of the Nehru era, when state leadership and considerations had resolved crises. The rungs of the ladder of command now dispensed with, all decision issued from the top. The results were detrimental to both party and country. In her grasp of the nuts and bolts of the machinery of power, so essential to control, Mrs. Gandhi exhibited a curious lack of overall vision, if power was to be vested in a community and not in the person of a single leader. She installed a strategy of command that depended entirely on personal loyalty. It did not train a leadership for the future, taking care to remove or subdue any sign of emerging leadership. Her vision stopped at the machine, and her unrelenting hold on it produced near-chaotic conditions in the states. Faction quarrels in Orissa forced Nandini Sathpathy (sent there by Mrs. Gandhi as chief minister in 1972) to quit. Kedar Pandey in Bihar and Ghanshyam Oza in Gujarat followed suit. In Madhya Pradesh P. C. Sethi fought the rebel faction in order to retain control as chief minister. In Andhra Pradesh where a separatist agitation started,

* The term "Center" is commonly used for the Union government (as opposed to the State governments).

Mrs. Gandhi's nominee faced rough weather. By 1973 faction fighting in many states was endemic, with state units in disarray and their leaders abandoning deteriorating conditions of law and order and economic decline while they sought the Prime Minister's intervention to keep their seats from rivals in their own party. Shaky on their own ground, each problem sent them hurrying to Delhi for orders.

The props and conventions of political behavior had been set aside by Mrs. Gandhi during 1969, and her own party felt the recoil. She was acknowledged leader over its mushrooming indiscipline, but did not seem able to prevent it. There was disgrace in the spectacle of the ruling party in its exalted, unrivaled position fallen into a snarl of schemes and intrigues. The *Patriot* lamented editorially in July 1973:

> While the Congress factions were busy cutting each other's throats, Ahmedabad witnessed a shameless outbreak of communal violence, a gruesome reminder to the ruling party that communal gangsters, if not the more unscrupulous elements in its own ranks, are ever on the prowl to exploit every unstable situation for their own ends.

In another July editorial the *Patriot* described the condition of the ruling party as an

> ... epidemic of petty factionalism that is spreading in the Congress from State to State, paralysing its organisational structure, benumbing whatever mind it had and threatening to create a mortal political crisis when the country is reeling without any sense of direction in a chaotic economic morass. ...

These indictments by a CPI-owned newspaper and supporter of the Congress were almost indistinguishable from the Right wing Jan Sangh organ, *Motherland*'s comment on Madhya Pradesh affairs:

> Mr. Sethi's personal fate or the outcome of the Congress faction fights, however, is of little concern to the people. What is really tragic is that the destiny of the nation should be in the hands of these morally sick leaders of a sick political party.

There was an increasing awareness of corruption at high levels. The public was convinced of authority's lucrative alliance with corrupt elements in the country, important smugglers among them, and with the "black money" that flowed from sections of industry.

It was finally the state of Bihar that showed the most dire effects of federal corrosion when, in 1974, the state government gave up all pretence at decision-making during a period requiring the most careful judgement and action.

Tension mounted within the Congress over its alliance with the CPI. The Nehru Study Forum considered it unnecessary and harmful to the party's image in the country. The Young Turk, Chandrasekhar, spoke scathingly of Communist "management" of the Congress, violently objecting to this new political elite, the control it exercised, and the Communist stamp that flourished under Mrs. Gandhi's umbrella. It was feared the extent of Indian commitment to the Soviet Union was cutting out other options when India needed wheat and skills. Yet the alliance with the CPI was officially and publicly affirmed in March 1973 when the CPI and the Congress took part in a New Delhi seminar organized by the Congress Form for Socialist Action, presided over by Congress President Shankar Dayal Sharma, to alert the people against "the Rightist counterrevolutionary challenge." Mrs. Gandhi ordered both forums to wind up when they clashed in open recrimination. But the tension continued.

As the bloom faded from the ruling party's image, disillusionment focused on two of its prominent figures: Lalit Narayan Mishra, Union minister for railways, and Bansi Lal, chief minister of Haryana. The 53rd Report of the Estimates Committee of the Bihar Assembly had recorded that L. N. Mishra and his family had made substantial fortunes out of contracts connected with Bihar's Kosi project. Specific charges of corruption and misuse of authority had been brought against Bansi Lal by Opposition leaders. These, addressed to President V. V. Giri, were contained in three documented memoradums, calling for an inquiry. As the demand for an inquiry gathered force during the 1972 monsoon* session of Parliament, Mrs. Gandhi gave the charge sheet against him to a subcommittee of the cabinet, of which D. P. Dhar, Kashmiri head of the Planning Commission, was an important member. It exonerated Bansi Lal and dismissed the charges. If Mrs. Gandhi was disturbed by the reputations of these colleagues she gave no indication of it. Her public references to them were warm and appreciative. The expectation that she would replace or reprimand them did not materialize. The impression grew that these were key figures in her confidence whose services could not be easily replaced. Her pa-

* Monsoon is rainy season. The monsoon session of Parliament is five or six weeks during July–August.

tronage of them made them flashpoints of a rising resentment. While L. N. Mishra, associated with fund-raising for the party, remained in the background, Bansi Lal, a cruder and more colorful political figure, was involved in open controversy and was known to have the prime minister's special protection in return for his staunch support and 291 acres of requisitioned land provided for her son's car factory in his state.

In her capacity as leader, Mrs. Gandhi apparently did not feel accountable to her party. She cultivated a monarchical remoteness, above and beyond the growing uproar of factionalism and criticism, untouched by and oblivious to it. Indeed she denied any interest in leadership. She had told the Congress Parliamentary Party on March 13, 1972: "I am not one of those who believe in leadership. My whole attempt is to create a society in which people do not need leaders." The society she was creating showed all the grotesquerie of the opposite trend. For those who had long known it, there was a peculiar pathos in watching the Congress, once a national movement inspired by high ideals, in its best days devoted to hard work and a constructive purpose, thus succumb. The idea of a leader as the focus of admiration and adulation was not new to Indians, a people more willing than most to follow a leader. But modern India's leadership had been built and based on professional excellence or on great example, not on the emblems or actuality of power. Mrs. Gandhi's citadel attracted an older simile, that of a reigning medieval monarch surrounded by the panoply of a court, its flattery, its intrigue, and the swift retribution that visits offendors. Backed by the modern machinery of state power in a country where the majority were uneducated and could be easily manipulated, her scope for the exercise of arbitrary leadership was almost unlimited. The pedestal she occupied, high above the party, served her well. Indicative of her lack of the common touch, her inability to tolerate equals, her trust of no one—failings of tragic proportion in ordinary life—it created the necessary regal distance between her and the party, her and the crowd, so that, though the muddy tide of corruption and confusion lapped at her, it could not overwhelm her. She could remain unsullied by it.

This became harder to do as questions rose and a storm broke in Parliament over the nonappearance of Maruti, her son Sanjay's car project, his failure to account for the delay and his personal financial gains from government contracts. There was critical comment in the press and talk in marketplaces and coffee houses, where most controversial issues and political scandal ended for dissection. Industry was called to account and penalized for failing to produce under a licence. No strictures had been served on the Maruti factory, built in record time at a period when building was handicapped by shortages of cement and other materials.

One newspaper, the *Hindustan Times*, was expected to withold both unfavourable comment and neutral assessment. K. K. Birla, its proprietor, and financial backer of Sanjay Gandhi, conveyed Sanjay's annoyance to the editor. B. G. Verghese replied on September 19, 1973, with his customary clarity and composure:

Dear Mrs. Birla,
Following your telephone call yesterday I checked through our file of items published on Maruti. According to our library clippings there is only one item recently published and this is an interview with Mr. Sanjay Gandhi published in the *Evening News* of September 5. This interview gave Mr. Gandhi an opportunity to project his project in the best manner possible.

Earlier in July we had published a news item about the automobile industry in which the opening reference was to Maruti.

Wing Commander Chaudhry of Maruti Ltd. sent us a letter discussing some of the points contained in our news report. This was published extensively. The clippings are enclosed. Some time later Wing Commander Chaudhry sent us a second letter apropos of nothing, which very largely repeated the points contained in his earlier letter. This we did not publish as it made no new point and came within a few weeks of the publication of the earlier letter.

I am, therefore, surprised that Mr. Sanjay Gandhi should feel that we have been unfair to him or his project. On the contrary we showed great forbearance in accepting the letters sent by Wing Commander Chaudhry although these were sent to us personally through a senior information official of the Prime Minister's Secretariat. This was very improper and is the kind of thing that arouses a great deal of suspicion, and lends credibility to the various public charges being made about official favours being bestowed on Maruti Ltd. . . .

With kind regards,
Yours sincerely,
(Sd.) B. G. Verghese

Verghese's editorship of the *Hindustan Times* was terminated on Sanjay Gandhi's order and with Mrs. Gandhi's knowledge and tacit consent. Actual dismissal was held up by the Delhi High Court's stay order and did not become official until September 22, 1975. Verghese's case became a cause celebre with a macabre twist.

The issue it raised— proprietal interference—gave a handle to the government's "diffusion of ownership" scheme and later its steps to "restructure" the press, while in fact the proprietor was carrying out the orders of Mrs. Gandhi's son. The government's claim that it wished to end the "monopoly" of the larger newspapers stood revealed as hypocritical when in 1976, K. K. Birla, publisher of the *Hindustan Times,* was made chairman of the board of directors of the *Indian Express* newspapers in obvious recognition of his services to the Gandhi family, with control over a larger newspaper "monopoly" than before.

Indian agriculture depends crucially upon the period of rain between June and September known as the monsoon. Its failure in 1972 was the beginning of a severe economic crisis laying bare the government's lack of program. Prices rose by 14 percent, essential supplies fell short, drought and famine gripped large areas. Constant and crippling power crises affected vital areas of public and private industry. The anxiety over food and unemployment set off agitations, often violent, at nine universities. These had to close for a time, including Delhi University and the prestigious Indian Institute of Technology in the capital. Government's announcements that disparities must end, "crash" programs would be launched for employment and agriculture, "big" business would be drastically limited in its scope of manufacture and would have to abandon the profit motive, got no further than cutting off existing initiative and performance. The excitement of bank nationalization had died away and with no clear credit policy had become a nonevent. The optimism following the Bangladesh victory was turning into shock and anger. Remedy, or even an attempt at it, seemed blocked by an atmosphere of moral decay surrounding and supporting political functioning at the highest level. No one expected purity of politicians, but the conviction that things had gone too far was not confined to critics of Mrs. Gandhi's party. Addressing a convocation of Jawaharlal Nehru University in Delhi, of which Mrs. Gandhi herself was chancellor, film actor Balraj Sahni, a star in the Left firmament, created a stir when he named Union and state ministers as corrupt. The sins of the undivided Congress looked pale and sedate compared with the lawlessness of Mrs. Gandhi and her lieutenants and their assumption of nonaccountability at the bar of any opinion.

In October 1972 a debate on fundamental rights began before a thirteen-member bench of the Supreme Court. Counsel for the petitioners who challenged the validity of the recent amendments was N. A. Palkhivala, eminent constitutional lawyer and authority on tax law. The government was defended by a galaxy of state advocates general in addition to the attorney general. The judgement, a mixed one, was delivered on April 23, 1973. The main issues before the judges were: (1) Can Parliament amend fundamental rights under its normal amending power consisting of a two-thirds majority in both Houses of Parliament? (2) Assuming it can, are there any areas affecting the use of these rights that the amending power cannot override? The majority of judges decided that fundamental rights can be amended by the normal amending power, but that essential features of the Constitution cannot be so changed. These, however, were not demarcated, leaving the fundamental rights in a gray legal area to be variously interpreted. A bulwark against possible dictatorship was heavily eroded, and the government's use of its mandate became a palpable anxiety.

The annual Congress session at Bidhan Nagar near Calcutta, held in December 1972 amid flourish and display during India's worst economic crisis, aroused comment, both despairing and caustic, from leading newspapers. Some of its severest critics were Congressmen themselves, the ebullient younger element, unawed and unsilenced, whose crusading fire had helped to raise Mrs. Gandhi to her powerful pedestal, and who had pinned great hopes on her for the fashioning of a clean, cohesive instrument to bring about change.

Key speeches at Bidhan Nagar took no searching look at the party's ills or the economic crisis. The Congress President, Shankar Dayal Sharma, spoke instead of "the forces of reaction eager to take advantage." Defence Minister Chavan called the violent agitations in Andhra Pradesh and Assam the efforts of Right and Left extremists to obstruct socialism: "We have to do everything possible to frustrate their machinations. They are not yet reconciled to the massive victory of the Congress in the last two elections." Mrs. Gandhi predictably declared: "We are with the people. Neither the capitalists nor the press can detract us from our path." This monotonous chant added thin comfort to what the *Tribune* editorially called:

> ... a year of less hope and more despair, of rich rhetoric and poor performance, of more bogeys and less realism in India. For Mrs. Gandhi personally and the Congress generally, it was in some ways the worst year since the historic split in 1969. Both were at the crossroads again, totally uncertain of the future.

CHAPTER NINE

Rhetoric and Reality

The ruling party had framed a national policy on agricultural land ceilings, with urban ceilings to follow, and had announced it would "extend the public sector" in areas where "state ownership is vital." These included coal, sections of foreign trade, and food grains. The Bidhan Nagar Congress session decided to eliminate the wholesale trade in food grains, making government the sole buyer of the wheat crop of April 1973 and the rice crop in October, through a government agency. Some chief ministers advised delay of such a massive operation that would need careful preparation, not only for procurement from the farmer, but for distribution over a vast population. These misgivings were hesitantly put forward and not freely aired in party councils, for fear that doubts about policy would mean a reactionary label and a black mark. An incomplete plan, conceived in haste, driven by the need to maintain a radical posture, resulted in long queues for bread in cities, the disappearance of grain altogether at intervals, and conditions bordering on anarchy in some areas. Discussing its failure, E. N. Mangat Rai[1] describes it as twofold: (1) Government made exceptions to its own monopoly, allowing retailers, and then consumers to buy privately, thus drilling leaks into the system. (2) An effective distribution system to ensure grain to the public was not created. The resulting panic put a strain on monopoly procurement that broke it:

> ... if government as the sole controller of grain creates a monopoly ... it must create a distribution agency for all persons to be fed. ... The responsibility to supply and the obligation by the consumer to accept no other supply were both lacking. In the absence of rationing, which provides precisely these twin points of security to system and consumer, there was a vacuum. The government met the situation by

99

allowing retailers to purchase limited amounts from the market to feed their customers, and by allowing customers to buy direct from the farmer for personal consumption. The farmer was convinced that he had not one buyer . . . for his wheat, but several. In places the consumer, when he could-not lay hands on supplies, panicked. . . . As the season advanced there were food riots, first in Nagpur, then in Bombay, later in Mysore. In Kerala education was shut down after students attacked grain trucks. Supplies were rushed to distress areas; the movement of "special trainloads" was publicized in the press and over the government-operated radio. There was drama about the movement of food. The wheat "monopoly" had become a shambles within weeks of its start. On 31 August Fakhruddin Ali Ahmed, the Food Minister, reporting to the party said that the government had purchased to that date 600–700,000 tonnes less than it did in a free market in the previous year. The buffer stock (of 9 million tonnes on July 1, 1972) had been reduced, after accounting for new purchases, to 4 million tonnes.

Some of the chaos could have been avoided if the experienced wholesale trade had been retained as government's agent and paid at a fixed price, as had been done in a streamlined operation following the Bengal famine of 1943 and continued for some years after independence. But policy-makers had now labeled the wholesale trade a "vested interest" and earmarked it for destruction.

As the government lost control of the food situation, a mixture of incentives and threat were belatedly held over the farmer, further confusing the takeover operation, and the country driven to import more than 6 million tonnes of grain at a high international price in the very year that self-sufficiency was to have been proclaimed. The rice crop takeover by the government, scheduled for October, was "postponed." The intention to take over the wheat crop of April 1974 was abandoned. Mrs. Gandhi's statement that the people would have starved but for government action did not explain why the action had been abruptly discontinued. She laid the blame for its failure on the bureaucracy's ineptitude. On July 29, 1975, when dictatorship had silenced dissent, efficiency was the government's proclaimed watchword and blame could no longer be passed on, Food Minister C. Subramaniam said in the Rajya Sabha, quietly disowning a past disaster, "The idea looks all right on paper. But taking over the entire surplus grains would burden the system, leading to its collapse. Instead efforts should be made to build up a public distribution system for specific areas."

This manifest economic failure was accompanied by a rude shock to stability in Uttar Pradesh, the country's most populous state, with the largest number of seats in Parliament, and Mrs. Gandhi's constituency. Chief Minister Kamalapati Tripathi was clearly not in control, as a lightning revolt of the Provincial Armed Constabulary (the state's special police force) succeeded to the extent of capturing arsenals and refusing to surrender. President's rule was imposed on Uttar Pradesh. The governor, Akbar Ali Khan's letter on June 12, 1973 to the president, reporting economic crisis and police revolt halted only by the army's intervention, spoke glowingly of the chief minister:

> You and your Government have been in touch with the recent happenings in the State. The power shortage and scarcity of essential commodities had already created considerable difficulties for the general public and the State government was trying to grapple with these problems, as well as with the growing student unrest, when it had to face quite a serious situation caused by some sections of the civil police and the PAC. The incidents of grave indiscipline on the part of the subordinate ranks in some companies of the PAC had to be dealt with firmly, and assistance of the armed forces of the Union Government had to be requisitioned to meet an unprecedented situation.... The voluntary resignation of the Ministry headed by Shri Kamalapati Tripathi has come in spite of his unchallenged leadership of the Congress Legislature Party.... I would like to place on record my deep appreciation of Shri Tripathi's record as Chief Minister, the crowning glory of which consists in what he has rightly described as his act of self-abnegation in the larger interests of the State and the nation.

This letter is perhaps unsurpassed as an example of the mythical air state governments breathed, remaining bland and benevolent towards such stark realities as "the power shortage and scarcity of essential commodities," "growing student unrest," and even the "unprecedented situation" of actual police revolt. A state seething with political and economic discontent headed by a chief minister known to tolerate corruption—twin evils creating a volcanic resentment against Congress power in many parts of India—appear to have left the governor blissfully undisturbed. It is possible Akbar Ali Khan was aware a more factual report would have angered New Delhi, placing him in a position of critic towards Tripathi, a favorite. With President's Rule, the legislature was not, according to normal practice, dissolved. No risk could be taken with the Congress majority, which showed signs of being heavily eroded if another election were held, and members of legislative assemblies (M.L.A.s) continued to enjoy their perquisites. Despite the governor's assertion of Tripathi's "unchallenged leadership of the Congress Legislature Party," the Uttar Pradesh Congress presented a classic picture of political talent and vigor kept in check by an ineffective leadership obedient to the Center.

This travesty of a governor's responsibility for assessment and report reached its climax with the dismissal of Kamalapati Tripathi's successor in 1975. H. N. Bahuguna, one of the state's younger politicians, was appointed chief minister in Tripathi's place on November 8, 1973. Bahuguna set about with energy, ambition, and drive to restore efficiency. His solid political base in Uttar Pradesh and his confident stride attracted unfavorable notice. He was reported as having less than the requisite ardor for Mrs. Gandhi and dismissed without cause in November 1975. No effort was made to cloak this executive order in constitutional guise. It had been preceded by the appointment of a new governor, Chenna Reddy, whose brief included a close watch on Bahuguna's "loyalty" to Mrs. Gandhi, a mission he took no trouble to hide, taking over executive functions in the process that were not within a governor's province. S. C. Kala reported in the *Times of India* on March 13, 1975:

> He [the new governor] has called officials of the intelligence departments of the State and Centre to report to him and also issued orders directly to State government officials. . . . The Governor, who is hardly discreet in his utterances, has often made remaks which betray his hostility to Mr. H. N. Bahuguna. . . . There is no doubt his behaviour has not been constitutionally correct.

On November 29, 1975 Chenna Reddy reported to the president simply that Bahuguna, who enjoyed an "absolute majority in the State Assembly, has tendered the resignation of his Ministry to me this morning. . . ." By this time the imposition of President's Rule on a state bore no relation to the reasons stated for it in the Constitution: the actual or imminent failure of constitutional government. In fact, the frequency and transparent unconstitutionality of its exercise had deprived it of its meaning. In an article "Misuse of President's Rule" in the *Times of India* (July 16, 1973), Ajit Bhattacharjea had commented: "Since Mrs. Gandhi became Prime Minister 7½ years ago, the Centre has invoked President's Rule 22 times to take over the administration of States. In the previous 16 years, after the Constitution took effect, these emergency powers were used 10 times."

Among the rising stars Mrs. Gandhi was to cut down from their heights before long were two Young Turks about whom a special splendor shone as they took up fighting positions to demand a clean and dedicated Congress. Mohan Dharia and Chandrasekhar (born in 1925 and 1927 respectively) had both come to the Congress via the Socialist Party, home of some of the most original intellects in the country. Like many of their generation now celebrities in politics, they had been student activists. Both were of the caliber a political party normally regards as leadership material. Dharia had charge of the party's election campaign in Maharashtra in 1962 and 1967. He had been elected to the Rajya Sabha in 1964 and 1970, and to the Lok Sabha from Poona city in 1971. Mrs. Gandhi had appointed him minister of state for planning in that year. Chandrasekhar had been a member of the Congress Working Committee since 1967. He was elected to the Central Election Committee in 1971, to the Rajya Sabha in 1972 and reelected to it in 1974. His immense popularity and political flair had won him elected party posts against determined attempts to defeat him.

A third rebel who incurred his leader's displeasure was Krishna Kant. He was elected to the Rajya Sabha in 1966 and reelected in 1972. During 1971–72 he was secretary to the Congress Parliamentary Party.

All three shared an independence of speech and outlook and a dogged disregard of whom these might offend. In the sea of conformity, even servility, around Mrs. Gandhi, they were irrepressible, identifiable, attractive individuals, each with a capacity to go far in the party. A child of privilege herself, with special courtesy and consideration shown to her as Nehru's daughter by the party and the country, Mrs. Gandhi had entered politics at the top and not through the rugged school of competition. Her insistence on her unique position revealed her insecurity on her pinnacle and her distance from the true metier and experience of the natural politician, which her inbred disposition did nothing to overcome. She felt safe with the mediocre, uncomfortable in the presence of outstanding political talent or personality, and threatened by aspiration that sprang from the ground and did not need her permission to succeed. It was simpler for her to deal with the elders in her party, no longer willing or able to do open battle. Any show of political virility alerted her to danger. To disagree with her was unpatriotic. In her own party it was to become lèse majesté.

In a country so diverse culturally, where the problems of poverty and integration demand solution, a charismatic leader may well be an insurance of political stability and the will to get things done.

Nehru had been one in his time. Mrs Gandhi, however, introduced authoritarian trends and ideas into the Indian polity very different from the values of her two predecessors. It is possible that, in her hunger for leadership and without the solid apprenticeship this required, she became involved in more than she bargained for—a complex human situation, not merely a political one—and that a turn away from freedom became the inexorable course in reducing the human to malleable material. By the end of 1973 India's political and constitutional future were uncertain, without any balancing assurance of economic gain. And this was the consequence not of a "people's" urge but of a particular character driven by its own urges, in search of fulfilment.

Power has been sought for a variety of reasons. Mrs. Gandhi was not unusual in thus using "the people." The people serve, especially in a society such as India, patiently and often passively as the raw material of power. It is the leader who invents, or authentically articulates, their demands. How he conceives and articulates them is a matter of his own belief and temperament. What he draws from them reflects in part what he himself is. Thus Mahatma Gandhi could get mass participation through an appeal to suffering and make it a platform for dynamic political action. Jawaharlal Nehru could sustain democracy partly by sheer faith, upholding a vision of the future beyond present difficulties, so crucial for the courage all voluntary effort needs. Indira Gandhi understood the leadership of India as a relation between the ruler and the ruled, a rigid formula that left out the noblest and richest possibilities in human development.

CHAPTER TEN

Jayaprakash Narayan

In March 1974, a student movement in Bihar, originating as a demand for educational reform, created, under the leadership of Jayaprakash Narayan, the conditions for a powerful political challenge to Mrs. Gandhi. Jayaprakash, the most unusual figure in Indian politics and for twenty-four years, 1930 to 1954, the most important in the age-group under Nehru, had a career more fully representative of India's three-cornered political tradition than any other Indian. Three streams—British liberalism, Marxism and Gandhism—met in it to evolve a personal philosophy.

The challenge to Mrs. Gandhi was led by a man as different in background, experience, and temperament from her as can be imagined. Jayaprakash was born, the fourth of six children, on October 11, 1902, into a lower-middle-class family in Sitabdiara village on the Uttar Pradesh-Bihar border, where his father was a revenue official in Bihar's canal department. There were few comforts at home but there was plenty to read. He saw a city for the first time when, aged twelve, wearing the villager's dhoti*, shirt, and flat cap on his head, he arrived in Patna to join school. Matriculating with high marks in 1919, he got a government scholarship of Rs 15 a month to Patna College. At about this time, he was married by arrangement to fourteen-year-old Prabhavati whose father, Brij Kishore, had helped Mahatma Gandhi collect data on indigo plantation workers in Champaran and had supported his Champaran *satyagraha* (civil disobedience) campaign.

Jayaprakash left college two years later when Maulana Azad and Jawaharlal Nehru made a stirring appeal to students at a public

* Garment worn by men in north India.

meeting in Patna to work for freedom. JP (as he was propularly known) wrote later:

> I . . . was one of the thousands of young men of those days who, like leaves in a storm, were swept away and momentarily lifted up to the skies. That brief experience of soaring up with the winds of a great idea left imprints on the inner being that time and much familiarity with the ugliness of reality have not removed.[1]

His family persuaded him to take his examination, due in a month, from the Bihar Vidyapeeth, a college just established for students who had walked out of institutions aided by the British Government, and later to continue his studies outside India. In 1922 he sailed for the United States with $600 which he would have to supplement with what he could earn. He told a public meeting in Patna on June 5, 1974:

> I worked in mines, in factories, in slaughter houses. I worked as a shoeshine boy and even cleaned commodes [toilets] in hotels. During vacations . . . three or more boys lived in a single room and we cooked our own food. After graduation I got a scholarship and three months later an assistantship in my department which made it possible for me to live in some comfort.

He spent seven years in America, his studies interrupted by a long illness and a variety of jobs, and attended four universities, leaving California (Berkeley) where he could not afford the fees, for Iowa, Wisconsin, and finally Ohio. Saul D. Ozer, a classmate at Wisconsin, told Nageshwar Prasad of the Institute of Gandhian Studies, Varanasi, in March 1968:

> I had never met a person who was more awake and intellectually alive to the implications of whatever anybody in that class said. He was always like an architect, developing his case and argument to its logical conclusion. And as a logician he was superb. . . . We all felt there was greatness in Narayan.

Ozer remembers JP as tall and strikingly handsome. When they entered the library, "it wasn't more than five minutes before every seat was filled with girls looking at Narayan." His habits were monastic. He did not smoke, drink, or date. He did, in his own words, try "to learn to dance at the Recreation Room. I didn't have enough time, and never became any good." At a farewell party given by his Indian friends in New York before he left for home, they insisted that he "at least smoke a cigarette before leaving the shores of the United States."

The certificates his professors at Ohio University gave him when he applied for a fellowhip in New York reveal the wholeness of his impact on them, and a sustained academic brilliance that seemed as much a trait of character as a quality of mind. Ajit Bhattacharjea lists three in his biography:

> Intellectually, it seems to me, Mr. Narayan ranks as high or higher than any student I have ever had. He is a careful and critical thinker, and a searcher after truth; of course he is a wide reader. He is, in every sense, a scholar in the making. (Professor L. E. Dumley, Sociology Department.)
>
> In his class work on theoretical psychology I think he is one of the brightest students I have ever had. My impression at this time is that he has in him qualifications which under favorable conditions will lead to an outstanding position as a social theorist. (Professor Albert Weiss, Psychology Department.)
>
> Perhaps Mr. J. P. Narayan's most remarkable trait . . . is his idealism. It infuses his daily life as well as his world outlook. It has been my experience in living with him to be surprised again and again by little unexpected acts of unselfishness. (Professor Richard Steinmetz, Campus and Communications Department.)

JP's Hindi biographer, Lakshmi Narain Lal,[2] lists three others:

> He shows distinctly an enquiring turn of mind and a critical capacity rare even in the better class of graduate students. He is a fine-appearing man, a thorough gentleman, and in my opinion, a thorough student. I have noted that he always has an interest in the larger and deeper problems of economics, rather than in matters of technical detail. . . . (Professor A. B. Wolfe, Economics Department.)
>
> His work with me is consistently A grade. He is openminded, eager to make intellectual contacts and has plenty of originality. In short, Mr. Narayan belongs to the highest class of graduate ability. . . . (Professor Charles A. Dice, Department of Banking and Money Market.)
>
> Mr. J. P. Narayan is a fine candidate for a Moral Leadership fellowship. He is one of the ablest students I have ever had, both keen and deep. His whole outlook is based on a desire to know how to do something to help society. . . . (Professor Millar.)

JP's American experience was both varied and profound. At Wisconsin, Polish-born American communist Abram Landy introduced him to the Communist creed and classics. Convinced that

Marxism was the solution for change in India, JP found its paradoxes hard to digest. Ozer called him: ". . . a strange mixture of Marxism and Gandhism. . . . He told me that the major thing that bothered him was the morality, character, integrity of the Communist. . . ."

At home he joined the Congress, not the Communist Party. The Salt March in early 1930 impressed him deeply with the discovery that, while the ideologues propounded ideology, Gandhi, with neither ideology nor manifesto, took the people with him. The Mahatma's mission, freedom without violence, transcended political programs, yet concerned itself minutely with the human springs of social and economic change. Stalin's excesses disillusioned and repelled JP as they did his contemporaries, Ignacio Silone and Arthur Koestler. Yet his belief in Marxism and his admiration for many aspects of the Soviet experiment remained integral to his thinking, even after a brief abrasive collaboration between his Congress Socialist Party and the Communist Party decided him against any further link with the Communists. Differences between the two became bitter in 1939, when the CPI justified the Soviet invasion of Finland. The partnership broke when the CPI joined the British government's war effort, ignoring the nationalist mood in India and the Congress demand for an assurance of independence before it would actively support the Allies.

Prabhavati had spent the years of her husband's absence at Mahatma Gandhi's ashram in Wardha. JP's Hindi biographer records:

> Seven years later, when JP returned, they began to live together; but Prabha's vow of *brahmacharya** and her involvement with Gandhi's programme caused its stresses . . . [JP's] intellectual bias was Western; rationalism was an unfailing yardstick, dialectical materialism a tenet. . . . On the public platform, Jayaprakash would tirade against Gandhi, subjecting his arguments to a searching scrutiny. Behind him on the same platform, Prabhavati quietly spun raw cotton on a charkha†. . . . Yet there was a strong emotional bond that held them together.

JP's association with Congress Party began in 1930. His intellectual caliber, integrity, and ardent commitment to freedom endeared him to Nehru, thirteen years his senior, while Kamala Nehru and Prabhavati were drawn to each other. When Gandhi launched

* Chastity
† Spinning wheel, symbol of Mahatma Gandhi's ideology, including economics.

civil disobedience in 1932 and the government arrested Congress leaders, JP took charge of organizational work until his own arrest in September. He had made enough impact on the party and the public by then to merit Bombay's *Free press Journal* headline: "Congress Brain Arrested."

His fellow prisoners in Nasik Jail were, like himself, impatient young men afire with ideas, eager to give the Congress a Leftward direction and a firm economic program. They inaugurated the Congress Socialist Party, a radical group within the Congress, in Bombay in October 1934. The CSP sought the involvement of the intelligentsia as well as the peasants and working classes. JP toured the country to promote its programs and explain its ideas. His first tract, *Why Socialism*, was published and widely read in 1936, while his four imprisonments during British rule added drama to his celebrity. His second arrest, in March 1940, for making a "seditious" speech at a strike meeting of steel workers at Jamshedpur, Bihar, provoked Mahatma Gandhi to comment in his paper *Harijan:* "The arrest of Shri Jayaprakash Narayan is unfortunate. He is no ordinary worker. . . . He has forsaken all for the sake of the deliverance of his country. His industry is tireless. His capacity for suffering is not to be excelled. . . ."

His nine-month sentence ended at the close of the year, but he was arrested again soon afterward. As organizer of strikes, particularly in the steel industry, aimed at impeding Britain's war effort, he was a special target for the police and a growing legend for the public. Detained this time in a prisoner-of-war camp near Ajmer, he and thirty fellow prisoners went on a month's hunger strike in protest against camp conditions. A roused public opinion succeeded in getting the camp closed and its inmates transferred to jails in their own states. JP was sent to Hazaribagh Jail in Bihar. On November 9, 1942, he and five colleagues scaled the prison's seventeen-foot wall and escaped. The Quit India agitation begun three months earlier, sparked by the arrests of Gandhi, Nehru, and other leaders, had led to violent uprisings in part of the country and caused major dislocations in transport and communications. The sensational escape from Hazaribagh thrilled patriotic sentiment, as did JP's underground activities. In hiding, he and Ram Manohar Lohia, who had escaped with him, raised a small guerilla band near the Bihar-Nepal border, printed militant pamphlets against British rule, and traveled in disguise to organize resistance all over India. With a 10,000-rupee reward for information leading to their capture,

JP was arrested in September 1943 (and Lohia soon afterward) and held until April 1946, a year longer than senior Congress leaders.

Crowds gave him a tumultuous welcome on the train journey home to Patna. In the popular imagination he was a hero, covered with a charisma and glory second only to Nehru's, and looked upon as his successor, though now their paths diverged. The socialists formed a separate party when the Congress took power at indpendence, though Mahatma Gandhi remained a link between the two. In February 1947, on the eve of separation, Lohia, CSP president, said at Kanpur: "The Congress is our home. Even when one leaves a home, it is not easy to deal badly with it. . . . It is our hope that as long as Gandhi lives, he will not allow the Congress to abandon its revolutionary goals."

Gandhi was killed in January 1948. His agrarian emphasis, belief in decentralization, and in revolution as applicable to caste, not class struggle, achievable through peaceful, not violent means, remained a rallying program for the socialists. The dead Mahatma continued to light the way with a fundamentally Indian Leftism and rationale, as against the Moscow-dominated CPI and a Nehru government that the socialists believed was overly influenced by Western economic concepts.

The Praja Socialist Party (PSP), as a merger of socialist parties was called after 1952, was invited by Nehru in 1953 to cooperate with his government. The move was dropped when JP wrote to Nehru, saying it would have no meaning if it meant strengthening his hands "in carrying out your present policies." The party's impact was weakened and scattered when Lohia broke away with his own splinter group in 1955, and later when JP withdrew to seek solutions to India's problems outside party politics. It was yet perhaps the most idealistic development in Indian politics. Part and parcel of the national movement and the Congress inheritance, it did not fall under the Congress spell. It rejected charisma in favor of argument, criticism, and thought. Contemptuous of the doctrinaire, it kept the pot of ideas boiling.

On a visit to Gandhi's ashram at Wardha in 1952, JP found the institutions around it were "in far greater touch with the people and their problems than any other group in the country." The following year he went on a three-week purification fast in his evolving search for answers, coming to the conclusion that, "The problem of human goodness is of supreme moment today . . . it has become patent to me that materialism of any sort robs man of the means to become truly human. . . ."³ On April 29, 1954, he announced his intention to work for Bhoodan, Vinobha Bhave's land gift movement, a section of the Sarvodaya movement begun by Gandhi's followers after his death. In 1957 he gave up his membership in the PSP, in order to give all his time to Sarvodaya: "To create and develop forms of socialist living through the voluntary endeavour of the people rather than seek to establish socialism by the use of the power of the state."

Though ostensibly this was a withdrawal from politics, it provided a broader canvas for creating awareness in the countryside, a labor intended eventually to raise political consciousness and teach people the meaning of their democracy. His basic involvement with politics remained, and his speech to the thirteenth Sarvodaya Sammelan (a conference of the organization founded after Mahatma Gandhi's death to carry on his ideas) in 1961 had a prophetic ring:

> It means, of course, that we do not belong to any political party, that we do not and shall not take part, directly or indirectly, in any political contest for position or power. But does it also mean that we are not concerned with what is happening in the political field; with the working of our democracy and its various institutions? If democracy were to be in peril, if there was danger of political chaos, of dictatorship, shall we sit back smugly and twiddle our thumbs on the ground that we have nothing to do with politics? Perhaps it is not understood clearly that our policy not to be involved in party and power politics is meant precisely to enable us to play a more effective and constructive part in moulding the politics of the country.

A development in Madhya Pradesh strikingly illustrated his reputation as a leader whose human qualities and moral stature were held in high regard. At the request of the dacoit (outlaw) leader, Madho Singh, he negotiated with the government for humane treatment for the dacoits in return for their voluntary surrender. On condition that they would not face the death penalty, four hundred dacoits laid down their guns and ammunition in a moving ceremony before JP and his wife.

The early 1970s had seen dramatic changes in prime ministerial style and behavior. Mrs. Gandhi's drive towards centralization, her concentration of powers in her own hands, and her frequent use of the new arbitrary arrest law (MISA, June 1971) gave notice of a growing authoritarianism. In 1973 JP wrote to members of Parliament, outlining ways to protect citizens' rights and democratic institutions. An organization, Citizens for Democracy, was set up by him for this purpose. In an open letter to youth, dated December 9, 1973, he urged a Youth for Democracy movement: "What form their action should take is for the youth themselves to decide. My only recommendation would be that in keeping with the spirit and substance of democracy, it must be scrupulously peaceful and nonpartisan."

In January 1974 a student revolt against food prices in engineering college hostels in Ahmedabad and Morvi, in Gujarat, erupted into a citizens' movement against scarcity and Congress misrule in the state. A wave of antigovernment demonstrations, comparable in size to preindependence civil disobedience, was brought under control by the Central Reserve Police and Border Security Force rather than the state's own police. An unknown member of demonstrators had been arrested and between 85 and 100 killed by mid-March, when Mrs. Gandhi was compelled to concede the outraged demand for the state government's resignation. The Gujarat mood stayed anti-Congress. A year and a half later an election in the state ended in the Congress Party's defeat.

The agitation in Gujarat had taken Mrs. Gandhi's government by surprise. The first sign of organized protest in Bihar found it prepared, equipped, and armored.

CHAPTER ELEVEN

The Bihar Movement— 1974

The year 1974 saw an outbreak of smallpox in Bihar, so neglected by an administration caught in the coils of political maneuver that it spread to epidemic proportions. And in that year Bihar demonstrated the damage an unconfident chief minister, dependent on Mrs. Gandhi and with no political strength of his own in the state, could do in crippling a state government's initiative and, in a crisis, rendering it irrelevant altogether. Matters came to a head on March 18, 1974, precipitated by two events.

The Students' Action Committee, representing several Patna colleges and youth groups, held a demonstration that day at the state assembly, demanding a reply to a memorandum on educational reform presented to the state education minister at the end of February. The police took brisk action. Students who crossed the barricades set up by the police were removed and thrashed. They retaliated by throwing stones, and the demonstration was dispersed by lathis and tear gas. (Lathis are long wooden rods, often steel-tipped, used by the police to disperse crowds.)

On the same day a mob carrying kerosene and rags set the building housing two newspapers, *Searchlight* (English) and *Pradeep* (Hindi), on fire, destroying machines, files, records, newsprint, reels and rotary. The police arrived two and a half hours after the fire started, too late to prevent damage. The editor of *Searchlight*, S. K. Rau, believed the fire was the CPI's revenge against his editorial policy, which was critical of the Congress-CPI alliance, and that the delayed arrival of the police was deliberate.

Three days of looting and arson followed, with the police firing indiscriminately on terrified running crowds. The Bihar government, under a chief minister and cabinet sworn in eight months earlier, seemed unable to bring the situation under control. Jaya-prakash Narayan issued a statement from his home in Patna:

> In any democratic country after such a monumental failure of admin-istration as Patna witnessed on Monday last, the government would have resigned. . . . Everyone talks vaguely of hooligans and goondas [ruffians]. Hooligans, of course, were abroad in large numbers. It also seems reasonably sure that those responsible for the major incidents of arson were outsiders, probably hailing from Bhagalpur, and had a certain measure of expertise. For one thing, some of the drivers of the hijacked buses seemed to be well-trained; for another, the incendiary used appeared to be more powerful than ordinary fire and spread very quickly . . . among those arrested are members of the Tarun Shanti Sena,* the Secretary of the local centre of the Gandhi Peace Foun-dation, and the editor of *Ayeena*. Those who believe in and work for peace are being punished for the violence of others.

On April 8, at the students' request, JP led a silent procession in protest against indiscriminate arrests and police excesses. It was greeted with flowers from silent spectators. He was seventy-one, in indifferent health and bereaved by Prabhavati's death the pre-vious year. He explained his decision to enter the fray after twenty years devoted to Sarvodaya as the only possible one, in the context of recent developments. Two days earlier he had said:

> Speaking for myself, I cannot remain a silent spectator to misgovern-ment, corruption and the rest, whether in Patna, Delhi or elsewhere. It is not for this that I at least had fought for freedom. . . . I am not interested in this or that Ministry being replaced or the [Bihar] As-sembly being dissolved. These are partisan aims and their achieve-ment will make no difference. It will be like replacing Tweedledum with Tweedledee. But I have decided to fight corruption and misgov-ernment and black marketing, profiteering and hoarding, to fight for the overhaul of the educational system, and for a real people's democracy.

The students had twelve demands, eight for minor reforms at the university and four relating to corruption, unemployment, scarc-ity of essential supplies, and the need for fundamental changes in the educational system. After March 18 these were headed by the demand for the Bihar government's resignation. JP explained this unorthodox demand: "The argument that people have a constitu-tional remedy in that they can change the government at the next

---

* A youth brigade recruited by Vinoba Bhave to work for the Bhoodan Movement.

election has no validity now in view of the distortions and abuses of our democratic institutions and processes."

The student's movement expanded to include the community. Committees were formed to organize processions, meetings, and bundhs (closures of business establishments to show their support) to demonstrate the strength of the popular demand for the state government's resignation. Nonviolence was the condition for JP's leadership. Violence, which could in any case be crushed, would, he said, give the Union government an excuse to launch a dictatorship.

> Everyone participating in and sympathetic with the movement must eschew violence in word and deed, whatever the provocation. It is a matter of gratification that by and large the movement has remained peaceful. That has been its strength. God knows there has been no little provocation and it is natural that young men should become excited and angry. . . .

Nonviolence gave the movement one of its slogans: "*Police hamare bhai hain: unse nahin ladai hai.*" ("The police are our brothers; we have no quarrel with them.") The state police responded with enough sympathy for the Bihar government to summon armed aid from Delhi, as the Gujarat government had done. In shaky charge of a faction-ridden party that had no confidence in his leadership and wished him replaced, Chief Minister Abdul Ghafoor had, in any event, to rely on orders from Delhi in handling the crisis that now threatened to unseat him and overwhelm the state.

On June 5, shots fired on a procession led by JP wounded 21 participants. He referred to this, as well as to an earlier incident, at a public meeting that evening:

> The government of Bihar distrusts its own police force. We have a fine army which has raised the country's prestige and respect. Can there be a matter of greater shame than that these brave soldiers should be used to fire upon their own people? Is there no way to understand and deal with a people's movement except bullets and lathis and jail? Are not the demands of the movement such as are readily acceptable?
>
> There was an incident a few days back. A bomb exploded in a room of a dak bungalow. For two days news of the incident appeared . . . after that it was hushed up. It is said that the men in the building were members of the Indira Brigade. Now, today, shots were fired on the procession from the flat of an [Congress] MLA, Shri Phulena Rai. The flat also houses the office of the Indira Brigade. The police raided the place after the shooting and some men were caught redhanded, while

some others managed to escape. You have learned about all the arms
that were recovered from that place. Our friends in the Congress want
to give us lessons in democracy, lessons in peace. I ask the officers,
who should be given lessons?

His reference to the "army" was to troops of the Border Security
Force, created for the country's defence, now brought into Bihar
and supplemented as in Gujarat by the Union government's Central
Reserve Police (CRP). The arms found with the "Indira Brigade"
in "the flat of an [Congress] MLA," indicated the currents at work
in Bihar at this time.

The Union government's attitude toward the Bihar Movement,
starting with its tough initial handling of a student demonstration,
followed by a wave of arrests under the government's arbitrary
powers, showed a surprisingly weak link in Mrs. Gandhi's political
and psychological armor. Her view of dissidence as unnecessary
here became a refusal, or incapacity, to understand and deal in
rational terms with rational demands. The movement became for
her a personal insult, and disproportionate anger was visited on it
when it became apparent that this was not a phenomenon that could
be controlled by police action.

JP's speech on June 5 saw the Bihar stir as the inevitable outcome of conditions in the country and an opportunity to channel
the enthusiasm of its young supporters into constructive work:

> Friends, this is revolution, a total revolution. This is not a movement
> merely for the dissolution of the Assembly. We have to go far, very
> far. In the words of Jawaharlal Nehru, the people still have to travel
> many long miles to achieve that freedom for which thousands of the
> country's youth made sacrifices. . . . Hunger, soaring prices and cor-
> ruption stalk everywhere. . . . Unemploment goes on increasing. . . .
> Land ceiling laws are passed but the number of landless people is
> increasing. Small farmers have lost their lands. . . . The government
> has taken the path of falsehood and violence. It has only one power,
> that of repression. Use the police. Use arms.[1]

JP understood "total revolution" as fundamental change affecting social attitudes and economic priorities. It included decentralization, with maximum power to village communities and in
towns the strengthening of institutions of local self-government.
The former development began soon after independence and was
followed in 1959 by *Panchayat Raj* for "democratic decentralization." Welcoming *Panchayat Raj*, Nehru had said: ". . . authority
and power must be given to the people in the villages. . . . Let them

function and let them make a million mistakes. Do not be afraid about it. We are restricted in our thinking and in our movement because of our way of thinking. Let us give power to the *Panchayats.*" Institutions of local government, chiefly municipalities, were already in existence at independence with a long tradition and experience. Both developments had been neglected or eroded during the past decade. *Panchayat Raj* had gradually lost its independence and identity under pressure from state politicans. Municipalities had suffered from continual interference, the pattern of governmental erosion at state level being repeated at municipal and local levels.

West Bengal exemplified the trend. Sivadas Banerjee, writing in the *Times of India* on February 14, 1975, noted there had been no panchayat elections in Bengal for more than a decade, and in as many as 72 out of 90 municipalities a poll had been due for four to twelve years. An example of direct interference by the Union government itself was its takeover in March 1975 of the Delhi Municipal Corporation, when it became clear that the ruling Congress would be defeated in the mayoral election due on March 24. The Delhi Municipal Corporation became the twenty-fifth (of thirty-two) corporation functioning without elected representatives.

JP's effort to reverse this trend in Bihar began with the setting up of "janata sarkars," informal "people's governments." These were to work in cooperation with government agencies where possible, and without their help, if necessary, in dealing with local problems and prejudices ranging over caste, custom, the fair distribution of commodities, and the settlement of disputes outside the local court or police station. Janata sarkars would also form committees at village, block*, and district level to make people aware of their importance in the voting process, set up candidates for final selection from each polling booth area, and act as watchdogs over booths at election time. Any future government would have to reckon with these "permanent organs of people's power." Bihar, JP hoped, would become the laboratory of an experiment for which the mood of the people now seemed ripe. "Total revolution" countenanced no violent change. The negative consequence of a violent revolution, he believed, was that

> power comes invariably to be usurped by a handful of the most ruthless among the erstwhile revolutionaries [inevitable] when power comes

---

* A block comprises about 100 villages.

out of the barrel of a gun and the gun is not in the hands of the common people. . . . That is why a violent revolution has always brought forth a dictatorship of some kind or the other. And that is also why after a revolution a new privileged class of rulers and exploiters grows up in the course of time to which the people at large is once again subject.[2]

He explained the need for "janata sarkars" to the All India Youth Conference at Allahabad (UP) on June 29:

In countries where democracy has developed an infrastructure there are many checks on those in power: the press, the academic institutions, the intellectuals. There is strong public opinion. We have no such structure and it will take time to develop. I wish to give the people's movement a revolutionary direction so that the people develop their own power to become guardians of democracy. My interest is not in the capture of power, but in the control of power by the people.

A conference to report on the progress of "janata sarkar" was held in April 1975 at Khadigram (near Monghyr, Bihar). I recorded some impressions of the conference.

Many delegates were young men, some clear and forceful, others later scolded by JP for not marshalling their facts better. There was some dolefulness, some enthusiasm, but mainly unvarnished reporting. It ranged over issues involving village justice, land, sugar, caste and custom. Considerable success was reported in setting up courts for the settlement of local disputes. . . . A delegate from Bhagalpur said that a temple that raised funds through gambling sessions and shared the proceeds with the police had been stopped from doing so. In areas where it had become customary to marry several wives, abandoning the previous one when a new alliance was contracted, the "janata sarkar" opposed this practice but got no cooperation. It then decided to put an immediate stop to it. Its members lay in wait for the drums of the marriage party. As soon as the culprit bridegroom arrived, his attendants were ordered to scatter, he was seized, put on a donkey and sent home. This, said the speaker with satisfaction, soon put an end to 75% of these "double and treble marriages."

There were complaints that city youths considered themselves special, and few would devote time to active work. Political parties tended to be disruptive influences, diverting attention to their own camps and activities and electioneering. Talk of elections was generally condemned as an obstacle to the steady groundwork of "janata sarkar." Aware that decent representatives must serve on their committes, one delegate disconsolately remarked that there were no decent fellows in the village so they had chosen "fairly decent" ones.

All of this had proceeded without confrontation with authority. But confrontation is planned by Jagannathan, veteran Sarvodaya worker, under whom the "janata sarkar" in the Bodhgaya region will launch a campaign for land backed by 5,000 women led by his wife. According to the books, a Hindu *math* there owns 7,000 acres. The largest permitted family holding is 40 acres, and the *math** can only own twice as much. It has formed 18 trusts to get around the law and has been notified by the District Magistrate that he will recognize only one of these. The matter is now in government's hands for a decision. It is further complicated by the fact that some lands donated by the *math* earlier, as Bhoodan, have since been sold and are now tied up in litigation—an example of the untidy snarl of land problems in Bihar, where the law remains on the statute books and is not put into effect.[3]

This was, by itself, no revolutionary breakthrough, nor any portent of dangerous uprising as understood by governments. But "janata sarkar" in the hands of experienced Sarvodaya workers who knew their territory and its problems might make more than a dent in specific areas and might even become a challenge to long-established local institutions or government agencies. Its danger to the status quo was its dedication to its aims, and a determination backed, in many instances, by a thorough knowledge of the problem it was attacking. Beyond this, it possessed neither the arms nor the belief in violence to make it dangerous. The worst a hot-headed encounter with opponents could come to might be a fist fight or the use of crude weapons, no great matter for local authority to control. Yet "janata sarkar" produced a shiver down the official spine. A government claiming an exclusive relationship with the masses and a record of service and sacrifice, with both these under fire could not but be put out by the growth of "people's" agencies outside it, at times in confrontation with it. The arguments used to discredit the development called it "foreign-financed" and subversive. It was stamped out with a singular ferocity under the Emergency after June 1975.

In early November 1974 Mrs. Gandhi told the Congress Parliamentary Party the Bihar Movement was aimed at her personally, to drive her out of office. She labeled it reactionary and accused it of support by the Anand Marg, an occult religious group with political overtones. JP answered these charges a week later, after a procession led by him on November 4 was severely mauled by the police and he himself was thrown to the ground under a volley

* Religious foundation.

of lathi blows:

> Whether the blows . . . were meant for me or not, is best known to the
> Prime Minister herself, for it was the Central Reserve Police which
> was wielding the lathis. . . . What is of great concern to all democrats
> is that if this is repeated, then the people will have no chance to give
> expression to anything that goes against government policies and ac-
> tions, however bad or evil such policies might be. . . . I am not sur-
> prised that while the common people are the target in action, truth is
> the first casualty in their [government's] campaign to defame the move-
> ment. . . . The Prime Minister also goes on repeating that the move-
> ment in Bihar is in the hands of the RSS and the Anand Margis. The
> RSS has, of course, been active in the Bihar Movement, not directly
> but through its members in the Jan Sangh and the Vidayarthi Parishad
> student wing of the Jan Sangh. But the Socialist party, the SSP, and
> the Old Congress and their youth wings, the RSP and the Marxist
> Coordination Committee are all fully involved and active in the move-
> ment. The CPI-M has not joined the coordination committee of pol-
> itical parties, but has extended full support to the movement. So has
> the Forward Bloc. Non-existent groups are repeatedly mentioned, but
> the active involvement of all these parties, a majority of whom are
> radical, is ignored. . . . The Prime Minster should at least know this
> elementary principle of politics that it is the function of opposition
> parties to try and dislodge the party in power.

That the Bihar Movement, except for the Jan Sangh, was backed
by parties of the left and centre was not, as JP then believed, "ignored" by the prime minister. Government's confrontation with it
was shaped, in fact, by this realization and the knowledge that its
support was both progressive and broad-based. If Mrs. Gandhi admitted it was a genuine symbol of the common man's distress, she
would have to concede a rising tide in the country against her. A
"reactionary" movement that was "foreign-financed" justified its
repression.

During 1974 the police were increasingly evident in civic
affairs. In January civil disobedience in Gujarat was met with
violence. In May a twenty-day railway workers' strike demanding
parity with other public sector workers was efficiently crushed.
Some 50,000 workers were arrested while negotiations were on
between their representatives and the management. Another 100,000
lost seniority and other benefits, or their jobs. The treatment of
these and others imprisoned for dissent gave awe-inspiring dimen-
sions to Mrs. Gandhi's display of power. An element of unreality

was added to her fight against the Bihar Movement when in November the Congress and CPI began a "counteroffensive" against the "conspiracy to defeat democracy."

On November 11 a CPI procession was given permission to march through Patna carrying weapons. A cluster of onlookers who jeered the marchers were savagely attacked. The Congress held its own procession at Patna on November 16 led by its new president, Dev Kant Barooah, attended by an imposing contingent of Congress M.P.s from Delhi and supervised by the prime minister's aide, Yashpal Kapoor. The railway minister, L. N. Mishra, had requisitioned trains to bring participants from other states and was on hand to welcome them. This set the pattern for Congress processions in different parts of the country, costly affairs backed by government's resources importing trainloads of participants, using jeeps, motorcycles, and sometimes elephants. They did much to deprive the Congress president's office of dignity and serious purpose, while the Congress-CPI's newly affirmed partnership against the "conspiracy to defeat democracy" looked both frivolous and macabre against the neglect of the actual issues the Bihar Movement had raised. The reprisals against it contrasted unflatteringly with the movement's nonviolence. Police muscle began to figure in political comment:

> Democracy cannot last for long if its existence depends upon the continuous use of the State's coercive power. The strength of Indian police and para-military forces, which are used against the people, has reached the level of our military forces. People have been fired at once in every 4 days since 1971. In such a situation mass agitation and even counter-violence remain the only democratic instruments for the defence of people's democratic rights against the creeping fascism of the State.[4]

> ... battalions of the Border Security Force, raised as a security line of national defence, have been permanently stationed in placid Bihar towns, hundreds of students and others have been arrested and put in jail without trial, and worse still, the news of the Bihar happenings is suppressed from the rest of the country. The question is, which is more dangerous, and therefore more reprehensible: the violence of an unpopular government in deploying para-military organisations against civil resisters or the acts of violence provoked by such developments ...?[5]

In October 1974 the Public Accounts Committee of Parliament

published government's police budget figures,* showing allocations had doubled in five years. The increase was accounted for mainly by the steady expansion of three paramilitary services under the Union government's control: the Border Security Force, the Central Reserve Police, and the Central Industrial Security Force. The budget figures did not include those of the intelligence agencies, the Central Bureau of Investigation (CBI) and the Research and Analysis Wing (RAW).

I visited Patna in November:

> I went to the Patna Medical College Hospital, part of which has been turned into a prison with barbed wire fencing and armed guards. The prisoners within needed no guard. They were in no condition to move, with such injuries as a bullet in the throat, an amputated leg and an assortment of broken bones. They had been wounded in the act of doing no more than walking in a peaceful procession. . . . In the prison section of the hospital, food and blankets were in short supply. So were injections, X-ray plates and blood. These emergency cases had had the misfortune of falling between two stools, hospital and jail, and did not seem to be squarely the responsibility of either.
>
> Bihar's jails, long overcrowded and notoriously lax in their observance of the jail code regarding food, clothing and prisoners' rights, cannot accommodate the swelling tide of MISA, DIR and other political arrests.[6]

It was plain that Bihar had become the scene of a spontaneous convulsion with repercussions far beyond its borders. Protest had been a feature of Indian politics. Strikes, processions, and demonstrations had been staged by interest groups and by every political party since independence, including the ruling Congress itself in states where Opposition governments were in power. Political protest was an accepted part of the system. Its origins in the national movement had given it an honourable stamp. It had been institutionalized by Mahatma Gandhi's highly organized nationwide satyagraha campaigns. Individual protest had acquired dignity and distinction with his own fasts. Agitation had vast numbers to draw on, and perhaps nowhere in the world had it drawn on so many for a variety of causes, from freedom itself to wage rises, state boundaries, and a ban on cow slaughter. Even against this

* Police budget figures of the Government of India:
  1968–69 Rs 726 million
  1971–72 Rs 1183 million
  1974–75 Rs 1560 million

background the Bihar meetings were extraordinary for their size and discipline, the more impressive because official policy was directed at obstructing them and preventing the surrounding population from arriving in Patna to take part in them, apart from the force used against them. Three-quarters of their participants were young, which may explain the ardent commitment, the quality of youthful outrage, and the special delight taken in defying authority that had forfeited public respect. From the Bihari villager, more comfortable speaking his own dialect than Hindi, to the city student, the Bihar movement had wide-ranging young support, and it seemed to find JP's credentials particularly apt and attractive. A brilliant modern mind that had consciously rejected power in favor of the "Gandhian alternative" of service, he was a combination of the ascetic and practical, intellect and action, passion and poise. His quiet rational tone at public meetings was more philosophical than political. He seemed a counter-leader, a prevailing moral influence rather than a personality, at a time when many believed the leadership cult at Delhi had been carried too far. The idealistic and unequal nature of the confrontation now begun appealed to the best in youth. It harnessed an energy growing restless and combative in a deteriorating economic situation and a political atmosphere of moral decline. And it gave an outlet to students who had till now seen no way but violence to change the scheme of things.

Apart from Bihar, active participation in it was limited to neighboring Uttar Pradesh. Its success can be judged by the UP government's investigation into nine eastern districts of Varanasi and Gorakhpur for signs of its influence and a report on anti-Congress sentiment or activity in the area. Its influence extended further afield, to universities in Orissa, Delhi, and Haryana. In November, in anticipation of JP's visit, Kurukshetra University in Haryana was closed by the state government, a number of students arrested, and the president and secretary of the Student's Union expelled for taking part earlier in a rally in Ludhiana, Punjab, in support of the Bihar Movement. Gujarat, though its own agitation had died down with the dissolution of the state assembly, gave the movement its sympathy and support.

Why did this extent and activity of an avowedly peaceful development panic the government or make Mrs. Gandhi feel gravely threatened on her pinnacle? The strong reaction it aroused in Delhi was never defined. Several reasons might be ascribed to it. The movement represented grievances that could not, now that they were being so remorselessly and publicly aired, be ignored. It could not be explained away as a reactionary or anti-people development. It looked, in fact, very much the opposite, the groundswell of a just indignation backed by profound public sympathy, if this was to be judged by the success of its programs involving public cooperation. Its calls for bundhs effectively paralyzed life in Patna particularly, with a near-total shutdown of trading and academic establishments, and rendered the administration ineffective at district and subdivisonal levels. Many in the Congress tacitly sympathized with it. Bihar had been a storm center of revolutionary agitation during British rule and the heart of violent protest during the Quit India upheaval. That this movement was nonviolent increased rather than lessened its impact. The use of force against it discredited the user, while it conferred a badge of courage on its victims. Yet a leadership caught in its own insecurity continued to use arrest, intimidation, and violence to suppress it, and to be confounded by its failure to do so.

For Mrs. Gandhi the movement presented major irritants. It was a rival claimant to the people's voice. The reputation it had brought back into focus had little to do with the politics of power, and much to do with character, virtue, and example. A personality reminiscent of Mahatma Gandhi's now occupied the center of the stage, and it had arrived there without benefit of political paraphernalia, legend, or lore. Next to it the cant and carnival lately surrounding Congress politics looked shoddy. A clear voice had broken through, and people were listening to it. Mrs. Gandhi was faced with the British government's dilemma in dealing with the Mahatma, who had been able to unite, inspire, and influence because of the human being he was. Unable to resolve her dilemma, she took a whole country to task for her failure, through action that proved to be the natural culmination of her style.

On December 3 the *Indian Express* reported Bihar's jails as "bursting at the seams with students and political workers" on the eve of the assembly's winter session. Ten Opposition and Sarvodaya leaders had been externed from the state. Barricades set up by the police extended into rural areas. Forty-three assembly seats were vacant, thirty-seven of these due to resignations in response to the movement. A harassed chief minister, the polite and inoffensive Abdul Ghafoor, obediently carried out Delhi's instructions while he tried to hold his factious party together and to prevent some members from resigning their assembly seats. Supporting the validity of the demand for the assembly's resignation, G. S. Bhargava commented in *Everyman's* on December 1, 1974:

> Richard Nixon had received a massive mandate in 1972, with all the States of the Federation except Massachusetts voting for him. Until June last, Nixon also used to argue that demands for his resignation, like the attempts to remove him from the Presidency, were anti-democratic because his mandate lasted until 1977.... It is an irony that Mrs. Gandhi who owes her pre-eminence today to the successful mobilisation of the people against the former managers of the Congress Party should pit herself against political participation by the people, which is the essence of the Bihar movement.

JP expressed it similarly in a letter to the editor of *The Illustrated Weekly:*

> ... do you also think that Mr. Nixon's removal from the U.S. Presidentship before his term expired was wrong and against democracy? And do you think that the *Washington Post* and the *New York Times* and many other American papers were wrong in launching the campaign against Nixon? Were they enemies of democracy? ... Some of the highest constitutional authorities in the world have said that, in such cases of misrule, the people have a right—and a constitutional right, mind you—to demand removal of the offending government or dissolution of the offending parliament....

Moscow's concern at the blaze of opposition to Mrs. Gandhi became apparent when Kitsenko, *Pravda* correspondent in Madras, made a stinging attack on JP and when, on December 4, the opening day of the Bihar assembly session, Soviet TV cameramen entered the assembly chamber contrary to the rule forbidding cameras in the chamber. Ilyashenko, chief of Soviet radio and television in New Delhi, said he was there "with the permission of the Government of India." In the storm of objection from Opposition benches, Soviet TV withdrew, and the Union minister for Information and Broadcasting, I.K. Gujral, called upon to explain the intrusion, denied having granted permission, saying only that the Soviet request had been transmitted to the Bihar assembly secretariat. But the Soviet weight behind the Congress-CPI campaign against the Bihar Movement was now an open fact. In December the Congress Party inaugurated a series of secret conclaves. Narora, scene of the first, was an Uttar Pradesh village about seventy miles from Delhi. Barbed wire, armed guards, and a thousand tents for military and police personnel, brought it into national prominence. Mohan Dharia, Union minister for works and housing, revealed, on March 17, 1975, in Poona that the Narora camp had been attended by Soviet embassy officials.

On 1 January the *Hindustan Times* commented editorially:

It was the tragedy of 1974 that development was subordinated to politics, while politics in turn has come increasingly to be influenced by black money and the economic underworld which has established an unfortunate nexus with the country's administrative and political echelons. . . . The Government has not improved its image by its reluctance to move firmly, swiftly and openly against every form of corruption. . . . It is essentially this sense of anger and anguish that epitomises the Bihar Movement. Mr. Jayaprakash Narayan has become a symbol whose true relevance extends far beyond Bihar. . . .

CHAPTER TWELVE

January to June 1975

The first six months of 1975 saw a crescendo of political activity, with Jayaprakash Narayan as its center. The main Opposition parties acted in concert in Parliament and in some state assemblies and backed common winning candidates in by-elections. A series of Congress reverses at the polls, climaxed by its defeat in the Gujarat state election in June, brought the arousal represented by the Bihar Movement into sharp focus. Yet the new climate was fundamentally different from that of 1967, when Congress had suffered its first major electoral setback. As a result of the 1969 split in the party, followed by Mrs. Gandhi's victory in the 1971 election, high hopes and expectations had been roused. These had not begun to be fulfilled, and the electorate was sorely disappointed. A mood of euphoria had been dashed to the ground by grave economic crisis and the government's inability to cope with it, by the scandal and strife within the Congress and its shielding of the corrupt, and by its apparent indifference to mounting despair. The prospect of an alternative was emerging in the form of a united Opposition. But the new atmosphere was also the result of a searing psychological experience. Those who voted anti-Congress in 1975 did so because its leader, member of a revered family—no stranger to the democratic faith—had revealed how far she could go in trifling with democratic institutions and in crushing dissent, a performance frightening in its implications for the country. In the cold political light of 1975, public sentiment, affection, and indulgence, long a source of strength and succour to the Congress, had given way to distrust in its leader's basic credentials. A rocky road had been traveled in six years, from assured political values to political extravaganza, from ethics to the lawless techniques of expediency and ambition, from open transactions to the politics of secrecy and violence. It was, in essence, the distance between Jawaharlal Nehru and Indira Gandhi.

Events between January and June, profound in their effect on the political landscape, are best described in sequence.

On January 2 at 5:50 P.M. L. N. Mishra was injured by a bomb explosion at a railway platform ceremony in Samastipur, Bihar. He died at Danapur, Bihar, at 9:30 next morning. The surgeon, R. V. P. Sinha, who operated on him at Danapur, later pointed out the inordinate delay in getting him to a hospital. The train carrying the wounded minister did not leave Samastipur until 8:30 P.M. Instead of being rushed to Darbhanga, an hour away, he was taken to Danapur where another forty-five minutes were lost while the train shunted from the wrong platform to the correct one. When he reached the operating table, six hours after the explosion, he was a case of "grave emergency," his injuries so advanced, "it was a herculean effort to start the operation."[1]

Other related information came to light: K. P. Verma, Counsel for Mishra's family, said in his evidence before the Mathew Commission appointed by the Union government, that the failure to provide security for the minister was "deliberate," in spite of the Bihar government's instructions in 1974 to all relevant departments that special security arrangements must accompany the minister's visits to the state. After the breaking of the railway workers' strike in 1974, Mishra had apparently feared assassination and had told some colleagues he suspected a political conspiracy against his life. A private detective had informed the Delhi police in writing of a specific threat, naming Samastipur and Darbhanga as probable danger spots. In these circumstances K. P. Verma claimed the arrangements at the railway ceremony had been extraordinarily lax.

Just before the assassination, leaders of the Jan Sangh, CPI-M, and BLD had called for an inquiry into a series of "mysterious [road] accident deaths" of men investigating cases with important political implications. These included D. K. Kashyap, connected with the Nagarwala case; R. D. Pandey, a deputy director of the intelligence bureau; Anil Chopra, collector of Daman, who had broken a smuggler gang; and recently, Ramanathan, a CBI inspector examining the improprieties of Congress M.P.s selling licences to well-known firms, an affair in which L. N. Mishra was implicated, and which was the subject of storm and stress in the current session of Parliament. Mishra's death by violence raised a flurry of fresh speculation about his role in the "licence scandal."

On January 7 All India Radio broadcast a portion of Mrs. Gandhi's speech at a condolence meeting organized by the Congress Party's Delhi unit. Her shrill accusation that Mishra's death was a "rehearsal" for which she herself was the "real target" was as shocking as her imputation of the crime to JP's movement. An edge of hysteria was conveyed to listeners more startling than the printed account of her speech. Bewildered listeners heard her strenuously disown the crime herself and decry attempts to link her with it: "Even Congressmen have been misled by these blatant lies."

The condolence meeting was converted into one of fervent support for Mrs. Gandhi. Its most vigorous speaker, H. N. Bahuguna, chief minister of Uttar Pradesh, said "fifty-eight crores [580 million] of people" stood solidly behind the prime minister. Mrs. Gandhi's own wrought-up accusation had the reverse of the effect desired. On January 8 the *Hindustan Times* editorial pointed out:

> ... those who have rushed to implicate Mr. Jayaprakash Narayan by proxy with the Samastipur outrage might recall earlier bomb explosions last May at the Bankipore [Patna] dak bungalow and the subsequent firing on JP's procession in Patna on June 5th from a government flat allotted to a Congress MLA, Mr. Phulena Rai, and occupied by workers of the "Indira Brigade" ... the use of bombs and firearms in Bihar is older than JP's movement....

There was open talk that a government agency was responsible for Mishra's death. Controversy over the minister had reached a peak in the licence case before Parliament, involving government in its most embarrasing collision with the Opposition. His death had come at a convenient time. Jyotirmoy Bosu's (CPI-M) statement in Parliament that Mishra's office and home had been searched immediately after his death to remove documents connected with Sanjay Gandhi's Maruti Company was not answered by the home minister. The extreme slowness of the CBI investigation created further suspicion of government involvement, while the prompt dismantling of the dais at Samastipur had destroyed primary evidence. A politician who dominated and manipulated cliques, had men and money to do his bidding, and aroused disproportionate loyalties and antagonisms, Mishra had reportedly refused to resign and had a devoted following in the party to back him up.

The event served to blur Opposition differences and feed a mounting fear. The CPI-M issued a statement on January 13 from Calcutta: "The semi-fascist and gangster tactics of the ruling party have been continuing for the last three years, and free functioning of all opposition forces, especially the CPI-M and other Left and democratic opposition, had become an impossibility. . . ." Marxist leader, Jyoti Basu, announced the CPI-M would, as a result, invite the Old Congress and the Jan Sangh to a conference to plan a broad-based movement in Bengal for civil liberties and free and fair elections. Each party would conduct its separate campaign but the three would be synchronized. There would be no truck, he added, with the CPI.

The CPI, also an opposition party, was not recognized as such any more. Its interests were too closely identified with the Congress. In a recent article, Mohit Sen had explained his party's objective as "unity and struggle vis-a-vis the Congress." The unity was manifest, the struggle was not. If the CPI had disapproved of the breaking of the railway strike the previous year, its disapproval had been in a low key. During the Soviet President Brezhnev's visit to India in 1973, the party had been told to back Mrs. Gandhi regardless of her policies. The Soviet investment in India was political and geographical, not ideological. The Indian record showed that the CPI harvest out of this alliance, abundant in its share and spoils of power, had not added favorably to its reputation. An eight percent bonus to workers made law in September 1974 (and applicable to 1973) was withdrawn by the government in 1975. The wheat takeover, fully backed by the CPI, had been discredited by its failure. The projected takeover of the rice crop had been abandoned. The nationalization of coal mines in 1973, authored by Mohan Kumaramangalam, became linked in the public mind with the Chasnala mine disaster in Bihar in December 1975, one of the worst in mining history. It was judged to be due to "reckless slaughter mining endangering mine safety" in order to increase production after nationalization. The party's direct influence on the Congress had dwindled after its chief spokesman in government, Kumaramangalam, was killed in an air crash in 1973. The Congress-CPI combine had less logic to commend it than the Opposition of varying political complexion now drawing closer together. Developments in Bangladesh, with Mujibur Rahman taking dictatorial powers, added anxiety and incentive to this process. That the war to release a much heralded "Sonar Bangala" ("Golden Bengal") from bondage—one that so exhaustively engaged India's soldiery, resources, and idealism during 1971—should have come to this was a reminder of what might happen next in India, with the Bangladesh government closely advised by India. The possibility of a dictatorship, with a sudden seizure of extra powers by Mrs. Gandhi, was widely discussed.

On January 19, at a youth rally in Patna, JP appealed to adherents of the Bihar Movement to enlighten people about the danger ahead and mobilize them to defeat any move on Mrs. Gandhi's part to thrust dictatorship on the country. Her outburst at the condolence meeting for L. N. Mishra, he said, showed she was realizing "people were losing confidence in her." Defending the multiparty membership of the movement, he said it had no labels. Members of the Jan Sangh and Old Congress had faced lathis and bullets and were in prison for their participation in it. He would not ask any party to leave it. Six weeks later (March 5), addressing the twentieth plenary sesson of the Jan Sangh in New Delhi, he said he wished to communicate the conclusion after a year's work with the Jan Sangh and the RSS, that he had found them neither reactionary nor fascist. Fascism was rearing its ugly head, but it came from another quarter. A similar caution was delivered by the CPI-M general secretary, P. Sundarayya, in Hyderabad on February 12. Denying his party had joined hands with the Jan Sangh or the BLD, he said the danger of fascism, however, was much greater from Mrs. Gandhi. It would not surprise him if she, aided by the CPI, repeated the Bangladesh development and called off the 1976 election.

The Opposition, though fragmented, had been a lively and talented presence in Indian politics. The combined votes it polled, even before the 1967 elections, its high point of achievement, had been more numerous than those polled by the Congress Party. Single Opposition parties or coalitions had formed state governments, at times under outstanding and admired leaders, as Annadorai of Tamil Nadu and Namboodiripad of Kerala. Accomplished Opposition speakers had exerted pressure on the Congress majority in Parliament and contributed to the quality and maturity of Parliamentary debate. The near-impossibility of dislodging the Congress even gave the enterprise a certain gallantry. The challenge called for discipline and dedication. Thus the Jan Sangh built up a student cadre, the Vidyarthi Parishad, a successful foil to the CPI's All India Students' Federation, and prided itself on the allegiance it commanded among the young. A quarter century of democratic opportunity had left the Opposition divided. When it surfaced after Nehru's death, it did so with a distinct regional bias. It took Mrs. Gandhi's autocratic tread to goad the Opposition to unity. In this it had an advantage it had not had before—the decay of the ruling party's image and its impotence on the economic front. Unwilling to give up party identities, the Opposition formed a single bloc in Parliament and some state assemblies and fielded common "janata" candidates for approaching by-elections. After the Emergency of 1975, prison and suppression furthered the process, with the Janata Party finally challenging the Congress in the national election of 1977. This development can best be understood in terms of a scene reduced by Mrs. Gandhi's style to a warlike confrontation between the Congress and other opinion, leaving no room for compromise or maneuver.

Yet there was more to Opposition unity than this. If Mrs. Gandhi's categorical style had broken with the whole texture of the Congress past, initiated alignment with the CPI at home and the Soviet Union abroad, and in the process fundamentally altered Indian politics and the working of Indian political institutions, Opposition parties had also undergone degrees of transformation. Some old stock images had changed and no longer applied.

The Old Congress, the rump left by the split, tainted at the time by accusations of conservatism and "bossism," and expected shortly to capitulate to the ruling party and disappear from the scene, had not done so. Its president, Asoka Mehta, once a leading theoretician of the Socialist Party, had always been associated with the Left. Its elder statesman, Morarji Desai, had acquired added stature as an honorable man in the hurricane of desertion and defection encouraged by the split. He stood out now as one of the last Gandhians, recalling receding values, a symbol of dignity in the muddy political landscape. The charge leveled by Congress radicals some years earlier that Desai's businessman son, Kanti, had used his father's position to promote his business, now looked meager next to Mrs. Gandhi's vigorous sponsorship of her son and the official apparatus freely used to assist him. The conservative taint had faded in view of Mrs. Gandhi's lack of radical, or credible performance, while her party's extortion and use of money on a scale as yet unparalleled had given "bossism" and "black money" a new life and dimension.

The Jan Sangh had since its founding been open to all communities. On this issue it had parted with the Hindu Mahasabha and, under the leadership of Shyama Prashad Mukherjee, had avoided the word "Hindu" altogether in its official title, using "Bharatiya" instead. Its espousal of Hinduism and Hindi as the dominant culture and language of India was, it claimed, based on statistical realities, Hindi being spoken or understood by 42 percent of the population, as against the next largest figure, 9.24 percent speaking Telugu. Its attitude toward these two issues had, of circumstance and necessity, become more tolerant, for religion ceased to be a profitable issue in politics once the fever following partition subsided, while the search for support in the south and among the Muslims produced a modified stand on Hindi. Mrs. Gandhi's angry militancy toward the Jan Sangh showed its front rank leadership up in a sober balanced light by contrast. Even the RSS, noted for militant activities in the past and denounced for its antisecularism and cultivation of the Hindu mystique, now contrasted favourably with the growing aggressiveness of the Youth Congress, protected when it transgressed the limits of law-abiding behavior.

The Socialist Party, always antidoctrine and experimental, felt vindicated in its demand for a redistribution of economic priorities and more decentralization. Mrs. Gandhi's drive for world recognition and her definition of "achievement" as victory in war and the explosion of a nuclear device did not accord with these.

The Old Congress, the Jan Sangh, and the Socialist Party found common ground with Congressmen who opposed the alliance with the CPI and feared the consequences of Mrs. Gandhi's present unyielding posture.

The CPI-M, its ideological purity intact, kept out of the Opposition bloc, but extended its cooperation where it thought fit. Battered by police action, its chief enemy was the "fascism" of the Congress-CPI combine.

Mrs. Gandhi had two choices. Influential members of her party were urging a reconciliation with the Opposition, and a basic program inviting the cooperation of all parties to meet the urgent needs of the population. She chose her second option, rejecting a conciliatory course. This meant the manufacture of a "right reaction" obstructing her, with which no talks were possible.

That the time had come for a new political combine, ignoring conventional Left-Right divisions, was apparent to the public, for the effect of jointly fielded "janata" candidates was immediate and electric. The Congress had already lost two by-elections when, in the third week of January, the Opposition won a spectacular victory in the important by-election to the Lok Sabha from Jabalpur (Madhya Pradesh). The seat had been a Congress bastion for fifty years, vacated by the death of Seth Govind Das, who had held it since his membership of the Central Assembly during British rule. The New Congress candidate was his grandson, Ravi Mohan, backed by the chief minister, P. C. Sethi, who put state transport (including helicopters) and resources to lavish use in the campaign. Mohan was defeated in all eight segments of the Lok Sabha constituency, all eight of whose assembly seats were occupied by Congress M.L.A.s—an anti-Congress wind the *Times of India* described as "a veritable tornado." The "janata" candidate, a virtually unknown gold-medal engineering student, Sharad Yadav, became Parliament's youngest member. Welcoming the victory, JP told an interviewer in Bombay on January 22 that the people's force now at work was more powerful than the "greatest and grandest alliance":

> The "grand alliance" seems to have become for Mrs. Gandhi the same kind of cry as Bonaparte had become for British mothers in those times. . . . Mrs. Gandhi makes herself out as radical and suggests she stands for policies and ideals of which Jayaprakash Narayan and the Bihar Movement are afraid. But the people of Bihar, or for that matter, the people of India, would like to ask her what she has done in nine years of her reign. What radical change has she brought about?

The Opposition's "janata" candidate won next at the Govindpura by-election (Madhya Pradesh). February brought further defeats for the Congress in two (Meham and Rori) out of three by-elections to the Haryana assembly. The victories of the "janata" candidates, one of them a young lawyer new to politics, were particularly galling to Chief Minister Bansi Lal who had compaigned extensively with several cabinet colleagues. The Barpeta (Assam) byelection to the Lok Sabha on February 20 revealed a degree of panic in the Congress Party and the government. The seat had been vacated when Fakhruddin Ali Ahmed was nominated to the presidency. Now president, he paid a visit to Assam timed to coincide with the Congress election campaign. The "janata" candidate, B. Goswami, with a dramatic lead of 41,000 votes in a constituency of 100,000 was declared defeated by 28,000—more votes than the constituency had—in favor of the Congress candidate. Goswami's messenger, on his way to Delhi to lodge a complaint with the Election Commission, was detained at Gauhati (Assam) airport and not allowed to proceed, though the ballot papers he was carrying as evidence bore the signature and seal of a presiding officer.

Mrs. Gandhi described the new wave as "certain outside forces" taking a deep interest in India's internal affairs, a theme she expounded for newspaper and magazine interviews, and in open and closed-door meetings with selected academics, businessmen, and other groups. Her remarks were repeated as part of the news bulletin, or following it, over radio and television. She did not support her statements with facts, figures, or precise information. Along with secret conclaves being held by the Congresss Party in parts of the country, her remarks shrouded the atmosphere in insinuation and vague menace, but presented no argument.

> Indira Gandhi's view of JP as a mere epiphenomenon or a shadow, or a puppet controlled by sinister forces is a typical attitude of the established reaction against the rising forces of revolution. . . . Each day a new scandal, a new Watergate that exposes the ruling party and the government confirms the absurdity of JP's caricature at the hands of our rulers. Almost all the forces of fascism, such as big business, black money, bureaucratic power, secret police etc. are all lined up against JP's movement, and on the side of the Congress-CPI alliance. Indian fascism will have a radical face, as is the case of many other countries in the Third World.[2]

The above comment, by no means isolated, represented the opinion of several distinguished nonpartisan commentators that Mrs. Gandhi was pursuing a neurotic line, unrelated to facts. In her view of a black-and-white, either-or world, peopled with elements "for" and "against" her, it is probable she could not see the situation objectively. The act of coming "down from the clouds," which her father had seen the need for years earlier, had never been accomplished. She had continued to be "extraordinarily imaginative and self-centred or subjective," and the line between fact and fantasy was one she was unaware of. "A great actor when he is acting, never forgets that it is all a game," Ignacio Silone wrote of the distinction consummate actors and politicians make between deceiving others and themselves. Mrs. Gandhi had, however, fully identified herself with the fictions she was playing. Her opening speech at the Jamaica Commonwealth Conference in May made admirable reading, showing a touching idealism divorced from her own reality: "I was brought up in an atmosphere where politics denoted neither power nor riches. . . . But as I look around I find that politics are taken to be the art of acquiring, holding and wielding power. International relations are said to deal with power equations among nations. . . ." It was precisely her expert use of the levers of power, her realization that its capture and continuance outside democratic channels depends on planning, conspiracy, surprise and ruthlessness, that marked her own success in the politics she herself had initiated—a far cry from the upbringing she had had when "politics denoted neither power nor riches."

The dictatorship in Bangladesh cast a shadow over India. On February 15, addressing a meeting of government employees in New Delhi at the Boat Club, JP reminded them they were permanent public servants, unlike the president, the prime minister, M.P.s and M.L.A.s, who were temporary, and that they should not obey illegal, immoral, or partisan orders: "Your loyalty is to the country, to the people, and to the Constitution, not to the Government, the Prime Minister or the Home Minister. Use your rights and do your duty without any fear." It was over half a century since Mahatma Gandhi had launched his first civil disobedience campaign in India. This appeal seemed to arise out of an even grimmer and more urgent need. In view of the adverse publicity given to this statement during the Emergency, and the excuse made of it to launch the Emergency, I quote my own comments on it in March 1975:

> Satyagraha is a moral principle, only employable when the cause is just. Its essence is that truth, be it represented by the individual or the mass, can shake an empire.... In a purely religious context the message of Christ on the cross is somewhat the same, for how could the suffering and death of one man save millions unless the truth he stood for had the power to affect and influence beyond him?
> ... In British times we broke laws we considered unjust, made by a government to which we did not give our allegiance. Today we have a Constitution and laws of our own making and a government elected through them, but one which almost daily violates them either in fact or in spirit. We ... do not wish to depart from either the Constitution or the laws, but to see that they are observed by those in authority. The aim of satyagraha today is to demand their proper observance. We are in the very curious position where the government of the country needs this reminder.
> ... the politician or his mouthpiece must be disobeyed when he plays fast and loose with the laws or with decent practices and conventions. The civil servant who is told to arrest 25 people who are squatting in a peaceful demonstration knows very well that there is no ground for arresting them, that the demonstrators are breaking no law, and that the executive order is arbitrary and unjust. In such a case the civil servant is not bound to carry it out. There are too many such

cases nowadays where the civil servant, particularly the young and sensitive, fresh from their training or their first experience of field work, and earnest about their responsibilities, are thrust into terrible situations of being driven to act against the law and against their own conscience. The ritual enactment of MISA must put this kind of strain on many an official conscience, as it must also on the police, who must at times be confused and bewildered at what they are asked to do. The ferocious use of force, or on the other hand the total absence of the police when they are urgently needed, are signs of confused, and at times unscrupulous executive orders.[3]

JP's appeal was bound to stir interest and controversy, especially when it was repeated on other occasions, and addressed to the army and police as well. He was interviewed[4] in Delhi in May:

Question: At Bhubaneshwer your appeal to the army and police have been described by the Home Minister as "treasonable," because it may cause disaffection in the armed forces and police. Can you explain the context in which your remarks were made? And what is the role you envisage the armed forces and police to play?

Answer: What I said at Bhubaneshwar about the army and the police, I have said earlier also at some places. Let me take up the army first. On March 3 I had said at the mass rally at the Boat Club, New Delhi, in the context of the possibility of some sort of authoritarianism scuttling our democracy, that the loyalty of the army was to the country, its flag and its Constitution. The Indian people have given themselves a democratic constitution of the parliamentary type. The President of India in his capacity as Supreme Commander of the armed forces is pledged to protect and uphold the Constitution of the country from authoritarian threats. If any party, government or party leader intends to use the army as a means to further their party and power interests, it is the clear duty, to my mind, of the army not to be so used. . . . If the rulers do venture to use the army to suppress a peaceful revolution, then the army should not allow itself to be so used. I have also decried sometimes the use of armed personnel to deal with civil disturbances, for which the civil armed forces, like the armed police and the paramilitary forces, should be enough. If all this amounts to committing treason, I shall not mind being prosecuted for this offence.

As for the police, the circumstances in which I have made references to them are these: Sometimes in the course of the [Bihar] Movement, the police commits excesses, no doubt under orders of superior officers. For instance, on November 4 last, when I, with a large number of students and citizens in Patna deliberately broke prohibitory orders, the Central Reserve Police personnel present were asked to lathi-charge. The demonstration was entirely peaceful. Not even a pebble was thrown by any demonstrator, and not a single policeman or magistrate was injured, and yet there was a lathi-charge. It would have been perfectly legal if we had all been arrested. But when there was no violence of any sort, in fact even when I was hit and fell to the ground, young men kept shouting the slogan *"Police hamare bhai hain, unse nahin ladai hai"* [The police are our brothers; we have no quarrel with them], a lathi-charge was wholly unjustified.

There have been hundreds of cases where policemen have been ordered by their superiors to commit illegal acts. Take the Calcutta incident of April 2. While thousands of hooligans milled around my car, hit it with sticks, reducing its sunshade to smithereens, and some of them got up on the hood and others on the roof, and jumped and danced on it, badly damaging the car, the police looked on disinterestedly. I saw Samar Guha MP being struck on the face with a stick just two or three yards from my car. Yet the police did nothing. Is it wrong in such cases to tell the police what their duty is? ... I consider it my duty to explain to the police that ... they must not obey orders that are illegal or go against their conscience.

Contrasting sharply with Mrs. Gandhi's overreaction to JP's open moral appeal was her government's silence on a pamphlet published by the CPI in 1974, setting forth the thesis that armies, properly infiltrated, can be used to overthrow governments, a strategy successfully employed by the Sovet Union later in Afghanistan. The following extracts from the pamphlet, *Political Role of the Army in Developing Countries*,[5] convey the argument:

> Communists have always attached tremendous significance to work in the army. During the preparations for socialist revolution in Russia, Lenin repeatedly emphasized the importance of propaganda and agitation among soldiers and officers, of establishing connections in the military milieu with the aim of training conscious revolutionaries among members of the armed services.[6]
>
> The role of the Army in safeguarding "internal security" has recently grown appreciably. Since "internal security" is not a purely military but also a political category, it has boosted the role of the army as a political, or to be more accurate, as an innerpolitical factor. This circumstance, which the officers and generals of the armies in Asia and Africa realise very clearly, could not but make them conscious of their new role in society, of their political advantages and possibilities.[7]
>
> The position of conspirators is always difficult. On the one hand the fewer people are initiated, the safer the conspiracy, but on the other hand the more of the military have promised their support in advance, the easier it is to carry out the coup and the greater are the chances of success. The example of a number of coups in Syria, Iraq, Ghana

and other countries confirms that for the success of a military coup it is insufficient for some individual military unit to take action . . . it is essential that they have the support of the commanders of the biggest garrisons, of those commanding over the majority of the armed forces . . . it is essential for the idea of overthrowing the government to be ripe in the minds of the majority of the officers in key positions.[8]

Mrs. Gandhi's refusal to draw a realistic conclusion from the "janata" poll victories and her relegating the national tide to "the forces of reaction" and "certain outside forces" amazed her younger colleagues. Leading radicals, Chandrasekhar, Mohan Dharia, and Krishna Kant, rejected this daydream utterly with the stern reminder that the Bihar Movement was a result of Congress failure to fulfil its promises. They made repeated forceful pleas for a national reconciliation and an all-party effort to tackle the country's urgent problems. The blank they came up against in Mrs. Gandhi, who adopted the simple expedient of no-response, was perhaps the first sign they had of a frozen irrationality in the leader they had so exuberantly raised to power.

Finding it difficult even to meet her for discussion, they continued their efforts to defuse the situation. Their independence released a long-dormant animation in their party. The steady hum of controversy and speculation—meat and drink to Congressmen until Mrs. Gandhi's rule—returned. In the new situation the Opposition could not be dismissed as unnatural, unpatriotic, or outcast. Contacts were resumed. The processes of give-and-take that people and parties live by were set in motion again. The nonpartisan record and integrity of JP gave these a more than political purpose. The time had come for a talk on fundamentals, an all-India debate long postponed. Mrs. Gandhi's displeasure struck Mohan Dharia first.

On March 1, 1975 Dharia, speaking at the Harold Laski Institute in Ahmedabad, had renewed his plea for talks between Mrs. Gandhi and Opposition leaders and strongly condemned the brutal treatment of youth demonstrations. He had also said "the CPI design to replace the tricolour with the red flag would be frustrated." In a letter of the same date, Mrs. Gandhi informed him: "It is not proper for you to continue in the Council of Ministers since your views are not in conformity with the thinking of the Congress Party." Dharia replied, expressing his astonishment at this abrupt dismissal. He tendered his resignation to the president and said he would explain it in the Lok Sabha: "Had the prime minister shown the courtesy of indicating to me her intention, either directly or indirectly, I would have immediately and willingly tendered my resignation." On March 5 in Parliament he denied the prime minister's charge of disagreement with party policies. Where his views on implementation or behavior had differed, he had repeatedly used party forums or conveyed them personally to the prime minister to make them known:

> On October 7, 1974 I personally conveyed my feeling that the continuance of persons with dubious reputations in the Ministry would erode the credibility of the government. . . . To adopt a callous attitude toward rising doubts in the public mind is easy, but to ignore them is very dangerous. . . . The period between 1969 and 1971 was one of making promises and giving assurances . . . 1971 should have been marked by the determination of the Congress and the administration to enter upon an era of performance. . . . I have been of the view that the cooperation of all such parties and people should be sought who are willing to contribute in the implementation of the policies in the interests of the common man.

Dharia said he had sent a letter and note to the prime minister on November 19, 1974, requesting a time-bound program of action. In a letter of February 26, 1975, he had further elaborated his views. Before writing it he had tried, from February 11 onwards, to get an appointment with the prime minister and had failed to get one. He did not know what greater efforts he could have made to keep her posted with his thinking.

Dharia's statement was heard by a rapt Parliament and warmly welcomed by his constituency. Instructions to Congressmen of Poona city and district to boycott a reception and public rally arranged for him were blithely ignored. Dharia's dismissal had enormously enhanced his reputation and brought him a wider celebrity. Opponents of Mrs. Gandhi within her party noted the fact.

On March 6 JP and Opposition leaders led a mammoth citizens' procession to Parliament and presented a charter of demands to the Speaker. The *Indian Express*, comparing its significance with Mahatma Gandhi's Salt March, reported that "when the head of the procession reached the Boat Club, its tail was still near [its starting point] the Red Fort," a distance of about five miles. JP addressed a public meeting at the Boat Club, announcing similar meetings at state capitals until April 6. The 6th would be observed as "Revoke Emergency Day"—(this referred to the war emergency declared in December 1971)—as it was becoming evident that the Prime Minister would use this emergency to call off the 1976 elections and declare a Bangladesh-type dictatorship. He categorically denied inciting the people or the army to revolt, and charged Mrs. Gandhi instead with wanting the movement to turn violent, so that she would have an excuse to crush it under a dictatorship. "You should not give her this opportunity." So far, he said, the Bihar government had killed 200 peaceful participants in the movement, yet they had the "temerity" to call the movement violent.

Delhi wore an armed look on March 6. A Marxist M.P. described it in the Lok Sabha:

> ... the entire police force of Haryana seems to have tumbled into the capital, and blank-faced policemen wielding anything from lathis and batons to rifles stood in their hundreds at every point. Between the Boat Club and Parliament House it was a human wall of policemen and one could not move an inch without being challenged.

Police barricades had been erected outside the prime minister's house, far from the procession's route. That morning the state-owned Delhi Transport Corporation cut its bus services from about 1200 to 336—explaining the stoppage as being caused by the need for repairs—to prevent citizens from joining the march. Haryana Roadways suspended all its bus services to Delhi. Private buses were halted and delayed at three points along the Gurgaon–Delhi route for checks "to prevent overloading." Trucks were denied permission to carry passengers to Delhi. Along with contingents of the state's police force sent to the capital, these measures brought Bansi Lal's militant authority and loyalty to the prime minister into flamboyant display.

At Ahmedabad (Gujarat) on March 6, seventy-nine-year-old Morarji Desai led a procession to Raj Bhavan and handed the governor a petition for an election to the state assembly, due following its dissolution in March 1974. It was given a rousing ovation along the way.

For the movement's participants the day had achieved a high point in corporate action that might now break through the authoritarian trend. The effect was, however, the reverse, as two state governments launched determined action to halt the spread of JP's influence and disrupt his public engagements. Evidence of incapacity to meet the situation politically, these measures inflicted more wounds on the Congress cause than on that of its adversary. The first incident took place in Orissa.

On March 8 the *Statesman* had editorially assessed substantial support for JP in Orissa because the state's Congress "has never been reconciled to the arbitrary manner in which Mrs. Sathpathy [chief minister] was foisted on it." She had made "as many enemies within the Congress legislature party as outside." "The Orissa government has done little to mitigate distress from drought and flood; the wheat procurement effort has almost collapsed; while ambitious promises on radical land reform have yet to be implemented."

Mrs. Sathpathy had set up an informal espionage system of young recruits to help keep official agencies informed of the extent and activities of JP's supporters. She had refused the Students' Union of Utkal University in the state capital permission to hold a conference and invite JP to address it on March 31. Relations between the Students' Union and the Orissa government had been strained since late 1974, when the university had been placed under a government administrator. The Students' Union had voted at the time not to allow any state minister on campus, a ban Mrs. Sathpathy now decided literally to batter down. On March 24, flanked by armed guards and accompanied by the state governor, Akbar Ali Khan (lately of Uttar Pradesh), she entered the university "smashing the human resistance put up by the Students' Union, with the help of outsiders displaying sticks, iron rods and knives."[9] One hundred Students' Union representatives barring entry to the campus were overpowered by a contingent of the Youth Congress and armed "outsiders." The Students' Union reacted by announcing its intention to hold its conference on schedule, saying it would be attended by 400 student representatives from the state's colleges and addressed by JP.

The Bengal government's action was more successful. On April 2 Congress and CPI youth organizations stopped JP's party on arrival at Calcutta University. Demonstrators climbed on his car and smashed the windscreen. Those who came out of the university building to receive him were surrounded, beaten, and had their clothes torn. The meeting had to be abandoned, but the orgy continued, as JP addressed a teachers' convention while the hall was stoned and glass panes broken. Coming out he faced a barrage of stones and missiles and was trapped with his companions for half an hour in his car before it was allowed to move. He told newsmen before leaving for Patna:

> I could have been killed. . . . I am sure this kind of thing could not have happened without the clearance of the Chief Minister and also of Mrs. Gandhi's government. . . . I don't think any single organisation

is strong enough to face this menace because the Bengal government is behind this menace. . . . I appeal to all parties in the Opposition, and all student and youth organisations in Bengal to bury their differences and join hands, and before anything else destroy the rising menace of fascism.

Methodical and open violence against workers of the Bihar Movement now appeared. On April 27 JP called attention to an incident in Arrah town in Bihar the previous week, when six of his student workers had had to be hospitalized, and twelve others had received injuries:

> It seems that the government, being unable to put down the Bihar Movement by the forces at its command, is hiring goondas and ex-criminals to do the job. . . . It should be a matter of joy for everyone in the State, whether he agrees with the Bihar Movement or not, that all through the time that the students were being beaten up they kept on raising slogans like "Hamla chahe jaisa ho, hath hamara nahin uthega" ["whatever the violence used against us, we shall not retaliate"]. I myself feel proud of these students. By their heroic and peaceful action they have set an example for others to follow.

In Delhi Morarji Desai informed the prime minister that, unless correct constitutional procedure were adopted in Gujarat and an election announced in the state, he would fast to death. He began his fast when Mrs. Gandhi replied the election could not be held until after the monsoon. She set no date. A reader's letter in the *Indian Express* on April 14 commented on this development:

> We all know that of late Mrs. Gandhi and the Congress have been losing political ground very fast. . . . In the wake of the JP movement which is giving her sleepless nights, Mr. Desai's fast has become another nightmare for her. Thus the only alternative left for Mrs. Gandhi, if she wants to hold on to power, which she obviously does very desperately, is to go the Mujib way. . . . People feel that there are ample indications that things are gradually being manoeuvred into such an eventuality. This is what makes Mr. Desai's fast very crucial. Had there been faith in the plighted word of the ruling party's spokesmen, Mr. Desai perhaps would not have staked his life for advancing the election schedule by a mere three months. But unfortunately he knows, as do others, that there is no such certainty about the promise held out by the ruling party. Hence the urgency to force the issue. (Ramadhar, New Delhi.)

Mrs. Gandhi announced an election in Gujarat in early June. The death by fasting of a veteran Congressman, once her father's cabinet colleague, might have provoked shock and outrage. Her own popularity, according to opinion surveys, was low. A reader's letter in the *Indian Express* on January 31, 1975 conveys the flavor of public disenchantment:

> With the kind of massive mandate and unstinted support the Prime Minister has received from the people, which has been the lot of very few politicians in history, any shrewd and sagacious statesman could have virtually converted the country into a veritable heaven. But she has failed miserably to deliver the goods. . . . If the Prime Minister is the repository of all dynamism, radicalism and wisdom . . . why should she at all have given quarter to this corrupt clique? Secondly, having somehow done so, why should she find it difficult to extricate herself from their clutches? It is indeed odd that some six years ago she required to be protected against the so-called "syndicate" which fettered her hands against the radical measures she wanted to take. Today she must be rescued from the inefficient clique that surrounds her and nullifies all her efforts. At this rate, some other hurdle may crop up tomorrow! (Badlu Ram Gupta, Sonepat Mandi).

Raj Narain's (Socialist MP) court case against her election to the Lok Sabha in 1971 was being reported in detail in the press, and her replies in court made ambiguous, evasive reading. The testimony of her agent, Yashpal Kapoor, did nothing to clear the air. His rise from average means and obscurity to sudden wealth and commanding political authority during the last few years had made him a highly controversial figure. In these circumstances Mrs. Gandhi was ill-advised to campaign in Gujarat herself, accompanied by the impressive paraphernalia of her official position. Dressed in a Gujarati-style sari, she called herself a "daughter-in-law of Gujarat." (Her husband, a Parsi, came from a Gujarati-speaking background, though his family had settled in Uttar Pradesh.) Her speeches carried the hint that Gujarat's need of central assistance for its fertilizer and other schemes would be judged against how the state voted. The Congress was defeated by twelve seats in an Assembly of 182, a particularly humiliating blow after the loss of every critical by-election in 1974 and 1975. The Opposition Janata Front, the largest single party, formed a government with the support of the Kisan Mazdoor Lok Paksh (KMLP), a group that had earlier broken away from the Congress.

The last election result was announced on June 12, the day of the Allahabad High Court judgement indicting Mrs. Gandhi on two corruption charges in the conduct of her 1971 elections, declaring her election invalid, and debarring her from holding political office for six years. The verdict was not unexpected. Yet it made a sensation. Much of the public argument and coffee house debate had revolved around whether the judge would, if he found her guilty, be fearless enough to indict the prime minister. Public opinion had been less concerned with "technical infractions" of the election law than with Mrs. Gandhi's scant regard for rules and proprieties in general and the uses she had made of authority over a period of years. Could judicial freedom survive this process? Justice Jagmohan Lal Sinha had been as much on trial as Mrs. Gandhi.

The news that Mrs. Gandhi had been unseated by the Allahabad High Court judgement was announced on All India Radio at 10:25 A.M. The police had prepared for the possibility by erecting iron barricades around Mrs. Gandhi's house and closing all roads leading to it, with heavy police patroling of the area. This left a clear field for rallies and "upsurges" in her favor while it prevented public demonstrations against her from approaching. The *Times of India* reported: "The capital wore the look of the days of the 1969 Congress split. In the afternoon of June 12th about 2,000 Congress demonstrators assembled near the Safdarjang Road roundabout shouting Indira slogans and *"Justice Sinha murdabad."* The report added that between 3:00 and 8:00 P.M. the prime minister came out of her house three times to address rallies at the roundabout. Each time she warned the gathering against internal and external threats to the country and said, come what may, she would stand by the people to usher in socialism.

The scene was, however, different in important respects from 1969. Some of her crucial supporters during the Congress split— the best known and most popular of the Young Turks—were now absent. By 1969 Mrs. Gandhi had antagonized and alienated the Old Guard. Six years later she had dissipated her credit with key radical supporters. In 1969 there had been risk and chance in Mrs. Gandhi's battle with her party. In 1975 she stood securely at the head of it through her control of its organization, while her command of the nation relied heavily on the country's intelligence and paramilitary forces.

There was one vital similarity to 1969. Realizing then that her chances of succeeding against her opponents in the party were not certain if she proceeded through accepted political channels and observed the political code, she had set conventions aside and turned to street agitation to create the drama of a leader demanded by the people. The High Court judgement debarred her from office. Correct procedure ruled that she resign her seat in Parliament and her leadership of her party with immediate effect. However the High Court had granted her a twenty-day stay order—a gesture of courtesy and accommodation to the party in power—to allow the Congress to choose another leader. Mrs. Gandhi turned this interval to account, once again through street agitation. The slogan "Death to Justice Sinha" and the burning of the judge's effigy gave it the drama of "the people's " judgement as against the court's. The drama continued with the stoppage of bus services for the public the next day and Delhi's entire transport system diverted to carrying demonstrators to Mrs. Gandhi's house. This major dislocation in the capital evoked very similar accounts in leading newspapers:

> The public transport system here was virtually paralysed today (13th) as hundreds of buses were unauthorisedly diverted to points near the Prime Minister's house to carry demonstrators affirming support and loyalty to her. Not a single DTC bus operated till 1 P.M. Some buses made their appearance around 2 P.M. By 5 P.M. only 380 vehicles out of 1400 were operating on scheduled routes. . . . There were heated exchanges between rival DTC workers' union representatives . . . workers of the union controlled by the CPI-M protested against the sudden dislocation of the bus services. (*Times of India*, June 15, 1975.)

> As DTC buses went off the roads this morning, leaving lakhs [hundreds of thousands] of commuters stranded, Congress volunteers were pouring into the capital from Punjab, Haryana and UP in buses and trucks, hired or comandeered by State units of the Party. This followed an understanding between Chief Ministers of these States who met here yesterday, that they would flood the capital with party volunteers to march to Mrs. Gandhi's house to demonstrate that the people were with her in this "hour of travail." . . . Over 200 DTC buses were used to ferry people from Gurgaon and adjoining Haryana areas to Delhi. . . . A resident of Akhumpur village told this reporter that five DTC buses visited his village to collect people, but all of them went back without a passenger. Only a handful of people from some areas went to Delhi to join the rally. The Haryana government also allowed DTC buses to enter its territory without road permits, in direct contrast to the March event when buses carrying people to Delhi from Haryana to attend Jayaprakash Narayan's meeting were stopped from proceeding to the capital. (*Indian Express*, June 14, 1975.)

> The mass upsurge, barring the DTC workers' rally, was in reality rag-tag bands of people hastily collected and carted in New Delhi Munic-

ipal Committee trucks and DTC buses that should really have been plying where they were needed most. Squatting on the grass behind banners prominently displaying their affiliations, the demonstrators stoically suffered the scorching heat, cheering listlessly as speaker after speaker rained a considerable amount of rhetoric and made blasphemous statements against the judge and judiciary. . . . For anyone not in the party of demonstrators and without credentials to prove his ranking as a Congressman, access to the roads leading to the Prime Minister's residence was barred. The security arrangements were the tightest they have ever been. . . . (*Hindustan Times*, June 14, 1975.)

The Opposition prevented from holding a meeting or demonstration near the prime minister's house, held one outside Rashtrapati Bhavan, condemning the dislocation of transport, the closure of many electricity units, and Mrs. Gandhi's resort to street agitation when facts and legalities went against her. The rumble in her own party grew distinct. Shambu Nath Mishra, M.P., issued a statement:

Nobody has ever been indispensable in this world and nobody can be made indispensable at the cost of morality, propriety, fair play and justice, and more so the honour of the country. If she herself wants to stick to the chair, a thousand excuses can be invented. If she is honest and sincere and has no lust for power, she must save the face of the country from the greatest ridicule of the world. . . .

Mrs. Gandhi could come back with honor and dignity, the statement continued, if her appeal against the High Court judgement succeeded. It was unfortunate that rallies and propaganda had been launched to whip up public opinion and prejudice the judiciary.

The Congress Parliamentary Party was openly divided on the issue of retaining Mrs. Gandhi as leader. Senior Congressmen, encouraged and emboldened by the High Court judgement, had advanced their claims. Mohan Dharia had already called for her resignation. A move to collect pledges of loyalty failed when many members refused to sign the blank sheet handed round. Some M.P.s vigorously objected to the burning of Justice Sinha's effigy and condemned this and other forms of rabble behavior. Others wanted to know for whose benefit the rallies were being staged.

On June 21 the executives of five Opposition parties met in New Delhi and passed a resolution:

The joint meeting of the National Executives of the Akali Dal, Bharatiya Lok Dal, the Congress (O), Jan Sangh and the Socialist Party is deeply perturbed at the stand taken and activities indulged in by Mrs.

Indira Gandhi in the wake of the judgement against her by the Allahabad High Court. . . . Mrs. Gandhi is not only sticking to her position but is resorting to means and methods repugnant to democracy to maintain herself in power . . . there has been an exhibition of mounting arrogance and a cynical disregard of moral values. It is against this terrible travesty and moral degeneration of the political structure that the people have to bestir themselves. The combined Executives appeal to the people to expess themselves fearlessly and massively through all the legitimate and peaceful democratic channels.

The national newspapers exhibited a rare unanimity, suggesting that the High Court verdict warranted Mrs. Gandhi's resignation. The *Tribune* in an editorial titled "Janata on the March" had gone further: "Today the Indira Wave or the Indira Hurricane is only a distant memory, and slogans like Garibi Hatao raise only Rabelaisian laughter. . . ." In its June 26th editorial, the *Tribune* said, "A claim to rule by staking it out on the streets must, and will, invite challenge. Already there is talk of civil disobedience."

Civil disobedience did not begin. The night it was announced by Opposition leaders, India came under the Emergency.

The enormity of the High Court judgement's blow to Mrs. Gandhi must be understood in terms of her assessment of herself as indispensable to the Indian scene. She considered herself more than a politician or a party leader. She believed she had played a role of glory and sacrifice in the struggle for freedom, even been classified a "dangerous" prisoner by the British. Her background, she was convinced, had endowed her with wisdom and instincts since childhood that no one else in the country possessed. That anyone should regard her as a politician, subject to normal political processes, was a gross impertinence and injustice. She had come to believe she was India. In 1975 "Indira is India, and India is Indira," the Congress president's slogan, became the party's refrain. At the party's annual session in December, the national anthem was followed by a new song *"Indira Hindustan Ban Gai"* ("Indira has become India"). By that time Mrs. Gandhi had passed "through the looking glass" into the full-blown exotica of make-believe.

Yet no political leader can be a creature of fantasy alone. The shrewd politician in him sees when the tide is running against him and no make-believe attends the concrete preparations he makes to master an entirely real challenge to his power. The High Court judgement and the Gujarat election result were incontestable realities. The Opposition gave every sign of improving its strength and support as the 1976 elections drew near. Public disillusionment with Congress performance centred on Mrs. Gandhi. None of this, however, is likely to have made the extreme step of declaring a second Emergency (an Emergency had been in existence since the Bangladesh war) necessary to Mrs. Gandhi if she had been sure of her own party's loyal support. But it was becoming clear that the move to replace her, now being discussed, would allow no easy return. A party far from bankrupt of leadership, in fact restless with aspiring leadership and with leaders smarting under blows to their pride and dignity, would use this opportunity to ease her out. Its brilliant rebel corps was waiting to do so. The Emergency was Mrs. Gandhi's second, and this time a literal coup against the opposition in her own party. Unless this had been so, the sweep of arrests during the night of June 25 would not have taken Congressmen from their beds, including Chandrasekhar and Ram Dhan, high office bearers in the party. More revealing, these arrests did not have the sanction of the Emergency provision of the Constitution. Mrs. Gandhi's cabinet did not meet until the morning of June 26 to take this decision. The president signed the proclamation on Mrs. Gandhi's orders during the night of the 25th. Clearly this sequence of events was intended to be a warning to wavering cabinet colleagues as well. By June 26 they had been provided with reinforced, heavily armed guards at their gates, and some with armed escorts, ostensibly for their own protection, when they attended official engagements. Without doubt preparations for the smooth transformation to dictatorship proceeded without the knowledge of Mrs. Gandhi's cabinet. They were made in consultation with selected aides and the police and intelligence network. Her own party was as much a victim of this lightning seizure of absolute power as opposing opinion outside it.

CHAPTER THIRTEEN

The Flowering of a Style

Mrs. Gandhi's pre-Emergency measures highlight her political technique. Power failures arranged for the night of June 25 prevented most morning newspapers from appearing on the 26th. Arrests made that night gave her the advantage of surprise attack over political adversaries, in both her own party and the Opposition. They also presented her cabinet with a *fait accompli* when it met on the morning of the 26th. The cabinet's "consideration" of a proclamation of Emergency, invoking Article 352 (1) of the Constitution, came many hours after the event, when police action had been taken and an efficient network of control established.

With its official proclamation, the Emergency went into smooth visible operation. Presidential ordinances, later converted into law, enlarged government's powers to arrest and imprison without trial. Meetings of more than five persons without permission were forbidden, an unrealistic ban in overcrowded market areas where the streets teem with human beings. It was rigorously enforced where it could be. Casual groups collected on streets and outside coffee houses were roughly dispersed. Delhi's most popular meeting-and-talking place, the crowded Janata Coffee House in Connaught Place, a people's venture set up to combat the rising price of coffee a few years earlier, was demolished. On the other hand, officially backed "spontaneous" demonstrations in support of Mrs. Gandhi sprouted like mushrooms and were enacted too often to even require permission from authority. The double standard of law already in evidence was now practiced quite openly. Posters of Mrs. Gandhi appeared in the streets, bazaars, and at thoroughfares proclaiming her the savior of law and order. Shop windows were required to display her picture prominently and to post a pledge supporting the Twenty-Point Program alongside. (On July 1, 1975, the prime minister had announced a set of economic programs that came collectively to be known as the Twenty-Point Program.) Delegations of teachers, writers, students, workers, lawyers, and trade union representatives were regularly summoned to her heavily guarded residence to congratulate her on the Emergency and endorse her program. Government's propaganda department claimed the police had obtained clues to secret hoards of arms and ammunition with the "discovery" of "weapons" in the offices of the RSS and found skulls in the offices of the Anand Marg, an occult group not connected with any Opposition Party. A connection was sought to be established in the public mind through film documentaries showing Jayaprakash Narayan and Opposition leaders addressing gatherings, alternating with rows of skulls being "discovered" by the police, and flashbacks to Hitler rallies and goose-stepping Nazis. These clumsy efforts tried to convey that something very sinister had been about to happen when the Emergency saved the situation. Anthony Lukas of the *New York Times* got the following official enlightenment about published pictures of wooden swords and staves found in RSS offices:

> I asked Om Mehta, minister of state in the home ministry, about this and he replied vaguely, "There were some metal swords too." Even with some metal swords, I asked, how could boys with staves pose much of a threat to a superbly equipped army of about one million men, the Border Security Force of about 85,000, the Central Reserve Police of about 57,000, and some 755,000 state policemen? "Well," Mehta said, "there were undoubtedly some rifles too." "Did you seize any?" I asked. "No," he said, "but they probably kept them at home. Don't underestimate these people's capacity for mischief."[1]

In a standard speech Mrs. Gandhi made, with minor variations, over the next twelve months to interviewers and different audiences, she claimed there had been a "plot" against established authority. The charge was never substantiated, and no one accused of conspiracy was brought to trial.* The more specific charges she repeated were: the Opposition wanted to remove her and the Congress Party from office; it wanted to weaken the nation; it was insignificant and had no following; the only following it had came

---

* The exception was George Fernandes, Socialist Party leader, arrested in June 1976, whom the government proposed to bring to trial.

from the press:

> It was necessary in order to avoid any trouble because it would have been their effort to provoke violence on our part. *If* they did something, that would not have created a good situation. So it was more to keep the peace. (To a Bombay weekly, July 8, 1975.)

> A large section of the press had identified itself with the Opposition. (To a group of editors, July 9, 1975.)

> In the last few years a consistent attempt was being made to weaken the fabric of the nation. (To members of the Lions Club and Lions International, July 19, 1975.)

> The Opposition had no support except the support of a vociferous section of the press. . . . These parties concentrated their entire energy on denigrating me and spreading the most baseless canards such as that I smoke and drink, which I do not do. (To members of the Nehru Youth Centres, July 11, 1975.)

> Sections of the press had become total partners of the Opposition front . . . Censorship of Opposition newspapers had become necessary. . . . In the process other sections of the press have also had to face inconvenience. (Interview with the *Sunday Times* and the *Observer*, July 12, 1975.)

> Reverting to the situation leading to the proclamation of Emergency, Mrs. Gandhi said there had been a steady effort to weaken "our system" since 1950. (To 7th biennial conference of State Anti-Corruption CBI Officers, July 1975.)

> A section of the press was anti-government and it was projecting only what was anti-government. . . . Newspapers were building up the Opposition. (To correspondent of West German daily, *Bild Am Sonntag*, August 10, 1975.)

> The press was not only a mouthpiece of the Opposition, but spearheading it too. (To Comex VII, September 23, 1975.)

> The Opposition had united for the purpose of forcing me and the Congress Party out of office. (Interview with NBC, published August 24, 1975.)

> The press, both Indian and foreign, were denigrating India. (At Bhubaneshwar, September 27, 1975.)

In a situation where no voice but her own could be heard, now that debate and dissent had been silenced, and there were no enemies at large, real or illusory, to react to, Mrs. Gandhi's utterances laid bare a complaining naiveté. She sounded aggrieved and perplexed that the Opposition should want her and the Congress out of office and that sections of the press should support the Opposition. Her answers to questions in an interview with NBC made her reasons for declaring an emergency sound no more rational:

> Q: You yourself say the Opposition is in a small minority. Why did you really have to move in the extreme way you did? We simply cannot see that there was a national emergency.
> A: Well, perhaps you're just too far away. Many things could not go on because a very few people, a handful of people, were disrupting it.
> Q: If you want to tell the world this, why not put the people on trial? You have a good court system. Why not let the world know what they were about to do?
> A: Firstly, our court cases go on for years and years. And it is very difficult to prove anything.
> Q: How much real danger was there that the armed forces would mutiny?
> A: I don't think that there was a real danger. But this sort of thing causes confusion in the minds of the people.

The home ministry's document "Why Emergency," placed before Parliament on its opening day, July 21, 1975, labored hard. The Opposition, it said, had held a series of meetings between June 21 and 25 to work out a "grand design" to dislodge Mrs. Gandhi and her government. On the 25th Jayaprakash Narayan had called on the army, police, and government employees not to obey orders they considered "wrong." He had urged the Chief Justice, A. N. Ray, not to sit on the bench to hear the prime minister's appeal against the Allahabad High Court judgement.

> Thus these Opposition parties had irrevocably embarked upon the path of chaos and anarchy and were soon to set about executing their grand design. . . . The true justification for the present Emergency under Article 352 of the Constitution is the preservation of the social interest in peace and order and the promotion of the public good.

The document listed as "unconstitutional" methods the railway strike of 1974, and the movements in Gujarat and Bihar.

Jayaprakash Narayan, arrested before dawn on June 26, and reduced to sudden, rapidly deteriorating illness in prison, wrote to the prime minister on July 21, 1975 from his solitary confinement alternating between hospital cottage and hospital ward at Chandigarh:

Dear Prime Minister,

I am appalled at press reports of your speeches and interviews. (The very fact that you have to say something every day to justify your action implies a guilty conscience.) Having muzzled the press and every kind of public dissent, you continue with your distortions and untruths without fear of criticism or contradiction. . . .

About the plan to paralyse the government. There was no such plan and you know it. Let me state the facts. Of all the States of India it was in Bihar alone where there was a people's movement . . . and you should know, if your ubiquitous intelligence has served you right, that it was spreading and percolating deep down in the countryside. Until the time of my arrest "janata sarkars" were being formed from the village upwards to the block level. Later on the process was to be taken up, hopefully, to the district and State level.

If you had cared to look into the programme of the "janata sarkars," you would have found that for the most part it was constructive, such as regulating the public distribution system, checking corruption at the lower levels of administration, implementing the land reform laws, settling disputes through the age-old custom of conciliation and arbitration, assuring a fair deal to Harijans, curbing such social evils as *tilak* [a caste mark worn on the forehead] and *dahez* [dowry] etc. There was nothing in all this that by any stretch of the imagination could be called subversive.

Only where "janata sarkars" were solidly organised such programmes as non-payment of taxes were taken up. At the peak of the movement in urban areas an attempt was made for some days through dharna [silent protest] and picketing, to stop the working of government offices. At Patna whenever the Assembly opened, attempts were made to persuade the Members to resign and to prevent them, peacefully, from going in. All these were calculated programmes of civil disobedience, and thousands of men and women were arrested all over the State.

If all this adds up to an attempt to paralyse the Bihar government, well, it was the same kind of attempt as was made during the freedom struggle through non-cooperation and satyagraha to paralyse the British government. . . . What right has anyone to ask an elected government and elected legislature to go? . . . The answer is that in a democracy the people do have the rights to ask for the resignation of an elected government if it has gone corrupt and has been misruling. . . .

. . . the students of Bihar did not start the movement. . . . After formulating their demands at a conference they had met the Chief Minister and the Education Minister. They had had several meetings.

But unfortunately the inept and corrupt Bihar government did not take the students seriously. Then the latter *gheraoed* [surrounded] the Assembly. The sad events of that day precipitated the Bihar Movement. Even then the students did not demand the resignation of the Ministry, nor the dissolution of the Assembly. It was after several weeks during which firing, lathi charges and indiscriminate arrests took place, that the Students' Action Committee felt compelled to put up that demand. It was at that point that the Rubicon was crossed.... Thus the plan of which you speak ... is a figment of your imagination, thought up to justify your totalitarian measures.

If there was a plan, it was ... announced at the Ramlila grounds by Nanaji Deshmukh on June 25 and which was the subject matter of my speech that evening. The programme was for a selected number of persons to offer satyagraha before or near your residence in support of the demand that you should step down until the Supreme Court's judgement on your appeal. The programme was to continue for seven days in Delhi, after which it was to be taken up in the States. And ... it was to last only until the judgement of the Supreme Court.... It goes without saying that the *satyagrahi* willingly invites and accepts his lawful punishment. This is the new dimension added to democracy by Gandhi. What an irony that it should be obliterated in Gandhi's own India. It should be noted—and it is a very important point—that even this programme of satyagraha would not have occurred to the Opposition had you remained content with quietly clinging to your office. But you did not do it. Through your henchmen you had rallies and demonstrations organised in front of your residence, and posters appeared in the city suggesting some kind of link between the judge and the CIA. When such despicable happenings were taking place every day, the Opposition had no alternative but to counteract the mischief ... by orderly satyagraha.

And why has the freedom of the press been suppressed? Not because the Indian press was irresponsible, dishonest or antigovernment. In fact nowhere, under conditions of freedom, is the press more responsible, reasonable and fair than it has been in India. The truth is that your anger against it was aroused because on the question of your resignation, after the High Court's judgement, some of the papers took a line that was highly unpalatable to you. And when ... all the metropolitan papers, including the wavering *Times of India*, came out with well-reasoned and forceful editorials advising you to quit, freedom of the press became too much for you to stomach.... It staggers one's imagination to think that so valuable a freedom as freedom of the press, the very life-breath of democracy, can be snuffed out because of the personal pique of a Prime Minister.

You are reported to have said that democracy is not more important than the nation.... It is a false choice you have formulated. There is no choice between democracy and the nation. . . . [Our] democratic constitution cannot be changed into a totalitarian one by a mere ordinance or a law of Parliament. That can be done only by the people of India themselves in their new Constituent Assembly, especially elected for that specific purpose. If justice, equality and fraternity have not been rendered to "all its citizens" even after a quarter of a century of signing that Constitution, the fault is not that of the Constitution or of democracy, but of the Congress Party that has been in power in Delhi all these years. . . .

You inherited a great tradition, noble values and a working democracy. Do not leave behind a miserable wreck of all that. It will take a long time to put all that together again. For it will be put together again, I have no doubt. A people who fought British imperialism and humbled it cannot indefinitely accept the indignity of totalitarianism. . . .

The prisoner received no reply.

The essence of the Emergency was the pinnacle of power—a position above the multitude, unacountable and unchallengeable—it sought to guarantee the prime minister. This was accomplished by three Amendments to the Constitution and an Act of Parliament. The 38th Amendement put the declaration of Emergency beyond the scrutiny of the courts. The 39th Amendment made election disputes relating to the prime minister, president, vice-president, and speaker nonjusticiable. This wiped out the Allahabad High Court judgement with retrospective effect and ensured a Supreme Court judgement in Mrs. Gandhi's favor. On November 7, 1975, a five-judge bench of the Supreme Court, with no legal option but to exonerate her, upheld her 1971 election to Parliament. The proposed 40th Amendment conferred complete immunity on the prime minister, president, vice-president, and speaker, in respect of past or future criminal offences. An Act banned the publication of "objectionable matter," making criticism of the prime minister, president, vice president, speaker, and council of ministers a penal offence. The inclusion of these other dignitaries resembled light musical accompaniment to the somber theme of prime ministerial power, finally established through a drastically amended Constitution in 1976.

The Emergency enabled Mrs. Gandhi to move toward an institutionalized control of the press and the Opposition. "Personally I am not for censorship at all, but the Home, and Information and Broadcasting Ministries have their own difficulties," Mrs. Gandhi said in an interview with a Bombay weekly. The policy she had instituted was, nevertheless, censorship, controlled by a chief censor at Delhi and his counterparts at state capitals. Among the newspapers shut down by the government on June 26 were the Jan Sangh's *Motherland* and Jayaprakash Narayan's *Everyman's*, with their last issues shredded by the police. The arrest of two prominent editors, among others, acted as a brake on the profession generally. Official reprisal for past criticism, at first directed at large-circulation papers and journals, narrowed its attack, until *Opinion*, a one-man protest paper that had flourished since independence in criticism of Nehru's policies was eliminated in August 1976. A series of steps including a "code of ethics" for journalists and editors, government nominees on newspaper boards, and the "voluntary merger" of India's four news agencies—PTI, UNI, Samachar Bharati, and Hindustan Samachar—into a single, government-regulated agency called Samachar, ensured government control of the news and docile channels for its transmission. The Press Council, set up in July 1966 "for the purpose of preserving freedom of the press and maintaining and improving the standards of newspapers and news agencies in India," was dissolved by ordinance on December 8, 1975. The council had recently defended some celebrated cases: the *Tribune* vs the Haryana Government, the burning of *Searchlight* in Bihar, and the dismissal of B. G. Verghese by the Birla proprietors of the *Hindustan Times*. With the establishment of Samachar, the government could "lift" curbs on foreign reporting in 1976, and permit a "debate" on pending changes in the Constitution, allowing newspapers to report limited opposition opinion on the subject. But the censorship mandate continued to operate. It covered the writings of Mahatma Gandhi, Nehru, and Tagore relating to freedom, and all news items and events adverse to government—for example, riots against sterilization measures, jailbreaks, satyagraha campaigns, and Opposition opinion. Whether a political opposition could survive at all became dependent on the ruling party's favor, when the amended Constitution in 1976 gave Parliament the right to pass laws overriding the fundamental rights, forbidding "antinational activity," and banning "antinational associations." Mrs. Gandhi had moved before this to bring the two Opposition governments, in Tamil Nadu and Gujarat, under central control, ending the last vestige of true federal functioning. Mrs. Gandhi's style and preference in this regard was aptly stated by Congress president, D. K. Barooah, at a party symposium: "The Central Government is the national government of India. All other

governments [i.e., in the States] are only municipal governments."
Neither Tamil Nadu nor Gujarat capitulated. The campaign mounted
against each, and the resistance it met lit for a while the last bright
embers of political opposition and federal vigor.

In Tamil Nadu the Dravida Munnetra Kazhagam (DMK) was
firmly established as the dominant political force in the state. On
July 12, 1975, Chief Minister Karunanidhi had addressed a mass
meeting on Marina Beach in Madras, declaring there was neither
an internal nor external threat to India and calling upon the vast
concourse to take a pledge to defend their freedoms. His public
speeches caustically directed at the Emergency were laced with
Tamil folk humor and biting sarcasm. On July 29 the police seized
all copies of *Murasoli*, the DMK's Tamil daily with a circulation of
30,000, for publishing "objectionable matter." But the party's hold
on the state was confirmed in December, with its conference at
Coimbatore:

> The biggest crowds ever seen in this industrial city of half a million
> thronged the 5-mile route of a long and colourful procession taken out
> by DMK. (*Times of India*, December 5, 1975.)

> The Coimbatore conference clearly did not look like that of a party on
> its last legs. The size of the gathering assumes importance when one
> considers that the DMK is a party without "glamorous" leaders, that
> runs against popular political currents, and that it has had a string of
> electoral defeats in the past 3 years. (*Statesman*, January 1, 1976.)

Karunanidhi was not the only obstacle to a takeover by Mrs. Gandhi
in Tamil Nadu. The enormous prestige of Kamaraj, elder statesman
of the Old Congress, stood in her way. Kamaraj, normally silent and
phlegmatic, had expressed his horror at the declaration of Emergency at a public meeting at Sholingar and in an interview with
students at Tiruvellore:

> I am shocked to hear that leaders have been arrested throughout the
> country. This state of affairs is not good for the nation. . . . What hap-
> pens in Delhi we are not able to know. The radio does not give correct
> news, newspapers are also not giving correct news. . . . Such an event
> has no parallel even under British rule, (Sholingar, June 27, 1975.)

> I feel as though I have been left in the jungle blindfolded. I cannot
> visualise the consequences of the Emergency. Can anyone even imag-
> ine that such an Emergency would be proclaimed. . . . During the 1971
> election I had expressed my apprehension that there was danger to

democracy. Mr. Karunanidhi and Mrs. Gandhi, who were then in alliance, scoffed at me. What I said in 1971 is happening in 1975. (Tiruvellore, June 28, 1975.)

Kamaraj's death on October 2 gave Mrs. Gandhi the opening she needed to suck the state's Old Congress unit into her own party. The effort had some of the ingredients of Kathakali, the ancient dance drama of the south, with masks, costumes, and color in full play, and great cymbal clashes punctuating the performance. Her spokesmen in Tamil Nadu announced that "certain outside forces, including some foreign powers, are at work in Tamil Nadu to scuttle the merger of the two Congress parties in the State." The Old Congress countered by suspending its state unit and instructing that no decision could be taken during the Emergency. A committee was set up in its place, headed by Ramachandran. On December 2, 1975, D. K. Barooah told a meeting at Tiruchirapalli: "If we fail to remove [Ramachandran] we shall be treacherous to the memory of Mr. Kamaraj." The *Statesman* account of the meeting read:

> The speeches were also notable for the frequent emotional references to Mr. Kamaraj; often many were seen wiping their tears at the reference. A number of policemen stood around the meeting venue to prevent any trouble from those opposed to the merger proposal.

The mixture of tears and truncheon over Kamaraj's dead body accomplished a kind of merger with a faction of the Old Congress. On January 31 a virtual occupation army in the form of Central Reserve Police contingents moved into Tamil Nadu, bringing it under control. A state assembly election was due. This could have been postponed by the Union government as the parliamentary election had been postponed and the DMK government, with its strength of 166 in a House of 234, given an extended mandate. Both these options and any semblance of constitutional action were discarded, as the Center's police moved in and Tamil Nadu was brought under President's Rule. On February 14, 1976, Mrs. Gandhi drove in an open car under decorated arches bearing portraits of herself and Kamaraj to open the Kamaraj Memorial at Guindy in Madras. She said the merger had been his "last wish." He had sent her a message about it, and she had wanted to come to Tamil Nadu to discuss it with him, but he had dissuaded her, saying this would give rise to gossip about the merger. "For me," she concluded, "it was a privilege to work with him. I sought his guidance and we discussed almost every matter of importance." Earlier, the newspapers had reported Kamaraj's gun carriage funeral attended by Mrs. Gandhi and her "great grief" at the loss of her advisor.

In an interview on February 29 with the New Delhi fortnightly *India Today*, Union finance minister, C. Subramanim, Once Kamaraj's cabinet colleague in Tamil Nadu, said:

> My own impression was that [Kamaraj] would have taken the plunge for a merger, but he fell ill. Then this Emergency came. He again became allergic to any decision taken during the Emergency, when his colleagues were in jail.

The *Democratic World*, political and economic weekly, offered its own unmistakeable opinion:

> [Kamaraj] never concealed his contempt for the many political fortune hunters who flocked to Mrs. Gandhi's party since 1969. . . . Given his reputation for principled consistency, it is difficult to believe that during his last days he changed his stand and decided to give his colleagues short shrift.

Gujarat's Janata Front government took six weeks longer to remove. Hitendra Desai, defector from the Old Congress, took the lead in the campaign against it and secured a flow of youth support for the Congress Party from the 1974 Gujarat agitation, helping it to an impressive victory in the panchayat elections. The Union government built a "case" against Gujarat on the issue of "clandestine" literature being produced in the state and the discovery of dynamite, allegedly being moved to Varanasi. The Janata Front died hard. In October, November, and December 1975, it won important civic elections in Rajkot, Baroda, Surat, Broach, and finally to the Ahmedabad Municipal Corporation, the largest civic body in the state. For the Ahmedabad election the bulk of Janata seats had been shared between the Old Congress (a constituent of the Front) and Majur Mahajan, the prestigious labor organization of textile workers started by Mahatma Gandhi. The Janata Front lost its majority in the State Assembly when its partner, the KMLP, was dissolved by defections on February 11. It was defeated on a budgetary demand in the assembly on March 12, 1976. The Congress Party secured defections of six corporations of the Ahmedabad Municipal Corporation and gained control of this important body soon afterward.

A third state, Jammu and Kashmir, maintained a discreet but definite distance from the Emergency. Sheikh Abdullah, restored to power as chief minister some months earlier, refrained from joining the chorus of praise around the prime minister. He spoke of a national reconciliation and on September 20, 1975 told newsmen, "If I can be of any use to the Prime Minister in this regard, my services are at her disposal." Resisting Congress pressures to merge his own party with the ruling party, he said the National Conference had waged the people's struggle against Maharaja's rule. It would keep its identity, and the Congress could merge with it, if it wished. He said at a public meeting at Lal Chowk:

> Power was handed over to me when the ship of State was on the point of sinking with the loads of corruption and maladministration. We are not obliged to those who vacated office in our favour. It is they who should be obliged to us because we are being obliged to carry the mess created by them. No one voluntarily gives up power. If someone does so, it is only to save himself from the deluge. My government is determined to root out corruption. Its extent and ramifications at the moment would frighten even the devil. The image of the Congress in the State is far from healty. But we want no confrontation with Congress.[2]

Kashmir, a sensitive border state, was paradoxically less vulnerable to "takeover" than Tamil Nadu or Gujarat. Its stability was vital to the country and Sheikh Abdullah was firmly in the saddle. At a public meeting in Udhampur on March 13, 1976, in what may have been an oblique reference to the massive security arrangements at the prime minister's meetings, he objected to police barricades separating him from the crowd. He said the worst that could befall him was an assassin's bullet, and he would prefer that to being kept at such a distance from the people.

Mrs. Gandhi had kept a group of Kashmiri Brahmins close to her. This preference for her community, and kith and kin, was climaxed by the emergence of Sanjay into the political limelight. The ease with which Sanjay was planted in the body politic was not, as it might have been in normal times, due to the respect Indians attach to family and tradition. Acceptance without demur by the Congress illustrated how thoroughly democratic procedures in the party had been gutted and the fear that now ruled out disagreement altogether. A party whose inner confidence had been shaken, and whose senior figures had been reduced to obedience, dully submitted.

Unlike his brother, Rajiv, a happily married airlines pilot and father of two, who stayed out of the limelight, Sanjay did not enjoy a reputation for modesty or pleasant human relations. A problem student, he had been withdrawn from boarding school and tutored at home to prepare him for the school-leaving examination, and later, had left Rolls Royce at Crewe before completing his training. Sanjay and brother had never known any environment but India's select Doon School and the prime minister's house (first their grandfather's at Teen Murti and later their mother's at Safdarjang Road), with all the privilege, prestige, and authority that went with it. Some of the most charming press pictures of the Nehru era had been of two enchanting children and three golden retrievers on the lawns of Teen Murti House. Sanjay had developed a taste for authority and a life-style lacking restraint. Much is forgiven a handsome young man, particularly a prime minister's son, and his escapades, which at one time included hijacking cars and coarse personal behavior, were generally ignored. He came to critical public notice for the first time as the recipient of government favor with no qualifications in education or experience to justify it, "suddenly heading a huge car manufacturing industrial complex involving an investment of ten million dollars, although his declared income for the year 1969–70 was Rs 748, [about $100]."[3]

The Emergency gave Sanjay wide scope for bullying command and vendetta. He already exercised authority without official position. He was now credited with ordering arrests and house and office raids. He gave direct orders to government officials and had squads of the Youth Congress to do his bidding. An aura of terror now attached to his name, and it was augmented by the enforced sterilization campaign conducted by him. By the end of the year he was given the status of a leading political personality, his arrivals in state capitals accompanied by official panoply to match his mother's. He was met by chief ministers and cabinet members, his visits elaborately arranged and attended by state politicians and officials. On a "surprise" visit paid by him to Patna on December 3, 1975, Jaggannath Mishra (brother of the late L. N. Mishra), Bihar's new chief minister, told newsmen "everyone was impressed by the simplicity of Mr. Sanjay Gandhi and his concern for the downtrodden masses." He made his official debut as "youth leader" at the Congress Party's annual session in December at Komagata Marunagar near Chandigarh, and was projected henceforth as one who "truly understood the aspirations of the poor," gifted with brains, business acumen, vision and compassion. Not surprisingly, the halo looked incongruous, and his new personality and importance had to be reinforced by a flood of rhetoric and bestowed with a new character. The following write-up in the *Indian Express* on February 12, 1976, in anticipation of his visit to Calcutta, is one of the more sedate examples of the lavish buildup provided for Sanjay through the media:

> Youth Congress leaders, Cabinet Ministers, industrialists, Rotarians and intellectuals are vying with each other to give him a big reception. Welcome arches are being erected at every turn of the ten-minute route through which he will be taken in a motorcade. At one point on the VIP road, a group of Sikhs will receive Mr. Gandhi with the bhangra dance, while at other points women will accord him a welcome in traditional Bengali style. The day-long programme is so packed with functions that Mr. Gandhi will be running from place to place to keep his engagements. The highlights of the programme are his address to a mass rally at the Shaheed Minar Maidan, the reception by the six Chambers of Commerce and two other business associations at Kala Mandir, and the luncheon meeting with the Rotarians. Never before have the Chambers of Commerce and the Rotarians from all over the State jointly welcomed any national leader or even a Prime Minister as they would be doing to Mr. Gandhi. At the meeting with the Chambers of Commerce, Mr. Gandhi will be answering questions by the country's top industrialists—an event of unique importance.

Sanjay's undefined powers ranged over a wide area, his activities including public meetings, interviews to newspapers and magazines, and conferences with ministers. On a visit to Bombay on January 11, 1976, Sanjay, according to a PTI (Press Trust of India) report, "spent over two hours discussing the economic and political problems of the country" with a group that included Bombay's Congress Party boss, Rajni Patel, Maharashtra revenue minister, Rafiq Zakaria, Union ministers V. C. Shukla and Bansi Lal, and "leading journalists."

Asked about the powers her son was exercising, Mrs. Gandhi replied in two interviews in October 1975:

> It is a big lie that the whole Emergency and so on is being run by or decisions taken by a small group including my son. (Interview with North German television, October 3.)

> This is a systematic campaign all over Europe and America, not just in Britain. . . . My family has been very much maligned and of course my son is not in politics at all. (Interview with the *Sunday Telegraph*, October 12.)

Private Indian comment on Sanjay's startling elevation at first favored the view that his mother, completely isolated from her colleagues' true feelings and beset by the actual and psychological hazards of autocratic rule, could now be sure of no one but her son. But this did not explain his natural assumption of arbitrary authority, which could more readily be understood in terms of special knowledge and information in his possession concerning his mother's political functioning. Crucially damaging to her credibility and the cult of her popularity, for example, would be any evidence of a carefully rigged poll in 1971, more believable in view of Mrs. Gandhi's subsequent behavior. His induction into the limelight served a useful purpose in projecting a new "pragmatism" while Mrs. Gandhi could continue to carry the "radical" posture: "I believe in anything that will help the poor. . . . This is a point on which there is no difference of opinion between my mother and me." (April 9, 1976.) On March 20, 1976 he declared that the "ideological struggle" of Right and Left had been started by "vested interests, the very forces that had supported the British in India, only to misguide youth."

Sanjay's anticommunism was an assurance to industry and the propertied class that they had nothing to fear, that no radical economic change would take place, an assurance borne out by events. The annual budget, by convention a closely guarded secret, became the subject of Sanjay's comments and revelations at a meeting of the Calcutta Chambers of Commerce in February 1976 and provided substantial tax relief for the upper class. The *Democratic World* commented on March 28, 1976:

> If the Finance Minister's budget proposals are any indication, India has no poor at all. If anything, the people who need succour the most are the rich. Else why should the man who has wealth of Rs 15 lakhs pay a tax only a quarter of what he was asked to pay earlier. . . .

Sanjay received Soviet recognition and blessing when he visited the Soviet Union with his mother and brother in August 1976. Soviet support for the Emergency had been announced when *Pravda* lauded India's "new economic plans" in July 1975 and Brezhnev told the 25th Congress of the Soviet Communist Party in February 1976 that the Soviet Union "attaches special importance to friendship with that great country, India . . . close political and economic cooperation with the Republic of India is our constant policy."

The Congress session in December 1975, a high point of the

Emergency, represented Mrs. Gandhi's style in full flower. Between the last session, almost unnoticed in the outcry of economic distress and the rising tide of Opposition opinion, and this one, Congress had suffered visible decline in reputation and popularity. In June it would have replaced Mrs. Gandhi with another leader. The declaration of Emergency obviated this need. With all crucial opposition eliminated via arrest, intimidation, and censorship, the one-party, one-leader idea could rise unhampered out of a leveled landscape as the single political presence. The session was celebrated as a "national" event representing "nationalism." D. K. Barooah declared the Congress a movement, not a party, and in February 1976, at a public meeting on Marina Beach in Madras, he said its doors were open to "all who believed in Indian nationalism, and were honest in personal and public conduct. . . . [Congress was] a brotherhood of patriotic Indians who fulfilled these two conditions."

"So far as I know," said Mrs. Gandhi on August 21, 1975, "force has not been used at all, not even in a small way anywhere." She repeated this in an interview with a Bombay weekly later: "There is no use of force and . . . there is no show of force whatsoever anywhere in the country. The truth is that the police have had less work since the Emergency than ever before."

Political arrests had been a feature of the past five years, beginning with the powerful assault on the CPI-M and expanding during 1974 to fill jails with multiparty dissenters belonging to the Bihar Movement. The treatment of prisoners had drawn international inquiry and reportage and aroused shocked comment in India. Government's budget for the police had doubled in five years. Mrs. Gandhi had no basis whatever for the statement she made. On September 19, 1975, it was announced that Delhi would have a sixth police district and its police force would be expanded by 900 men. Brutality figured large in suppressing protest and extorting bribes, and torture became an instrument of vengeance. The number of citizens arrested during the months following the Emergency was not revealed. Estimates by some Opposition parties, based on the number of their workers arrested, along with state government figures quoted from time to time, put the arrests at 110,000. There was no way of making an exact assessment.

For the majority, "preventive detention" meant punishment in primitive conditions continually strained by waves of new arrests, a policy designed to enfeeble or break opposition while the

Emergency lasted. The prime targets were the Jan Sangh and the CPI-M, both with a strong following and influence in the academic and professional world. But the Emergency also gave Mrs. Gandhi a unique opportunity to stamp out "janata sarkar" and other aspects of the Bihar Movement. Specific cases of force used against prisoners and terror exercised by the police were brought to her notice and that of the home ministry, as well as to the president of India. There is no question that she was informed about these, and it is hardly credible that she was in ignorance otherwise of the enormities and excesses of the police state she had established.

On October 22, six leading Socialist Party M.P.s wrote to the prime minister: "We have already addressed a few letters to the home minister regarding the ill-treatment of the political détenus in various jails. We have not received any reply to these letters so far."

The letter listed, among others, the following examples:

In Muzaffarpur Central Jail in Bihar where a large number of professors and political workers are detained ... a lathi charge was made on September 9, 1975 by the jail authorities and criminal convicts were let loose on them. A large number of them received injuries, some of them serious. ... We are seeking your intervention not only because the Home Minister did not reply to our letters earlier, but because we feel that political detention should not amount to punishment.[4]

On May 24, 1976 Mrs. Alice Fernandes, mother of George Fernandes, Socialist Party Chairman and trade union leader, then underground, wrote to the president of India with copies to the prime minister and other members of the central and state (Kerala) government:

Sir:
It is with a heavy sorrow-stricken heart that I am writing this, further to my letter dated May 12, 1976 (copy enclosed for ready reference), with the hope of obtaining justice at your hands. ...
On Saturday, May 1 at about 9 p.m., my 44-year-old second son, Lawrence Fernandes, was taken away from our residence by the police, on the pretext that they wanted t interrogate him about the Habeas Corpus petition filed in February ... by my third son, Michael Fernandes (an officer of the Indian Telephone Industries and a trade union leader) who has been detained without trial under MISA in prison since 22 December 1975. After keeping up this pretext for about an hour, the police began questioning him about the whereabouts of my eldest son, George Fernandes, and then subjected him in a most

inhuman, reckless and ruthless manner to third degree methods of physical torture, going on with this torture into the small hours of the morning until 3 a.m. Besides beating him with clubs (until five of them were broken to pieces) they used a banyan tree root to clout him with and booted him and slapped him. They also used vulgar language in abusing him and our family, and threatened him that if he did not reveal the whereabouts of George Fernandes he would be thrown on the railway tracks and killed under a moving train, leaving no evidence of their hands in his death. They were actually preparing to do so about 3 a.m. when his physical condition had deteriorated to an almost irreparable state. After thus reducing him to a condition of physical, mental and nervous wreck, he was kept in solitary confinement until May 20, during which period he was subjected to further torture and interrogation. He was kept without food for 3 days and was not given proper food on other days, nor allowed cigarettes. During all these 20 days he was allowed bath only on 3 days and made to remain in the same clothes in which he was when he was taken away on treatment. He was taken to different doctors and hospitals, each time under a different and false name, impersonating him as a police officer, for treatment to keep him alive. On one night a doctor was brought to the police station itself for treating him.

On May 9 my son was taken by police car 300 kilometres away to Davengere, and on May 10 produced before the magistrate there, as though arrested in Davangere on the previous day. He was tortured and kept in a closed lockup there until May 11, and then brought back to Bangalore. . . . He was refused lawyer's help and not allowed to contact home or anybody else either by letter or by phone. He was not allowed newspapers and kept in solitary confinement. He was threatened with dire consequences if he reported to the magistrate or anybody else about his torture. Finally on May 20 he was produced in the Second Metropolitan Magistrate's chambers during lunch time and then removed to the Bangalore Central Prison where he has been detained in a cell meant for condemned criminals, or for convicts who are mentally unsound, or under punishment for violation of jail rules.

In addition to oral complaints, I had lodged written complaints, sent telegrams and letters to all concerned from the highest to the lowest level of authority, but without any result and without even acknowledgement, and the whereabouts of my son, Lawrence, had not been informed to us. On May 20, upon being informed by a lawyer, I went to the prison, and although I waited along with the lawyer from 6:45 p.m. to 7:30 p.m., I was not allowed to meet my son. On the 21st after waiting for over 3 hours, from 10:45, I was taken at about 2 p.m. to the cell to see him. I found him looking dead. He was unable to move without two persons helping him about, and then too with great pain and limping. His left side is without use, as if crippled, and both his left leg and hand are still swollen. He is in a mentally and physically wrecked condition, and is unable to talk freely without faltering. He is terribly nervous and mortally afraid of the police, of anyone in khaki uniform, of the approaching sound of anyone walking with shoes on, or of any other person, all of whom he fears to be interrogators and tormentors. . . . As if to deal a further blow, yet another page was added to this sordid, inhuman act by serving on him in the prison in the afternoon of May 22 an order of detention dated May 21, signed by the Commissioner of Police, detaining him under MISA.

Whatever I have stated here is on the basis of what the family could gather from Lawrence during the visits to him in the cell. . . . I urge upon you in the name of all that is good in civilised conduct of human beings and their governments, and in the name of justice, to order a thorough judicial enquiry into this barbaric torture, and take suitable action against the concerned authorities. I also urge that he should be transferred to a good hospital, and specialist medical and psychiatric treatment be given to him, and daily visits to him by the family allowed so that he may regain his mental and physical health and become a human being. . . .[5]

In August 1976 an *Indian Express* editorial referred to the deaths of twenty-two prisoners while being interrogated in lockup. The fact was quoted from a government-instituted enquiry in Uttar Pradesh.

Mrs. Gandhi's most celebrated prisoner was served with more subtle punishment. Jayaprakash Narayan came close to death in the care of government doctors and the country's two premier, government-owned, medical institutions, the All-India Medical Institute at Delhi and the Post-Graduate Institute at Chandigarh. Released in mid-November 1975 and brought a week later to Bombay's private Jaslok Hospital, his doctors expressed surprise at his kidney collapse not being diagnosed and treated much earlier. This dramatic deterioration contrasted sharply with his condition immediately prior to his arrest. JP had been on strenuous tours, addressed mammoth meetings in the intense heat and dust of May and June, without any adverse effects except fatigue. On his release, when facts concerning his illness became known, his condition gave rise to the chilly joke: "The British just put you in jail. But if they put you in jail now, you'll find yourself tied to a kidney machine for the rest of your life." JP was released following a letter from his brother, Rajeshwar Prasad to the prime minister, which described in detail the systematic deterioration, month by month, in the prisoner's condition, at times bed-ridden and unable to move without help.

Rajeshwar Prasad's letter, drafted at his request with my help in the second week of November 1975, reads:

Madam,

You are aware that I am the brother of Shri Jayaprakash Narayan.

I have been meeting him every month since July '75 in Chandigarh.

In July and August I found him in dubious but not serious ill health. He had been suffering from low blood pressure, low blood sugar, and had feelings of nausea.

In September I found that he had lost all appetite, was not able to eat or relish any food. He had become very weak.

In October, when I met him on the 5th, he told me that he had a severe pain in the stomach. A few days before I met him the acuteness of the pain had subsided, but the pain was persisting, and investigations and examinations were going on by the doctors to find out the cause. At that time he was in the hospital. His condition had deteriorated. He was very weak and his loss of appetite persisted.

Subsequently in the later weeks of October our other relatives met him. They found that he had been transferred to the hospital ward for better medical care and attendance. They found him completely bed-ridden and on a liquid diet.

I met him again on the 7th of November. I found that he was now able to move about in the room, but he had to be supported during his movements, such is his weakness. He was still on a liquid diet. And what is most alarming is that even after such a long period, and in spite of several so-called thorough examinations and investigation, the disease has not been identified. He is not even told what medicines are being administered to him.

His general condition has fast deteriorated during these three months. Swelling in the legs is still there. Two toes are bent. There is some trouble in the eyes, apart from the fact that there are swellings below both the eyes as big as hanging pouches.

I have very serious apprehensions that if his condition continues like this he might not survive for more than two months. This is causing us the greatest anguish. I have not discussed my anxiety with JP, nor mentioned that I would be writing to you, but I feel I must apprise you of his condition so that you can make your own assessment. Apart from the great personal tragedy that his loss would mean to our family, it is for you to decide whether it would be in the interests of the Government if JP dies in jail.

Yours truly,
Rajeshwar Prasad

Morarji Desai, aged eighty, a prisoner in one of Haryana government's circuit houses, took the precaution of refusing to eat any cooked food, except what was on occasion provided by his family.

Arbitrary arrest, with the denial of appeal or trial, created the fear necessary to obedience, while censorship kept people ignorant of events and opinions adverse to government. Both were indispensable to a state of affairs where drama substituted for the real and arduous process of governing. Ministers carried out "surprise" visits to their departments to check on punctuality and much was made about getting to office on time. Orders to retire at fifty were served on "officers with a bad reputation for integrity." Government made examples, via arrest, intimidation, and "tax raids," of "economic offendors." Overnight clearances of selected localities and sterilization drives based on quotas that were indifferent to age and whether or not a man was married and had any children at all went into operation. It soon became clear that achievement not based on sound programs was illusory and could not be sustained. In a free market, economy prices would fluctuate. The low price of vegetable oil in the summer of 1975 had been the result of bumper crops of mustard seed and groundnut already in the market, while low grain prices were made possible by a good monsoon. No artificial low price level could be maintained, and prices gradually took their course, with new high levels registered in a range of goods from kerosene and cooking gas to vegetables, fruit, and bus tickets. Violent uprisings, with hundreds killed and imprisoned, erupted in fury against evictions and sterilization at Turkman Gate, Delhi, in April 1975, and the following year in Uttar Pradesh and Maharashtra. Continuing arrests and repeated official references to the forces of disruption, made it clear that a large and politically conscious country could not easily be reduced to submissive conformity. Government's anticorruption measures acquired a spuriousness as the drive against economic offendors became linked with its own political opponents, and action to clean up the administration left the power structure around Mrs. Gandhi intact, including those whose reputations had attracted the greatest public anger and criticism. Bansi Lal was appointed Union defence minister, while L. N. Mishra was enshrined for posterity on a postage stamp. At a ceremony on his fifty-fourth birth anniversary, the prime minister called him "a shining example of bravery and courage and readiness to make the supreme sacrifice for the cause of his country." D. K. Barooah announced a statue of the late minister would be put up in the capital. Drama accompanied a scheme for the voluntary disclosure of wealth, promising tax evaders immunity from punishment or probe, and yielding government Rs 250 crores in tax revenue. The fact remained that the tax department, armed with drastic powers under the Emergency, could have attained its object more respectably, without showing leniency to the corrupt.

The language in use contributed to the atmosphere of bad theater. Emergency perorations abounded in repetition and cliché. Political heterogeneity had accustomed Indians to every kind of political speech. From the flights of early Bengali oratory to the thoughtful evocations of Nehru, a tradition had been shaped. The speeches of trade unionist, district politician, student and worker, radical and conservative, had reflected a whole political development. Public speeches and political expression, now limited to the Congress-CPI combine, filled the air with verbal gunsmoke. The once dignified addresses of governors repeated it: "The tide of fascists and reactionaries has been repulsed but we must not be complacent." (Governor of Punjab, August 14, 1975.)

A joint statement issued by the Congress and CPI units in Bihar on August 2 warned people against complacency over "the inactivity of reactionary conspirators. . . . They want to utilise the present economic distress of the people to instigate them in support of their diabolical venture . . . the counter revolutionaries fondly hope that the 21-point programme will fail so that they can engineer their sinister conspiracy once again."

D. K. Barooah referred to L. N. Mishra as "a symbol of our struggle against the dark and sinister forces of fascism." This trend displayed its full psychosis at several "anti-fascist" conferences organized by the Congress and CPI. The first, held on September 11, 1975 at Town Hall, Amritsar, made much of human skulls and weapons found by the police and said fascist forces had gone underground to create chaos and destroy democracy. At the last, in Patna in December, advertised as a "world anti-fascist conference" D. K. Barooah spoke somewhat obscurely of "the dark forces of neo-imperialism and eastern racial arrogance which were combining in a sinister attempt to snuff out the light of democracy in this part of the world." Vested interests in India and abroad, he said, felt deeply hurt and frustrated by Congress policies and had combined for a most vicious and violent onslaught on the party. Not much research was required, the Congress president declared, to spot the international forces behind this conspiracy. On February

10, 1976 in Trivandrum, a session of the CPI's national council stressed vigilance against "the sinister conspiracy of imperialism and its monstrous agencies."

Mrs. Gandhi's own statements sounded strangely fantasy-laden:

> I am such a meek and mild person. (To Paul Saltzman of *Macleans Magazine*, Canada.)

> I am a very humble person. (To Mauritius Broadcasting Corporation, October 4, 1975.)

> Hundreds of thousands of poor and humble people of India will rise in revolt if any harm were done to her. (To a news conference at Bhubaneshwar, September 27, 1975.)

> Had this [Emergency] been a question about me as an individual I would have been least concerned, but it involved the Prime Minister of India. (Radio broadcast, November 10, 1975.)

> The verdict of the Allahabad High Court did not cause any disturbance to me, nor was I tempted to take any decision or steps because of it. (December 27, 1975.)

> Until the age of 13 or 14 I hated people, some but not many, one or two, e.g., the police. But after 14 or 16 I cannot remember having hated anyone. . . . I am not at all concerned with things like achievement, success, failure. (*Hindustan Times* interview, February 7, 1976.)

> I am not the Prime Minister because I like power. I want to serve the people, and their service is the only thing I have before me as my life's mission. (Public meeting, Durgapur, March 3, 1976.)

In January 1976 the Congress Party celebrated Mrs. Gandhi's "dynamic decade" of power. The directorate of advertising and visual publicity released a book, *A Decade of Achievement 1966–75*, and the president opened a "Decade of Achievement" exhibition. Vidya Charan Shukla, information and broadcasting minister, declared that more had been done during Mrs. Gandhi's decade than during the last thousand years.

As against the fulsome self-congratulation of Emergency language and its sharp attack on invisible antagonists, actual tragedy was met with subdued vocabulary and casual approach. Patna was flooded in the third week of August 1975. On November 23, Suman Dubey reported in the *Indian Express*:

> . . . it is hard to come by evidence of government-sponsored rehabilitation in this city. . . . Where rehabilitation is under way . . . it is

mainly through the efforts of private voluntary agencies. . . . The condition of roadside dwellers, such as along Serpentine Road opposite the Circuit House, is the worst of all. With the cold of the winter settling in, all these people have for shelter are four bamboo boles supporting a thatch or piece of tin or pieces of cloth. . . .

A mine disaster of shocking magnitude at Chasnala on December 27, 1975 killed 372 workers. A warning by the Central Mining Research Station nine months earlier, that the mine was unsafe, was ignored. Rescue was delayed and the operation confused. A request for high performance American pumps was cancelled. On January 11 the UNI reported that five Indian pumps had developed "working difficulties" that day, five high capacity Polish pumps were yet to arrive, and only two Indian and two Soviet pumps were working. On January 19 when the first rescue attempt could be made, there was no sign of life in the mine. The minister for steel and mines, admitting 372 deaths, told the Lok Sabha that conditions in India were better than in some countries, and everything possible would be done to improve mine safety.

In terms of development, the Emergency accelerated the priorities of Mrs. Gandhi's decade, during which the total assets of the twenty largest industrial houses increased by 150 percent, while industrial production, savings, capital formation, and investment in the public sector generally declined. Liberal terms and support measures were provided to domestic and foreign big business and export promotion; foreign exchange reserves rose with incentives to nonresident Indians to maintain foreign exchange accounts in India; and, despite the government's proclaimed policy of self-reliance, it sought and accepted unusually heavy aid from abroad. In contrast, there was no corresponding push on land reform. By mid-March 1976, 136,000 acres had been distributed to the landless—only 3 percent of the approximately 4 million surplus acres estimated under the July 1972 guidelines, and whose distribution was to be completed within a year of the Emergency. In eight states 62,300 bonded laborers were identified, and 55,583 released, though the actual number of bonded laborers in these states was believed to be about ten times larger than identified. (The term "bonded labor" means a kind of economic serfdom, in which the servant, due to extreme proverty or indebtedness, is driven into a situation where he works for no pay and is exploited in various ways by his employer.) Those identified as bonded laborers were released from this situation. Workers fared badly with 700,000 laid off during the first year of the Emergency, while a freeze was imposed on the labor movement. Trade union activity became hazardous; pressure was brought to increase workloads; and militant workers were jailed or victimized. Both Congress and Communist trade union leaders were compelled to voice their opposition. Evidence that the Emergency had ill served the working class was the seething discontent that erupted and had to be met as soon as freedom was restored, greatly hampering the new government, which was committed to human rights. The Emergency does not appear to have brought any improvement of substance for the mass of the people, while it did deprive them of their right to organize or protest. Even the runaway inflationary trend, arrested to an extent, was probably more a response to normal economic factors rather than an achievement of the administration. The more prosperous enjoyed the benefits of cheap labor and a frozen labor situation. There was little indication of a move toward a more egalitarian order.

The longest constitutional amendment Bill in the world revealed the Emergency's true rationale. Boycotted by the Opposition, it received the Emergency Parliament's sanction at the end of 1976 and established the institutions and powers of authoritarian government.

An individual's headlong will and urge to power had transformed the government and politics of India. The setting for personal rule had now been consolidated by the Constitution.

CHAPTER FOURTEEN

Why Mrs. Gandhi Called an Election

The Constitution of 1950 allowed the government, under conditions of emergency, to postpone elections to Parliament for a year at a time. Mrs. Gandhi took advantage of this provision to postpone the election due in March 1976 for one year. In November 1976 she announced a further year's postponement. Her November decision and its sudden reversal on January 18, 1977 when she announced an election for March revealed once again personal temperament rather than orderly political process as characteristic of the style she had brought to Indian politics. Like her declaration of emergency, the new decision appeared to be intimately connected with her estimate of her own political fortune and now, in addition, that of her son's.

Mrs. Gandhi had declared an Emergency when her party's future was at a distinct crossroads. In the preceding months the Congress had suffered stunning defeats in four out of five by-elections at the hands of the Opposition combine, known as the Janata Front, that was produced by the Bihar Movement. These defeats had been climaxed on June 12, 1975 by the Front's victory in the Gujarat state election. While by-elections and state elections are not always pointers to major change on the national scene, the emergence for the first time of a united Opposition as victor showed a new weight in politics that could not be ignored. The Congress might be returned to power in the next election, but not since 1967 had its credit been so low. If it was returned with a greatly reduced majority, it would pave the way for Opposition governments in several states, and the breakdown of its monolithic rule at the Center and states since 1971–72. The Bihar Movement, apart from securing the cooperation of four political parties, had been a potent force in intensifying political awareness in the countryside and organizing new sections of the population against the Congress. It had also stirred the conscience of Congressmen and driven high office-holders in the party and the government to forthright criticism. By June 1975 the cracks in the Congress were plain to see, but it was plainer still that Mrs. Gandhi had a fight ahead of her to retain control of it. For those now grouping against her, she represented the autocratic structure that would have to be dismantled if the Congress were to recover the confidence of its own rank and file, as well as mass sympathy and backing. The Allahabad High Court judgement invalidating her 1971 elections to Parliament for two violations of the election law gave the Congress a quiet opportunity to replace her, without any tinder being lit over the event or appeals to loyalty and emotion being launched. The citadel of power she had built did not permit a normal open debate about a change in leadership. But Chandersekhar, Mohan Dharia, Krishna Kant, Ram Dhan, and others had already made their views public and had become the focus of admiring attention. This admiration was reinforced by the wall of unspoken resentment her style of leadership had brough into being. The astute and ambitious among her rivals in the party bided their time for the denouement that now seemed inevitable.

Mrs. Gandhi's characteristic recourse to "spontaneous" rallies arranged at her residence—this time to condemn the High Court judgement and uphold her as the people's choice—and her effort to stir and inflame feeling in the capital was drawing little response. The routine had staled. Small, straggling groups, rounded up with difficulty from Delhi and its environs, sat polite, patient, and bored in the enervating heat, listening to the now familiar claim to unique sacrifice, ancestry, and position. The signs, for any temperament not comfortable with the democratic process and the change it now seemed certain to bring, were ominous. Against an impending possibility of checkmate, Mrs. Gandhi declared an Emergency and launched a police state, with one gesture disposing of her opponents in and outside her party and immobilizing the gathering opposition to the Congress. What were the factors, nineteen months later, that influenced her to risk an election?

The element of risk now seemed small, as far as a Congress win was concerned, for it had held the stage without competition for those nineteen months. During that period Mrs. Gandhi had disciplined the dissidents in her party through arrest or its threat.

She had successfully introduced, and systematically pushed, the idea of dynastic rule, a thing she would have found difficult if not impossible to do in normal times. The Opposition was severely handicapped by nineteen months out of the public gaze, with no chance to make its views heard, while the government, with its monopoly of public meetings, demonstratons, and media control, had been able to keep up a steady barrage of accusation and condemnation in extreme language against it. Some Opposition leaders were crippled with illness in long confinement. The chairman of the Socialist Party, George Fernandes, was not granted release to stand for election and had to do so from jail. For thousands of party workers, release from jail would mean first of all the urgent rehabilitation of their families, often reduced to severe hardship with the sole wage-earner in prison. For the Opposition as a whole, the process of reassembling, collecting funds, and preparing for an election would be painful. The censored press—its independent editors dismissed or silenced—had daily assured Mrs. Gandhi of her popularity. It is certain she believed the election would be a formal affair renewing her mandate.

There were other hopeful signs for a ruling party victory. The emergency had benefited by two good harvests when grain had been abundant and its price comparatively stable. With about 80 percent of the average Indian budget spent on food grains, inflation in the basic needs had been kept in check. High inflation in the West at this time had provided Indian exports with a noticeably improved market, and these had fetched better prices, adding substantially to India's foreign currency reserves, as had the government's belated measures against smuggling and tax evasion.

As against these advantages, the prices of many goods had risen and there were signs of shortage. Protest had remained alive, confirmed by expanded police vigilance and continuing arrests. The law courts had tried to act as a brake upon the government's arbitrary behavior and to uphold prisoners' rights. In Delhi and Muzzafarnagar, Uttar Pradesh, there had been large-scale and bloody riots against forced sterilization and peremptory eviction. And vigorous objection to the constitutional amendment package, giving the prime minister virtually unlimited powers, had erupted when the government modified the ban on public meetings to permit a degree of debate on the amendments. The outcry against the amendments, not confined to the intelligentsia and the cities, was heard in the countryside. The Indian villager had come to rely on the court system for redress of wrongs. Courts took time, but he could expect justice from them. Under the new dispensation, the powers of the courts to deal with land and other specific categories of cases was to be reduced or eliminated. For land cases, government tribunals were to be appointed. Small landowners and the landless feared that local vested interests and government bosses would end all impartial decision-making.

A combination of these plus and minus factors may have decided Mrs. Gandhi to go to the polls while she had complete control of the situation and before affairs, in the shape of man or nature, took an uncontrollable turn.

But the election appears to have been necessary for another reason. Mrs. Gandhi had used the emergency to bury the scandal surrounding her son's business ventures and to raise him to an exalted status surrounded by the obeisance due to a hereditary heir apparent. Though he had no official position or political experience and was not even a primary member of the party, Sanjay was hailed as the leader and inspiration (even though he was not official president) of the Youth Congress. A concerted drive was launched to swell the organization's membership, to provide him with a following personally loyal and beholden to him and to empower the organization with independence of authority and action. Mrs. Gandhi introduced the new perspective at the annual session of the Congress in Gauhati (Assam) in December 1976, when she praised the exemplary role of the Youth Congress and spoke of its importance for the country's future. Sanjay had, since the Emergency, been a force to reckon with in political and administrative decisions in Delhi and in the states, and in December 1975 he had been escorted with fanfare into the party limelight at the Komagata Maru annual session at Chandigarh, but even earlier there were strong indications that Mrs. Gandhi had succession in mind. On September 19, 1975, in a speech to educators, she had denied allegations of vast powers in her hands and said that nowhere in the world had the head of government less power than she had. "Every decision," she said, "has to go through a number of levels." In the same speech she continued. "But I may not be alive. What happens then? What is the next rank? Who is going to carry the fight forward?" In normal democratic procedure who would this be but the next democratically chosen leader and his cabinet? Why, with less power any head of government in the world, did Mrs. Gandhi then raise the question of what may happen after her?

The rise and projection of Sanjay in the face of his reputation and the bitter resentment against his arrogant use of power during the Emergency reveal a curious yet classic flaw in his mother's otherwise tough political armor, without which it is conceivable that Mrs. Gandhi's experiment in dictatorship might have survived an election, or at least not ended in her own humiliating defeat at the polls. Her refusal to acknowledge the facts about Sanjay's behavior and transactions had been an emotional blind spot. She now seized the moment to consolidate his future so that, if she died within the next five or six years, his power base would be secure. The 1971 Parliament, a body largely subservient to her individual authority, had secured her own power base. The 1977 Parliament would ensure Sanjay's if it brought in a majority of his handpicked supporters.

As soon as censorship was suspended for the election, campaigning permitted, and the fear guaranteeing obedience and silence lifted, it was obvious this strategy could not be employed. A political avalanche in support of the Janata Party had overtaken opinion, with huge crowds walking miles to listen in pindrop silence to Mrs. Gandhi's recent prisoners. Another impending development fast followed, with a break in the Congress led by Jagjivan Ram and his formation of Congress for Democracy, and its electoral alliance with the Janata Party. Jagjivan Ram gave as his reason for silence thus far that, had he made his intention clear any earlier, the election would not have taken place, and he would probably never have been heard of again—reasons the public considered valid, judging by the enthusiasm and support his breakaway received and his own election to Parliament. In these circumstances further erosion in the Congress could not be risked, with elements in the party known to be antagonistic to Sanjay's domination. The original list, heavily weighted with Youth Congress names, had to be abandoned and a majority of the old candidates brought back.

Yet Sanjay's rise had been made possible by the police state, and it could have been consolidated within it. He himself, according to her statement in a post-election party meeting, had advised his mother against an election. Why then did she decide to hold an election?

The answer may lie in the complexity of human personality. India's leader, from 1966 to 1977, had been a woman whose childhood, education, and family tradition had provided her with unusual opportunitites for training in democratic ideals, yet whose own temperament had never felt entirely comfortable with this inheritance. The stages of her career as prime minister made it plain she was not a democrat by belief or instinct. She firmly believed in her own indispensability. Concessions, compromise, and discussion signified weakness to her, and opposition jarred and angered her. She needed the constant assurance of acceptance and loyalty to feel secure. Psychologically she seemed incapable of settling down into the routine of conducting the business of government, doing the homework practical decisions required, or understanding that in a democratic country the leader is fallible and dispensable, besides being mortal. She had watched democracy and indispensability successfully at work in her father's lifetime and had assumed the combination would be hers by right of birth. When it did not appear to be so, she looked for reasons outside the pale of fact or logic. As a child she had imagined herself a Joan of Arc, a liberator of her people with the forces of a foreign power ranged against her. As an adult she continued to see herself as a martyr. Though, as Nehru's daughter, she had from the start an assured and prestigious place in the party and became the choice of its senior leaders for its highest post, yet she imagined vested interests obstructing and threatening her and used argument to seize and retain absolute control. She saw enemies in the normal democratic process and frequently claimed she was in physical danger from the Opposition. She gave extreme labels—"fascist" and "reactionary"—to her critics and to a genuine mass movement, Gandhian in method and program, led by a nationally revered figure. Finally, she assumed dictatorial powers under the cloak of an "emergency" on unproven accusations of conspiracy against herself and her government.

Democracy was not Mrs. Gandhi's style, but it remained an insistent craving. In a world where leadership had to be one of two kinds, coercive or persuasive, she could not resolve her dilemma and fell between the two, debasing democratic values and destroying the system while repeatedly avowing her dedication to it. The confusion gave her pronouncements during the Emergency a ring of unbalance. With tens of thousands of citizens jailed without charges or trial and her critics outlawed and silenced, she could calmly and convincedly repeat, "I am a democrat." The repetition carried that element of yearning we often have for what we ourselves are not and cannot be.

Why should democracy have been a craving in such a character at all? It was part of India's British connection. It had been the heart and soul of India's struggle for freedom, recalling much older values in the soil. It had been fundamental to her father's philosophy and the letter and spirit of his government. The modern Indian imagination could not easily set democracy aside. It was a specter that haunted Mrs. Gandhi. She longed for a democratic image and never admitted to having any other. It was an image an election could only strengthen and brighten and a continuing Emergency could only tarnish. She did not doubt that the outcome of the election would be favorable to her party and to herself. But it might also achieve the deeply desired establishment of Sanjay as her successor.

India's sixth national election to Parliament was transformed by the events of the Emergency to a referendum on a single issue: Would Indians give the Congress Party a mandate to continue the form of dictatorship established by Mrs. Gandhi in June 1975, or would they choose to return to a rule of law and the restoration of civil liberties? Of an electorate of 320 million, roughly 60 percent voted a new party to power, reducing the Congress for the first time since independence to a minority. Significantly, Mrs. Gandhi and her son, along with the ministers who had represented unpopular policies—V. C. Shukla (information and broadcasting), H. R. Gokhale (law), Bansi Lal (defence)—went down to shattering defeat at the polls. George Fernandes, who had to contest from prison, won by one of the largest majorities of any candidate.

The election made history for other reasons. The Janata Party that defeated the Congress was inspired and led by the most unusual figure in Indian politics since Mahatma Gandhi. Jayaprakash Narayan's return to national prominence as leader of the Bihar Movement in 1974 had the profound impact it did because it restored the breath of idealism to the political controversy and revived echoes of an age of grand striving still fresh in Indian memory. Though he had been long regarded as an impractical idealist and visionary, it was his supremely practical accomplishment to unite the Opposition and guide it to victory on the issue that the masses need both bread and freedom, and there is no separating the two.

The election opened the way for two political processes stunted by Mrs. Gandhi's style and techniques of governing party and country: the natural development of the post-Nehru leadership within the Congress, and the natural development of an opposition as a growing challenge to the Congress. The myth of indispensability was quietly disposed of at the polls, and a path was opened for a new, perhaps unknown leadership of the Congress. With the vote in favor of the Congress concentrated in the south, for the first time since its birth its center of power might shift to the south. The expanding political awareness of the electorate had first made itself felt with significant Opposition victories in 1967. It was reflected in the Opposition's by-election victories in early 1975, while the 1977 elections reflected the new preference in the mass vote. The *Indian Express* editorial of March 22, 1977, entitled "Finest Hour," called attention to this mass awareness, not a small, tidy, city elite, when it wrote:

> The average Indian voter had demonstrated his maturity in exercising his franchise and has taught a lesson to rulers who might be inclined to take him for granted as a passive and pliable pawn in the game of power politics. Indian democracy will never again be the same after the traumatic experience of the last two years. No future government, however large its majority in Parliament, can afford to assume that it can drive a coach and four through the Constitution and the laws, make inroads on the liberties of the people and hope to escape nemesis from an outraged people. It is significant that the people's vote went against Mrs. Gandhi despite all her warnings that her defeat would mean plunging the country into chaos. . . .

The election's immediate achievement was the restoration of a legitimate political process, more important in the long run than the question of whether the coalition it had brought to power would survive. The electorate's rejection of the dictatorship Nehru's daughter had established was a vindication of Nehru's own passionate conviction that his countrymen must live and grow in freedom.

CHAPTER FIFTEEN

Leadership Style

As a member of the Congress Working Committee, Mrs. Gandhi made her debut into politics at the highest level. Her first responsibility admitted her to the rarefied atmsophere of policy and program, the top level of decision-making, without exposure to the processes leading up to it or encountering in a systematic way the lower levels, where practical experience of an organization is garnered through a daily brush with its sentiment and its problems. Policy and decision were seen by her as handed down. The ultimate attitude of a party dependent on the goodwill and votes of an electorate has to take note of local situations, personalities, and compulsions. The "executive suite," setting Mrs. Gandhi at the uppermost layer of confabulation without a thorough education in the levels supporting it, looked to her like an easy exercise in authority. On gaining ascendancy in her party, she took, of deliberation, steps to dismantle the effectiveness of the "process," establishing, as she gained control of the machine, a single omnipotent command. This left her no possibility of learning from a complex developing organism, and her concept of leadership as "pinnacle" authority unaccountable to any forum perpetuated a great gulf between her and the party. No connecting links could, except as temporary devices, span the gulf, since these had to be reshuffled to prevent local seats of power from developing. The loyalty she demanded thus became an affair of change and chance. Loud and repeatedly expressed, its expression often had no meaning, a fact she was well aware of, for flattery, unless it was accompanied by subservience, was quickly detected and disposed of by her. The stripping of H. N. Bahuguna's chief ministership in Uttar Pradesh in 1976 is a classic example of Mrs. Gandhi's treatment of allegiance when it came from a sturdy and popular politician with roots of his own. Rival power in the states was not permitted to surface by so much as a flicker. But even an assumption of indispensability to the prime minister in a more subordinate capacity was unwelcome and could be met with reprimand or suitable action. Favorites at court could not count on remaining so, hence Mrs. Gandhi had no sincere inner circle to rely on. The atmosphere and intrigues of a medieval palace prevailed. Similarly, she created a situation where she could not depend on the loyalty of her senior cabinet colleagues. From these, her one-time equals, public statements or other signs of allegiance were extracted. An abject example was that of Y. B. Chavan (then minister for external affairs), when, on March 8, 1975 in Sholapur, Maharashtra, he told Congress workers he had no political ambition and no stake in the prime ministership.

Chavan had been in politics all his life. An activist in the Quit India agitation, a respected chief minister of Maharashtra, an able and popular Union defence minister during the Indo-Pakistan war in 1965, this was for him a pathetic act of submission, showing how senior Congressmen of recognized ability had been humbled in obedience to the leadership cult. On January 19, 1976, unable to attend a Congress Party symposium in New Delhi to praise Mrs. Gandhi's decade, Chavan took the precaution of explaining his absence by letter, setting forth in it the standard florid tribute for her "amazingly firm and far-sighted leadership." The letter ended: "Apart from the fact that you have grown to the stature of a leading world figure, what is important for me is that you have grown to become a symbol of the hopes and aspirations of millions of Indians. As one of them, I wish you many more years of achievement at the helm of the nation's affairs."

A more significant rival cut to size was Jagjivan Ram, then Union food and agriculture minister, who was assigned the task of justifying the Emergency in the Lok Sabha on its opening day, July 21, 1975. As the government's mouthpiece, Jagjivan Ram's speech contained the compulsory homily to the prime minister and such stock phrases, clearly not his own, as "the nefarious plans of the [railway] strikers were dashed to the ground." Brought up in the hard school of untouchability, Jagjivan Ram had known no easy road to power, and much was expected of a man whose command of a substantial untouchable vote could have carried weight in his equation with Mrs. Gandhi. Jagjivan Ram was a contender for power when the move to replace Mrs. Gandhi after the Allahabad High

Court judgement began with the Congress Parliamentary Party collecting signatures supporting the election of a new leader.

These two men, playing the waiting game, missed their opportunity and evidently found it preferable, in their sixties, to continue where they were than to suffer total political eclipse or arrest. If they tried earlier to dislodge Mrs. Gandhi through intraparty maneuvers, there were definite limits on how hard they could try in circumstances where surveillance had become pervasive and routine. Once a police state was openly established, they could not try at all. The average man of any nationality feels fear and caution when there is reason to feel it. A picture comes vividly to mind of Chavan's arrival at the French Embassy's National Day reception on July 14, 1975, accompanied by seven gunmen. Wearing bush shirts that distinguished them from the invited guests, who wore "lounge suit or national dress" as specified by the invitation, they made no attempt to hide the pistols bulging from their trouser pockets. They clustered around Chavan, and their presence quickly put an end to normal conversation. Chavan, of genial and pleasant disposition, looked drawn and strained by the "protection" he was receiving. The glitter of naked power during the early months of the Emergency served as a businesslike warning to Mrs. Gandhi's senior colleagues and ended all political surmise and conjecture about their own possible future roles.

An extraordinary range and depth of human encounter might have served Mrs. Gandhi as "education" for the political process during her father's lifetime, through the ebb and flow of Nehru's relationships, intimate and public, with individuals and the mass. Her own temperament set limits on this opportunity. No miracle of "love and affection," so eloquently described by Nehru as his cherished gift from the Indian people—a transforming personal and political experience for him—could come her way and work its mutuality. A heritage of devotion, waiting for her, changed in her hands to the public's awe and fear of her. Politics was for her, therefore, the very antithesis of the experience it had been for her father, for whom even a mass meeting was people, and one he addressed as such. Mrs. Gandhi's meeting with the masses was gradually reduced to a formal encounter. Her public personality, compared at first with her father's, lost this resemblance as it took on the aura and exaggerations of The Leader. Her mass meetings were accompanied by increasingly heavier management, armed security, and distance from the crowd that gave them an artificial

aspect of "performance" alien to Indian politics. At one time undeterred by situations of risk, she showed less confidence as she
abandoned democratic procedures and relied on her intelligence
and police. A government officer, referring to Mrs. Gandhi's visit
to Ludhiana, Punjab, some months before the Emergency, said she
had needed more security than Linlithgow, unpopular British vice-
roy during the 1942 Quit India upheaval. In 1974 the contrast between her meetings and the vast spontaneous crowds drawn to
Jayaprakash Narayan's public engagements was particularly strik-
ing. Remote from the seat and emblems of power, with nothing but
his personal reputation to attract the crowd and with authority
mounted against him, JP represented an abiding urge: the desire
for a leader whose life was his message. Mrs. Gandhi thus missed
the crux and essence of leadership in India. More and more her
eminence had to be buttressed, arranged, safeguarded from natural
political processes, from the moons and tides of Indian politics in
particular. She could not permit any natural development, in her
party or in the country, that might unseat her. The following she
commanded progressively shed its thoughtful, enlightened, dis-
criminating sections and was reduced either to the cynical camp-
follower or to the "lamp post" variety, those whom she had raised
to office out of mediocrity or obscurity and who were not troubled
by indpendent thought or the critical faculty. Prestige and following
in India had taken note of the kind and quality of human being,
rather than the temporal power, if any, he wielded. The Emergency,
establishing a police state and eliminating civil liberties and opposing opinion, illustrated Mrs. Gandhi's total retreat behind the
barrier of force.

Talented and abundant political leadership has been a feature
of modern India, an outgrowth of the national movement, for thirty
years a training ground under Mahatma Gandhi. The Congress was
the only liberation movement in Asia to successively convert itself
into a political party and provide stable government in the post-
independence era. But the leadership phenomenon has extended
to the Opposition. Gifted men of the Right and Left, with a high
degree of individualism, have been able to capture the Indian
imagination sufficiently to show election results and form state governments. In the Indian context, state leadership has constituted
impressive power, backed not only by large numbers but by the
culture, language and economics of a region. Against this canvas
Mrs. Gandhi stands out as the only manufactured leader, consis-

tently built up through the media and other channels and relentlessly imposed on the Indian mind through a campaign of emotional appeal and outcry resorting to her father's name. The campaign of manufacture was extended to her son, Sanjay, imposed on the nation in an exactly similar way but without even the slim credentials Mrs. Gandhi brought to her job. Her ceaseless drive to establish herself as India's exclusive leader has revealed the fundamental anxiety and weakness in her position, driving her to measures that a genuinely mass-based, psychologically secure leader would never have needed to take.

Considered a master of political technique, Mrs. Gandhi has in fact demonstrated classically by her career the failure of political functioning, and its substitution, when failure endangered her political survival, by "direct action" or outright authoritarianism. She became prime minister through the party's traditional method of consensus, one she fully endorsed and cooperated with at the time. She discarded consensus when it went against her in her party's choice of a presidential candidate for the country and abandoned political ethics altogether in her support of another candidate. Unsure of her continuance as leader of the party, she used street arousal as a technique to proclaim herself the "people's" choice. Both these tactics depended for their success on moves outside her party, her cabinet, and accepted political standards. Six years later, faced with the Allahabad High Court judgement and the Congress Parliamentary Party's move to replace her, she responded swiftly with the Emergency, imprisoning and outlawing opposition, both within and outside her party.

The absence of disciplined political functioning shows up, too, in Mrs. Gandhi's remarkable indifference to the cultivation of good comradeship and goodwill with her partymen, ordinarily of great importance to a democratic politician. At turning points, in 1969 and 1975, when her future was in the balance, she fought a bitter battle to the kill, leaving no scope for compromise, no detail to chance. At both stages, the people who had started out as her supporters—the ruling clique of the Old Congress who had raised her to power in 1966 and the radicals who had backed her in the Congress split in 1969—became baffled and astonished by her behavior in the course of events and finally, in self-respect, unable to accept it. Indifference to party opinion is highly unusual in democratic politics, where differences of opinion must be faced and accommodation sought and where a politician's future is linked to his party's acceptance of him. Yet, though Mrs. Gandhi destroyed her credit with two entirely different groups, she did not on either occasion suffer the political consequences thereof.

In the light of the Supreme Court order in Balraj Madhok's case for an examination of ballots cast in the 1971 elections, the midterm election can no longer be ruled out as a category of successful "coup" staged by Mrs. Gandhi. Many who would not have considered an election fraud of any proportion conceivable in India, or any respectable leadership capable of resorting to it, have had time to think again during the years that followed, when Mrs. Gandhi's uses of power did not allow ethical considerations to stand in her way. She showed herself unburdened by conscience, scruples, or soul-searching. Her profound belief in her own indispensability adds weight to the argument that she could not risk getting less than a two-thirds majority at the polls and solved this dilemma matter-of-factly and efficiently though artifice. In this way she also ensured a docile majority for any future plans. The Congress Party in Parliament that came into being with the midterm election accepted almost without demur the constitutional changes after the Emergency—Mrs. Gandhi having taken the precaution of jailing its dissident members beforehand—though the party outside Parliament did not uniformly accept them. The Opposition view—that fundamental constitutional changes could only be considered by a constituent assembly elected for the purpose and could not in any case be steered through a parliament that had outlived its five-year mandate—could be ignored altogether.

All of this, while it may be termed "politics" in a broad general sense, is far from accepted political behavior in a democratic framework and is wholly alien to established principles and practices in India. The Emergency climaxed her failure as a politician. Coming upon the decay of her personal and political image, her shock at the High Court judgement, and her party's series of defeats at the polls during 1974 and 1975, it rang down the curtain on the political process altogether, sweeping from sight the issues of corruption, political scandal, and economic mismanagement for which she and her party were being indicted.

There appears to be no logic in a situation where a party leader in a parliamentary system thrives regardless of opinion in the party, where she not only ignores party support but alienates it, ultimately imprisoning those who seek, through legitimate democratic channels, to elect another leader during the breathing space provided by the High Court for this purpose. Yet this form of illogic has been a consistent factor throughout Mrs. Gandhi's career. Her sources of power have resided outside party forums and, if we are to include the 1971 elections as selectively rigged, outside the electoral process. Her emphasis has been on control of the party machine and money and of men through it. Her expansion and use of intelligence and paramilitary forces has taken the place of ordinary administration. The art and tasks of real governing have diminished correspondingly as her individual power grew. The transition to dictatorship was not made overnight. It was the last step in a steady erosion of democratic procedures. The ground had been prepared—politically, administratively, openly and clandestinely—for the final tilt.

If Indian events provide no clue to Mrs. Gandhi's behavior, some logic must be sought outside these to explain both the manner and the success of her functioning. Since 1969 the Soviet Union had thrown its immense prestige and support behind the leadership of Mrs. Gandhi. Beginning with denunciations of "rightist reactionaries" in her party who were said to be blocking radical policies, a tide of forceful official Soviet comment had buttressed, exalted, and defended Mrs. Gandhi against Indian opposition to her, a vocal flourish surrounding the solid political-cultural-economic scaffolding erected by the Indo-Soviet Treaty of 1971. The Bihar Movement and Jayaprakash Narayan's leadership were savagely attacked by *Pravda*, while on July 21, 1975 *Pravda* lauded "India's new economic plans." Admiration for Mrs. Gandhi was pointedly expressed by Leonid Brezhnev at the 25th Congress of the Soviet Communist Party in Moscow in February 1976. Compliments traveled both ways with great regularity. On April 6, 1976 Bansi Lal, new defence minister, expressed "a sense of deep gratitude to the Soviet Union for appreciating our special problems and difficulties." Government denials in India's censored press were particularly significant as confirmation of events and policy. On July 24, 1975 K. R. Ganesh, Union minister for petroleum and chemicals, "denied here today the presence of any Soviet experts in Delhi to help the Union Government." Ganesh said "the Rightist parties had started a whispering campaign after the proclamation of emergency that 100 Soviet experts were working in Delhi and that the Soviet Union had assured the Government of all assistance." Thus the Soviet presence as an armored escort to Mrs. Gandhi's leadership may provide a logic to her otherwise puzzling and irrational behavior. This logic had a life of its own, unaffected by the CPI's ups and downs in prestige, power shares, and ideological thrust in its relationship with the Congress, with Mrs. Gandhi, and after the Emergency with Sanjay Gandhi. Though the CPI noticeably lost influence and became increasingly disillusioned with the ruling party, the Soviet ballast remained undisturbed.

Mrs. Gandhi's attempts to explain why she declared an emergency based on a charge of "conspiracy" to dislodge her and her government, unsupported by evidence or argument, transparently lacked truth and credibility, while they revealed her far from healthy or rational frame of mind. The alarm she raised over internal and external threats to the country, over the country's unity and its economic problems, had no basis in fact as a justification of emergency. No crisis but that of Mrs. Gandhi's own political survival necessitated the Emergency in 1975. That it was a coup for self-protection was borne out with omnibus amendments to the Constitution, giving legal definition and sanction to authoritarian power, and with the fevered campaign to promote a dynastic succession, leaving no shade or shred of democracy to impede Mrs. Gandhi's design.

In contrast, genuine crisis conditions have been met and resolved by Indian leadership in the past through genuine practical measures that took no toll of existing freedoms. Independence itself brought a formidable quota of crises: partition murders on a mass scale, whole transport systems paralyzed when essential supplies could not be moved, huge movements of population throwing the new nation's unity and stability into grave jeopardy, anxieties accompanying the integration of the princely states into the Union, the 1947 war in Kashmir, and the continuing pressure for solution in Kashmir. There followed periods of flood, famine, and crop failure, Communist insurrection in Telegana, Naga insurgency, the Chinese attack, fevers aroused by the linguistic states, problems of law and order. At no juncture had the leadership seized on any of these very real crises to shut off democratic processes and end freedom.

Nehru, who could with ease have become a dictator, utterly rejected the idea, believing that India's people, long exploited and deprived, needed growth and nurture in freedom and expression, that, while dictatorship and conformity might achieve the military grandeur and destructive potential necessary for great power status, they seldom achieve the basic requirements of life and dignity faster than a free society, and that freedom, far from being a luxury for the affluent, is a fundamental human aspiration, even more necessary to those who have little else and from whom much is required in courage and endeavor. Thus the Indian people were led between 1947 and 1966 within the framework of consent into a very different dimension of life and expectation. Nothing less than a revolution took place under Nehru, with defined programs and definite steps toward a socialist order. The base India stood on when Mrs. Gandhi came to power—whether in industry and agriculture, or the confidence created by free political institutions— was the result of the Nehru years. The problems India was then facing were those arising out of change. Mrs. Gandhi's style resulted not only in a very different political order, culminating in dictatorship, but in the destruction of a vital human process, without any assurance of compensating economic gain. Inheriting a flourishing enterprise, she halted it and reversed its direction.

The most unusual aspect of India's political system has been the nature and quality of its leadership, committed to serve and safeguard the liberties of a people not yet experienced enough in the exercise of freedom to defend free institutions for themselves. India's leadership before Mrs. Gandhi was among the world's most sensitive, civilized, and humane. Her two predecessors treated their task of guiding the millions of an underdeveloped nation as an adventure of faith and trust, in circumstances where dictatorship would have been the cruder and more facile choice. Mrs. Gandhi's recourse to dictatorial power was a reflection of her own temperament and not of any new need in the Indian situation. That she succeeded in establishing it is not surprising. The twentieth century in Europe provides ample example of nations with far better and older opportunities in education, economic development, and political experience who fell prey to totalitarianism. That Indians, who in 1947 had their first opportunity in centuries to live as free human beings, responsible for themselves, should have so succumbed is not strange. The tragedy of this situation was Mrs. Gandhi's betrayal of a trust.

The style that had crystallized in the Emergency remained basic to an understanding of the woman who would become prime minister again in 1980.

CHAPTER SIXTEEN

The Janata Government Assists Mrs. Gandhi's Return

The midterm election in January 1980 returned Indira Gandhi to power just two years and nine months after her decisive defeat. Her party, now known as the Congress-Indira, had come into being on January 2, 1978, with herself as its president, following serious disagreements within the Congress party about its future course of action. The controversy centered on Sanjay Gandhi, who had enjoyed unlimited power during the Emergency and had been ranked the country's most important leader after his mother. Congressmen who had impassively watched Mrs. Gandhi's autocratic progress woke suddenly to the prospect of a hereditary leadership. More immediately, since it was clear that Sanjay's unpopular acts, chiefly his campaign of compulsory sterilization during the Emergency, had been a major cause of the party's defeat in 1977, he would have to be cut to size if the electorate's confidence were to be regained.

Emotion and calculation met in Mrs. Gandhi's rejection of this counsel. The youth wing of the party had received her special blessing during the Emergency, specifically because it was Sanjay's developing power base. The beginning of a youth cult associated with him had been a means of legitimizing him as her heir. The original list of candidates for election to Parliament in 1977 had contained a majority of his nominees. Sanjay was the central consideration in her plans for her party and the country. He had advised her against holding an election, and the party's debacle had increased her reliance on his opinion. Her defeat had brought a decensored critical press to life and a surfeit of hostile books, some by her former admirers. The opinion that travels with the tide had settled around the new government. Stunned by her defeat and convinced her career lay in ruins, she expected succour and support from her own party. The dissenters in it, who had been silent through the Emergency, looked like deserters.

Mrs. Gandhi's aunt, Vijaya Lakshmi Pandit, had been as shocked as her niece by the humiliating verdict in Rae Bareli and had broken down and wept when she received the news. Though she had come out openly against the Emergency and had campaigned against the Congress during the 1977 election, the issues she had fought for had been, for her, strictly political and not to be confused with her abiding devotion to her family. It was inconceivable to her pride that the electorate should have returned such a verdict against her brother's daughter, even though she believed it had rightly defeated her party. Uncertain of her welcome, she called on her niece in July 1977, four months after her defeat, accompanied by her daughter, Mrs. Rita Dar.

> Indu broke away from the circle [around her] and came toward me. I put both my arms around her and kissed her. She also kissed me and then Rita. She looks terribly worn out and ill and was trembling when I embraced her. We went in and sat on a sofa and I put my hand over hers which was really shaking. She was obviously trying not to cry. I began by saying that she should understand that I had been compelled to work against Congress in the election because the events of the last few years leading up to the Emergency, and then the Emergency itself, were a negation of all the values which both she and I had been taught to live by. Throughout the Emergency I had some contact with the underground and knew something of the horrors that were being perpetrated on those whose fault was that in some way they had opposed the government. But even this did not upset me so much as the dreadful manner in which men and women submitted and denigrated themselves for fear of jail or of losing their jobs. This was unforgivable and my own self-respect demanded that I should protest. The moment the opportunity came I did so. I worked with conviction for the restoration of civil liberties and human rights, and when these were vindicated, and the "haramis"* who had misguided her had been beaten, my conscience was at ease. . . . For you, I said, there is great sorrow in my heart and though the law must take its course I am with you to help you in any way I can. She was crying and said, "What can I say?" "Don't say anything." I replied, "Let us talk about the family." Then the children came in and Maneka and Rita carried the conversation most of the time. Rajiv was on flight and

* A rascal, Literally, one who betrays his salt.

Sonia had a sick headache. Sanjay was in the garden and he didn't come in.[1]

If Mrs. Gandhi had second thoughts about the Emergency, her public utterances gave no indication of it, and there was no visible crack in her public poise and composure. She defended Sanjay's role. If there had been errors and enormities, they were the fault of overzealous officials. This posture should have come as no surprise to her party. As prime minister she had held the reins of power close to her, afraid that vigorous regional and local leadership would weaken her own authority, until finally the Emergency had confined effective decision-making to a small, unofficial retinue, referred to by the press as her "caucus," that took its orders directly from her household. She had turned instinctively to her own Kashmiri community in her selection of key advisers. Fame, admiration, and elected majorities had done nothing to relax her dependence on the talisman of birth and family. She had seen no impropriety in promoting her son's business ventures through the prime minister's secretariat and relevant ministries. An entrepreneurship that Sanjay had neither the qualifications nor experience to pursue had proceeded automatically on the assumption of special privilege amounting to royal prerogative. His failure to produce the car he had been licensed by the government to manufacture, or to honor the terms of his license, had elicited no comment from her.

Sanjay took charge of the active core of the newly formed Congress-I party. It was understood that Indira Gandhi was its leader until Sanjay could take her place. Those who objected to this scenario remained in the existing Congress. If the Congress-I itself had members who did not subscribe to the "family" mantra (a chant prescribed and repeated in the course of worship), they must have realized that the logic of a Congress named Indira must result in the special claim of her decendents to lead it. The party would remain a family preserve so long as it did not raise the standard of revolt, and this was not a thing a party so recently restored to power on the strength of Indira's name alone would do. Mrs. Gandhi had correctly assessed the feudal factor as the lowest common denominator in the social fabric, and the only way to install family power in a democracy.

In a curious reversal of roles, Sanjay Gandhi now became his mother's mentor. It was Sanjay who launched a militant confrontation directed against the commissions of inquiry appointed by the Janata government to investigate illegal and suspected criminal conduct during the Emergency and against the courts trying cases against him. In cooperation with a section of the Janata leadership, he brought about the government's collapse in July 1979. The election that followed gave the Congress-I 351 Lok Sabha seats out of 525 for which polling was held, and 42.5 percent of the total vote cast, with 55 percent of the electorate voting. Sanjay was elected from Amethi, where he had lost in 1977. Mrs. Gandhi contested two Parliamentary seats (the Indian Constitution allows a candidate to stand for election from more than one constituency, though he can represent only one constituency in Parliament, or in a State Legislative Assembly.)—Rae Bareli in the north and Medak in the south—and won both by big majorities. She resigned the Rae Bareli seat and, drawing on close personal support, chose a young relative rather than a candidate from her party, to stand for by-election to the constituency. Arun Nehru was elected from Rae Bareli. After Sanjay's death he became secretary of the Sanjay Memorial Trust, and though he was not the party's official treasurer, its funds were channelled through him.

Several factors contributed to this remarkable turn of the tide in Mrs. Gandhi's favor, none more than the Janata government's failure to fulfil its pledge to bring to justice those responsible for Emergency excesses. The Janata government, India's first national alternative to the Congress, consisted of a merger of five parties. It took office on March 24, 1977, buoyed by the high hopes of a euphoric electorate, jubilant in its release from the fear and repression of the previous twenty-one months. The new government's priorities were broadly defined as the restoration of civil liberties, with changes in the Constitution to undo the damage of the 42nd Amendment; the punishment of those guilty of crimes during the Emergency, "from the highest political authority to the lowest functionary of the government"[2]; and the charting of a new economic direction favoring the rural sector and decentralisation as a means of bringing economic opportunity, the fruits of development, and the governing process nearer to the people. Civil liberties were immediately restored, the process of amending the Constitution*

---

* On May 9, 1980 the Supreme Court struck down Section 55 of the Constitution (42nd) Amendment Act 1976, which gave unlimited powers to Parliament to amend the Constitution. The Supreme Court decision meant that the Constitution could not be amended in such a manner as to destroy its basic or essential features or its basic structure. It also reasserted the primacy of fundamental rights over directive principles of state policy. Mrs. Gandhi's government is considering whether it will appeal this decision before a larger bench of the Supreme Court.

begun, and economic priorities mapped out†, but the mechanics of bringing the accused to justice revealed the fatal flaws and weaknesses of a system whose essential scaffolding had been shaken by neglect and abuse. Mrs. Gandhi, the architect of the Emergency—itself a violation of constitutional and cabinet authority, in the manner and for the reason it was proclaimed—remained the Janata government's main dilemma. The question of how to even begin dealing with her misuse of power came no nearer solution in a situation where the government's five constituents were locked in a struggle for control of their party. This was further complicated by intense personal rivalries among its three senior leaders, two of whom—Charan Singh and Jagjivan Ram—had been bitterly disappointed when Morarji Desai was chosen prime minister by consensus. Divisions in the party began to appear as the election victory faded, but Charan Singh virtually wielded the scissors that took the government apart.

Dissatsified with the Home portfolio, he carried out the precipitate arrest of Mrs. Gandhi on October 3, 1977, without sufficient evidence to convict her. Her immediate and unconditional release by a magistrate was the first step toward her political rehabilitation, while the government was condemned for its ill-prepared move. On April 9, 1978, Charan Singh resigned from the Janata Party's national executive and parliamentary board. His open attacks on the government led the prime minister to ask for his resignation from the cabinet on June 30. On July 12 he withdrew his earlier resignation from party posts as a gesture of conciliation, yet on December 23 he celebrated the defiant strength of his independent political base—the middle caste peasantry of north India—by holding an impressive rally in New Delhi. On January 24, 1979, he rejoined the cabinet as finance minister. Six months later he crossed the floor of Parliament to join an advance contingent of thirteen

† The draft of the Sixth Five-Year Plan, prepared during the Janata regime, noted that, with 40 to 60 percent of India's people still living "below the minimum acceptable level of living," "the most important objectives of planning have not been achieved, the most cherished goals seem to be almost as distant today as when we set out on the road to planned development." It held past planning responsible, which had devoted "an unduly large share of resources" to "production which related directly or indirectly to maintaining or improving the living standards of the higher income groups." The benefits of even government investment in the infrastructure "have accrued largely to the relatively affluent . . . the concentration of economic power has increased. . . . Within the Corporate sector the assets of the bigger corporations have increased more rapidly," while in the rural areas "the land reform measures had no visible impact on the distribution of rural poverty."

supporters who then achieved sixty-two more defections and formed a party known as the Lok Dal. The exercise showed how ephemeral Janata unity had been. It also demonstrated the fragility of a parliamentary system the conventions of which had been ignored or debased during the past decade. The manner of the Janata government's fall showed that the Union Parliament now reflected the same stratagems for upsetting or augmenting numerical strength as state legislatures had long done. The price of defections had increased, but the practice itself had lost its shocking edge and was settled deep and pervasive as the Indian dust into the fabric of elected assemblies.

On July 26, 1979, Charan Singh became prime minister as head of a coalition government, consisting of the Lok Dal and the Congress, whose continuance depended on the crucial support it had from the Congress-I. No sooner had he been installed than Mrs. Gandhi's party withdrew its support in a calculated move to escalate a constitutional crisis that had begun with the Janata government's resignation. The Congress-I emerged the chief beneficiary when President Sanjiva Reddy announced a midterm election. In his pursuit of prime ministership, Charan Singh became the pawn of a shrewder tactician, Sanjay Gandhi.

The question of how to deal with Mrs. Gandhi might have been resolved in one of two ways. As an ex-prime minister, she could have been pardoned and the law allowed to take its course with those of her aides who were found culpable. This would have had the advantage of bringing the curtain down with dignity over a traumatic period of history. The second alternative was to put her on trial before a specially constituted tribunal for the unjustifiable declaration of Emergency and the subsequent drastic amendment to the Constitution by a Parliament whose validity had expired. Either course would have had the overwhelming mandate of the election result. Intimidation, imprisonment, police savagery, and the lawless acts of her son and her aides were fresh in public memory. Mrs. Gandhi herself seemed to expect summary punishment at the hands of the men she had imprisoned without trial—a measure of her own failure to recognize the return of normal conditions and democratic functioning. The new prime minister, Morarji Desai, paid a courtesy call on her, and his government, which was committed to restore the rule of law, was particular to refrain from any act or suggestion of vendetta.

The Union government appointed several commissions of inquiry to investigate Emergency excesses. The chief of these was the commission appointed on May 28, 1977, under a retired chief justice of the Supreme Court, J. C. Shah, with extensive terms of reference:

   (i)   Subversion of lawful processes and well-established conventions, administrative procedures and practices, abuse of authority, misuse of power, excesses and/or malpractices committed . . .

  (ii)   Misuse of powers of arrest or issue of detention orders . . .

 (iii)   Specific instances of maltreatment and/or atrocities on persons arrested . . .

 (iv)   Specific instances of compulsion and use of force in the implementation of the family planning programme . . .

  (v)   Indiscriminate, high-handed or unauthorised demolition of houses, huts, shops, buildings . . .[3]

It was also asked to "recommend measures which may be adopted for preventing the recurrence of such abuse of authority, misuse of power, excesses and malpractices."

Under Indian law a commission of inquiry may be appointed to look into matters of public importance. It is a fact-finding body, with no judicial powers of punishment. Its findings determine whether cases can be framed and the judicial process begun. The Shah Commission's first interim report was delivered to the government on March 3, 1978, the second on April 7, and both were presented to Parliament on May 16. The third and final report was delivered on August 6. Their most important finding was that Mrs. Gandhi had imposed an internal emergency "in a desperate endeavour to save herself from the legitimate compulsions of a judicial verdict against her."[4]

> . . . There is no evidence of any breakdown of law and order in any part of the country—nor of any apprehension in that behalf; the economic condition was well under control and had in no way deteriorated. There is not even a report of any apprehension of any serious breakdown of the law and order situation or deterioration of the economic condition from any public functionary. The public records of the times, Secret, Confidential or Public, and publications in newspapers, speak with unanimity that there was no unusual event or even a tendency in that direction to justify the imposition of emergency. There was no threat to the nation from sources internal or external. The conclusion appears, in the absence of any evidence given by Smt.

[Mrs.] Indira Gandhi or anyone else, that the one and only motivating force for tendering the extraordinary advice to the President to declare an "internal emergency" was the intense political activity generated in the ruling party and the opposition, by the decision of the Allahabad High Court declaring the election of the Prime Minister of the day invalid on the ground of corrupt election practices. There is no reason to think that if the democratic conventions were followed, the whole political upsurge would in the normal course not have subsided. But Smt. [Mrs.] Gandhi in her anxiety to continue in power, brought about instead a situation which directly contributed to her continuance in power and also generated forces which sacrificed the interests of many to serve the ambitions of a few. Thousands were detained and a series of totally unwarranted actions followed involving untold human misery and suffering . . .

The nation owes it to the present and succeeding generations to ensure that the administrative set-up is not subverted in future in the manner it was done, to serve the personal ends of any one individual or a group of individuals in or near the Government."[5]

Mrs. Gandhi reacted spiritedly to what she called the persecution launched against her and her family. In a nationwide campaign, carried to London in November 1978, she expressed fears of being jailed and, after the hanging of Zulfiquar Ali Bhutto in Pakistan, that this might be her fate. She was in fact sentenced to a brief token imprisonment. On November 21, 1978, the Privileges Committee of the Lok Sabha held her guilty of breach of privilege and contempt of the Lok Sabha, for obstructing four government officials from collecting information for a question on Maruti (her son's car project) in 1975 and for instituting false cases against them. On December 19, 1978, the Lok Sabha expelled her and sentenced her to imprisonment until its prorogation a week later, on December 26.

The government's leisurely handling of the Shah Commission's report did not bear out Mrs. Gandhi's acute anxieties. The Committee of Secretaries,* where it was referred for processing and recommendations, gave as its opinion that no penal action was possible against Mrs. Gandhi, but that she could be disenfranchised. This left the government in a quandary about a course of action against her, though it began to deal variously and ponderously with the other cases arising out of the report, instituting "prosecutions",

* A Secretary is a senior civil service adviser to the government.

"departmental proceedings" and "remedial actions," "all in accordance with law and after careful examination of each case."

In May 1978 a prominent Janata member of Parliament, Ram Jethmalani, urged the creation of a special court to try Mrs. Gandhi. The prime minister reluctantly agreed under mounting pressure from the party, but said he would seek the Supreme Court's advice first. However, a private bill to set up a special court was introduced in Parliament on August 4, 1978. On December 1, the Supreme Court approved its provisions, with two modifications: (1) the bill should not be restricted to misdemeanors from an arbitrary cut-off date (February 27, 1975 as proposed), and (2) the government should not appoint the special court judges, who should be appointed by the chief justice of India and the chief Justice of the High Court, from among present High Court judges. Not until January 9, 1979, did the government introduce its own bill in Parliament, incorporating the Supreme Court's modifications. It was passed by the Lok Sabha on March 9, 1979, and by the Rajya Sabha, with two changes on March 21. The Lok Sabha reconsidered and passed it on May 6, 1979.

Two special courts were set up and hearings began on June 14, 1979. The misdeeds of the Emergency had now been reduced to twenty-one first information reports* resulting in four cases, two before each court. Rapid disposal of even these seemed unlikely as the Janata government's disagreements became more public and its future uncertain. A decade of political encroachment on the judicial system had severely affected the detachment and integrity of judges. Quick to respond to Mrs. Gandhi's election victory in January 1980, the special courts declared themselves illegal soon afterward. Justice Jain of Special Court Two announced on January 15, 1980, that "the creation and establishment of this court and the declarations and designations to try the said cases were not made in accordance with the provisions of the Constitution and are therefore of no effect and confer no jurisdiction on this court." A month later Justice Joshi claimed similar grounds for winding up Special Court One. The *Indian Express* commented editorially on this phenomenon on February 20, 1980:

> The circumstances attending the demise of the Special Courts must strike public opinion as rather odd. It took Justice Jain six months and

---

* The F.I.R. under Indian Penal law is the original complaint made by an aggrieved person or institution in regard to an alleged offence.

Justice Joshi a month longer to come to the realization of their lack of jurisdiction on an obscure technicality. It is not the Act creating the Special Courts that the two judges have found ultra vires. What invalidates the Special Courts, in their opinion, is that the Ministries of Home and Law which purported to exercise the powers under the Special Courts Act were not specifically allocated these functions under the rules of business.

In March 1980 Mrs. Gandhi's government appointed a panel headed by S. M. H. Burney to decide which, if any, cases launched by the Janata government following the Shah Commission's findings should proceed. Burney, who had been secretary to the ministry of information and broadcasting during the Emergency, was not expected to be neutral in his assessment of the cases before his panel. Cases against Mrs. Gandhi, Sanjay Gandhi, and V. C. Shukla, minister for information and broadcasting during the Emergency, were excluded from the panel's review. But, with important personnel changes in the investigating agencies and the appointment of a new public prosecutor, these were dropped by the courts on grounds of insufficient evidence. An example was the *Kissa Kursi Ka** case.

Kissa Kursi Ka was the title of a film held up for release in 1975 because its main protagonist, a politician whose party symbol was a "people's" car, had a likeness too close to Sanjay Gandhi for official approval. The film's producer filed a writ petition in the Supreme Court on June 11, 1975, and on July 18 was directed to surrender its prints and negatives to the government on the understanding that they would be kept safe. The prosecution case held that Shukla, appointed minister on June 28, 1975, banned the film and, in a raid on the film laboratory in Bombay on August 7, seized all material connected with it. This was brought by train from Bombay to the prime minister's house in New Delhi in thirteen trunks on November 10 and taken from there to Sanjay Gandhi's factory in Gurgaon near New Delhi, where it was destroyed between November 10 and 24. The Supreme Court ordered the government to screen the film before it on November 17. The screening never took place.

On February 27, 1979, after an eleven-month trial, the district and sessions judge in Delhi convicted Sanjay Gandhi and V. C.

* *Kissa Kursi Ka* means "the Story of the Chair, the "chair" representing office and status.

Shukla of entering into a conspiracy to destroy the film under cover of the Emergency. Each was sentenced to two years' rigorous imprisonment and fines of Rs. 10,000 and Rs. 25,000 respectively. In the course of the trial Sanjay had been found guilty of tampering with evidence and attempting to suborn the prosecution's witnesses. A three-man bench of the Supreme Court had cancelled his bail and sentenced him, on May 5, 1978, to one month in custody.

Sanjay appealed against his conviction, and the Supreme Court commenced hearing the appeal on November 26, 1979. It had been heard only in part when the court recessed for Christmas. When hearings were resumed, Indira Gandhi was in power. A. G. Noorani writes:

> It was a piquant situation. The government prosecuting Sanjay Gandhi was headed by his mother. A conviction would have disqualified him from membership of Parliament and sent him to prison. Co-accused Shukla would have suffered equally. In India the Government controls the prosecution agency to a remarkable degree. But the matter was now at the appellate stage before the highest court in India."[6]

Yet Noorani points out, the highest court in India did not see fit to take notice of the new public prosecutor's handling of the case, when he disposed of a record that ran into 6,500 pages, filling 20 volumes, and a 300-page judgement, in fifteen minutes. On April 11, 1980, the Supreme Court allowed the appeal and quashed the convictions of Sanjay Gandhi and V. C. Shukla.

The Shah Commission report had been printed in eleven regional languages. Mrs. Gandhi's government stopped its distribution and sale, endeavoring to insure that a public record of the Emergency would be obliterated and the consequences of suspected criminality buried. Three hundred tapes of the commission's hearings lodged with the home ministry have apparently vanished without a trace.

The "commitment" demanded of it by Mrs. Gandhi after 1969 had made deep inroads into the tradition of an independent civil service, and the Emergency had dealt ruthlessly with those who questioned arbitrary orders. The Janata government inherited a deeply demoralized bureaucracy. In circumstances where Mrs. Gandhi, as the months passed, appeared to be making a comeback, the bureaucracy, acutely sensitive to political pressures, showed little inclination to act even on vital information it received, as the following curious account[7] discloses.

Soon after the 1977 election, a van left Mrs. Gandhi's residence for her farm near Mehrauli, on the outskirts of New Delhi. A woman laborer employed for construction work on the farmhouse later told her village pradhan (headman) of valuables buried with the help of laborers at six places on the premises and a steel cabinet buried in the farmhouse itself in a room where the flooring was not yet complete. The pradhan, who had supported the Janata party during the election, took the story to C. V. Narasimhan, director of the Central Bureau of Investigation (CBI) in the last week of May 1977. No action was taken, but the pradhan persisted in his efforts to interest someone in authority. On receiving the information in June 1978, Prime Minister Morarji Desai asked the Intelligence Bureau (IB) to corroborate the story. The IB, no longer able to locate either the laborers or the contractor who had hired them—inquiry revealed that several of the laborers were reported to have died—decided to verify the story with the use of a metal detection device. The son of a head constable in the bureau was sent to the National Geophysical Laboratory in Hyderabad for training in metal detection. On August 31, 1978 he was smuggled into the farmhouse for two hours. Readings were positive and were conveyed next day to a meeting attended by a galaxy of the administration's most important officials: the cabinet secretary, the home secretary, the chairman of the central board of direct taxes, the director of the CBI, the special director of the CBI, the director of the IB, and the joint director of the IB. The Intelligence Bureau officers urged an immediate raid on the farm. The others were reluctant to take action. The finance minister decided to postpone the raid until November 6, 1978, the day after the Chikmagalur by-election to Parliament, which Mrs. Gandhi was to contest. On November 5 it was further postponed without explanation until December 29. In mid-November the Intelligence Bureau sent a memorandum to the cabinet secretary and the home secretary, listing information they had obtained about the Gandhi family's secret accounts, but the bureau was told the raid would remain scheduled for December 29. The IB placed the farm under surveillance but was ordered to withdraw this after two weeks, as it might bring the government unwelcome publicity. On December 28, the raid was postponed to January 5. On January 4 it was indefinitely postponed.

On January 8, 1979, the IB posted surveillance at the farm again and urged the home secretary to order the raid immediately, since the matter had now reached the newspapers. At 8:00 A.M. on January

19, an informant on the farm telephoned the IB to say that two young men, who had arrived by car (licence number DLY-1) half an hour earlier, were digging in the grounds. The information was conveyed to the home secretary, who, in no hurry, called a meeting in his office for 11:00 A.M. to discuss the advisability of a raid. While the meeting was in progress, another message from the farm said the diggers had loaded a large steel cabinet into their car and left. The informants followed the car but did not search it, though they were empowered under the Income Tax Act to do so. They watched it enter 12 Willingdon Crescent, Mrs. Gandhi's residence.

The home secretary's meeting ended at 1:30 P.M., having decided to raid the farm. The raid commenced at 4:00 P.M. and discovered nothing. Later enquiries revealed that only the last remaining items had been dug up on January 19. Most items had been removed immediately after the IB's surveillance was lifted on December 23. The newspapers carried pictures of the infructuous raid.

A bureaucracy, unwilling or mysteriously unable to deliver results, with even the intelligence agencies at cross purposes with each other, was partly the reflection of a disunited government. but the delays and ineptitude in carrying out the government's policy of rectifying the wrongs of the Emergency were symptoms of a more serious malaise affecting the very guts of a civil service in a democratic society. The fate of the process was finally sealed by the two special court judges, followed in rapid succession by other judges who uniformly dismissed the cases before them soon after Mrs. Gandhi's election victory—acts which may have lasting implications for the future of democracy in India.

There is another aspect to the slow progress of prosecution. Prime Minister Desai was committed to the meticulous application of legal procedures with all their latitudes and insisted these be followed, no matter what the political cost to his government. This view, fundamental to his own approach, also represented the swing of the pendulum away from the arbitrary powers and shortcuts of the Emergency to democratic procedures and the rule of law. A united government, determined to see these through, would have emerged stronger in public estimation as a result. Its vacillation branded it weak and incompetent. Its collapse erased the legal processes it had begun.

Mrs. Gandhi's by-election victory in Chikmagalur, on November 8, 1978, made it clear she was once again a factor to reckon with in Indian politics. Her public relations were assiduous and fault-less. From jail she sent a bouquet of flowers to Charan Singh for his birthday, presented to him on the dais before he addressed his spectacular peasants' rally on December 23, 1978. She took an el-ephant ride to Belchi in Bihar to establish her presence where violence against Harijans had taken place. She attended diplomatic receptions in New Delhi, and newspapers noted that she prayed at shrines in different parts of the country. She lost no opportunity to hold the Janata government responsible for the caste and com-munal incidents and the police violence she claimed were on the increase. Writing in the *Economic Times* on September 20, 1979, Prem Shankar Jha cited home ministry figures and police records of the past decade to refute her charges, saying that "the truth was considerably at variance with Mrs. Gandhi's version of it."

> In her speech Mrs. Gandhi expressly used three unimpeachable in-dicators of social tension and the degree of violence used to repress it. These were the number of police firings and casualties resulting from them, the number of communal incidents; and the extent of vio-lence against the Harijans. A fourth indicator, the extent of labour un-rest, was implicit in her repeated accusations that the Janata was ru-ining the economy. Unfortunately for her not one of these indicators supports her contention that the tensions are rising and that the nation faces a crisis.

Her campaign to rehabilitate herself was assisted by ample funds and support. Leading business houses had maintained their links with her, and these were strengthened as the Janata govern-ment's future became doubtful. Just before the 1980 election the capital witnessed an unusual stir of diplomatic activity in her favor.

On October 9, 1979, Mrs. Gandhi and Samjay joined the mourn-ing multitude at Jayaprakash Narayan's funeral in Patna, and laid a wreath on his bier. For thousands of youthful followers of the Bihar Movement this was the final irony. Yet the public at large found it no more ironic than the presence at the funeral of former ministers of the Janata government who now sat in the Opposition, in betrayal of the pledge they had taken to remain united to prevent the return of authoritarian rule.

The death of Jayaprakash Narayan, whose call for "bread with freedom" had brought five opposition parties together in 1977 and led them to victory, removed the last great figure of the liberation struggle from the national scene. Had the Janata party broken on ideological grounds, a realignment of political forces might have forged a strong Opposition. Its chaotic and unprincipled demise left political disarray within a system whose soundness even the elite—its main beneficiaries—were beginning to question. The political adventurer found little to obstruct him, and an impatience with law, convention, and procedure marked the style of the new breed the January 1980 election brought into politics. Members of the Congress-I, elected to the Uttar Pradesh legislature in the state's election in May 1980, did not wait for the formal allotment of their accommodation, but stormed into the legislators' hostel after breaking open the locks with their revolvers.

CHAPTER SEVENTEEN

The President Confers a Bonus

Addressing a public meeting at Shivaji Park in Bombay on September 10, 1979, Mrs. Gandhi said the Janata party had led the country to "utter ruination" and that the economy had degenerated. Two months earlier, on July 12, 1979, George Fernandes, minister for industry, had defended the government during a no-confidence motion in Parliament:

> We have been in power for only two years and three months so far and we could not have shaken the Himalayas ... (but) I want Honourable Members to realize that so far as the economy is concerned, all their arguments are hollow. In terms of output, in terms of production, in terms of growth, the Janata government's performance is an excellent performance. We are proud of that performance.

The conflicting statements of Indira Gandhi and George Fernandes are better understood against the effects of the budget presented by Charan Singh in February 1979, after his reentry into the cabinet as finance minister.

Figures reveal a well-cushioned economy during 1977–79 under a finance minister, H. M. Patel, who administered his portfolio with moderation and competence. The year 1977–78 had been a peak season for grain production with a record output of 125.6 million tonnes (13 percent above previous performance). In June 1979 the buffer stock of food grains stood at 21.4 million tonnes, 50 percent higher than at any time before. An additional 12.5 million hectares were brought under irrigation, and there were substantial increases in the use of fertilizer and the production of commercial crops. Consumer industries, many with a base in rural areas, showed significant growth. After the spiraling inflation of 1973–74

(20.2 percent) and 1974–75 (25.2 percent—the highest up to the time of writing), prices were comparatively stable. Foreign exchange reserves had doubled, rising to Rs 530 million by early 1979, as against Rs 286.3 million, the highest figure during Mrs. Gandhi's prime ministership. Exports totaled Rs 1,109.5 million and imports Rs 1,280 million, in each case Rs 200 million more than during the two years of the Emergency, which Mrs. Gandhi had used as an argument for economic gains.

Professor Raj Krishna of the Planning Commission, assessing the economic situation in a three-part article, "Performance of the Economy" in January 1979, wryly concludes:

> The recent positive performance of the Indian economy, without authoritarianism, and in spite of floods and labour unrest, is in sharp contrast with the performance of the Indian polity, particularly in respect of the maintenance of unity at the top, and the physical protection of the weak at the bottom of the polity. Most national leaders do not even seem to know many facts about the performance of the economy, for all their songs are burdened with 'non-performance'. Since considerable performance has materialized without the leaders even knowing about it, they can obviously claim no credit for it, and they could not have contributed to it. . . . History would perhaps offer few similar examples of the leadership of a great and vast nation so busy with petty personal quarrels that they are utterly innocent of the very encouraging economic events occurring around them.[1]

The unity move intended to strengthen the Janata Party and government that brought Charan Singh back to the cabinet on January 24, 1979, proved abortive. Politically it failed when Charan Singh broke with the party in July, and economically its consequences were far-reaching. The budget became Charan Singh's opportunity to unfurl his own flag of leadership and reach out in preference to his own particular constituency—the "large farmers" who had profited most by the new techniques, some requiring costly inputs, in agriculture. They now formed a powerful political lobby and dominated the northern countryside, sometimes in confrontation with lower castes, the Harijans and the landless. The budget, which was technically the Janata government's, actually represented Charan Singh's sectional interest—at the cost, as it turned out, of the rural poor and the urban working class, as well as the middle class.

On March 1, 1979, under the heading "A Political Budget" the

Indian Express editorial noted:

> The savage tax imposts proposed, which are estimated to net a record of Rs. 665 crores of additional revenue . . . are so constructed that they are likely to have an opposite impact. . . . The stark fact is that the proposals are highly discriminatory in their nature and incidence, the main target being the urban middle class. . . . [Mr. Charan Singh] has sacrificed revenue of the order of nearly Rs. 125 crores by excise reductions on certain inputs of interest to large farmers. . . . An extremely facile reason presented in justification of additional excises on a large number of consumption items is that this will price the products of big industry out and allow small industry to enter the market. . . . The danger of the economy getting stuck in the mire of stagnation, instead of advancing on the path of development, would appear to have become very real.

The four months from August 1979 to January 1980 registered the highest prices since independence. An erratic monsoon stopped suddenly in mid-August. The century's worst drought brought brutal suffering to human beings and livestock. The severity of the economic crisis overshadowed election issues. A determined government could have taken remedial measures when the monsoon failed, but the Lok Dal-Congress coalition, hurridly fashioned out of opportunism and now embroiled in election preparations, could provide neither relief nor sense of purpose. It was inevitable that the mass of the electorate were unable to distinguish between the caretaker coalition and the previous (Janata) regime. No mysterious change in mass psychology accounted for the reversal of the mandate at the polls. The Congress party had had thirty years of uninterrupted rule when Indians had had no alternative in a national election. The 1980 election, like that of 1977, gave them a choice. On each occasion they rejected those immediately responsible for their troubles.

Disenchantment with the Janata and its successor government strengthened Mrs. Gandhi's position in a campaign that took her to 384 of the Lok Sabha's 525 constituencies, projecting her as the only clear answer in a muddle. She promised stability, curbs on prices, and "a government that works." Her natural energy was fueled and fired by the obsession that failure this time would bring not only political oblivion, but possible legal action against her and her son, as the cases against them approached conclusion. The campaign became as profoundly personal a mission as it was political.

Deteriorating economic conditions were preceded by a prolonged constitutional crisis. The steps President Sanjiva Reddy took to resolve it made his announcement of a midterm election both controversial and suspect. On July 10, 1979, Y. B. Chavan, leader of the Congress, the main Opposition party in Parliament, introduced a no-confidence motion against the Janata government. Normally a routine affair, routinely defeated when a government enjoys a substantial majority, this one had unexpected results. Morarji Desai was compelled to resign as defections led by Charan Singh's followers began. The initiative passed to the president, who, in accord with convention, asked the leader of the Opposition to form a government. The invitation was a formality. Chavan, with only 75 M.P.'s, was unable to do so. The president next asked both Morarji Desai (with 203 M.P.'s) and Charan Singh (now with 76) to submit lists of their strength in the House within forty-eight hours. Only Mrs. Gandhi's assurance that her party would back Charan Singh can have persuaded the president to include him in this exercise—though it is not clear why he cut short the extension he had given Desai to prepare his list and, in a surprise move, called on Charan Singh to form a government, directing him to seek a vote of confidence in Parliament within three weeks. A positive vote for the Lok Dal-Congress coalition government led by Charan Singh needed and relied on Mrs. Gandhi's continued support. The Congress-I now withdrew this, leaving Charan Singh without the crucial count he needed. Isolated and anxious to keep out his rivals in the Janata party, he drove to Rashtrapati Bhavan (the official residence of the president of India) on August 20, 1979, without facing a vote of confidence, and advised the president to announce a midterm poll. The president complied. The communique he issued on August 26 was silent on two points. It did not explain why he had not invited Jagjivan Ram, who had replaced Morarji Desai as the Janata party's leader, to form a government. With Y. B. Chavan in Charan Singh's coalition government, Jagjivan Ram was now the leader of the Opposition and merited the invitation in that capacity. Nor did the communique explain why the president had accepted Charan Singh's advice to dissolve the Lok Sabha and call an election. Constitutional experts he had consulted had informed him he was not obliged to accept the advice of a prime minister whose strength in Parliament had not been tested. Moreover, Jagjivan Ram enjoyed an established reputation for constructive compromise, which Morarji Desai had, during this crisis, forfeited. The conclusion was inescapable that Jagjivan Ram had been ignored precisely because, with 203 M.P.'s behind him, he would have had no difficulty in getting the additional support he needed to form a government. The midterm poll desired by Mrs. Gandhi, who saw it as her opportunity to return to power before legal processes against her and her son matured, would then not have been held at all. On Sept. 2, 1979, the president declared he always took decisions according to his conscience and in the name of Lord Venkateswara, deity of the Tirupati temple.

The *Indian Express* quoted N. A. Palkhivala, authority on constitutional law, whose advice the president had sought, on August 23, 1979:

> The President's decision to dissolve the Lok Sabha is, to use the language of studied moderation, unjustified to the point of constitutional impropriety. The dissolution of the House, when it had finished only half its term, should have been the option of the last resort and constitutional propriety dictated that the President should have acceded to the request of Shri [Mr.] Jagjivan Ram, leader of the Opposition, and of the single largest party in Parliament, that he be given an opportunity to form a government.

The *Times of India* commented on September 5, 1979:

> President Sanjiva Reddy has been quoted as having said that he was not "under pressure from anybody" and that whatever he has done is "based on the dictates of his conscience". The reference is clearly to his recent decision to deny Shri Jagjivan Ram an opportunity to form a government, to dissolve the Lok Sabha and to ask the Charan Singh Cabinet to stay on in office till the poll next December. It is possible that the ugly rumour of the President having allowed himself to be blackmailed has reached him and that he has thought it necessary to repudiate it. But whatever the provocation, Shri Reddy has enunciated a doctrine which is highly dangerous. . . . He has to be guided by the Constitution, and not by his conscience.

In these circumstances the opinion gained widespread currency that the president's action was the result of inducement to use his "conscience." The suspicion was so strong and pervasive that the Janata party for a time considered impeaching the president if it was returned to power.

A pall of degeneracy and decay enveloped New Delhi, with even the president's image under a cloud. The Janata party had badly tarnished its own with its disintegration. More damage followed when Morarji Desai, on resigning the prime ministership, did not simultaneously relinquish his leadership of his party in Parliament as convention required, thus creating a tense and unpredictable situation within the party and complicating the constitutional crisis. The public mood was cynical—and, as election turnouts revealed, apathetic—as the lines were drawn for electoral battle.

The arrival of the vice president of the Supreme Soviet in India on August 10, 1979, on an eleven-day goodwill visit, should have interested political observers in an age when the big powers critically influence the affairs of nations in manifold ways. His presence, to observe the eighth anniversary of the Indo-Soviet Treaty of 1971, was not remarkable, but a visit of this duration by a figure so high in the Soviet hierarchy at the height of a political crisis, when there was in effect no government in New Delhi, was not normal. The presidential announcement dissolving the Lok Sabha and calling for a midterm election was made on August 22. The Soviet visit at this time also, is of special note in terms of the developing situation on the subcontinent, which culminated just before the Indian election in the Soviet Union's military entry into Afghanistan, and in the support it needed and received from the new Indian government after the election.

After a curious initial aloofness immediately after independence, the Soviet Union established cordial relations with India, including cooperation in the development of vital areas of the Indian economy. The Indian navy has been built largely with Soviet aid, and Soviet ships enjoy facilities at several Indian ports. Under the Indo-Soviet Treaty of 1971, the two countries share security concerns, though the treaty covers a wider area. Mrs. Gandhi has a friendly personal relationship with Soviet leaders and has established an identity of interests with the Soviet Union in matters relating to the subcontinent that reached its zenith with the birth of Bangladesh in December 1971. The relationship has traveled far since Sir Girja Shankar Bajpai, secretary general, ministry of external affairs, wrote on February 6, 1948, to Vijaya Lakshmi Pandit, Indian ambassador to the U.S.S.R. who herself was never received by Stalin:

> The silence from Moscow over Gandhiji's death persists. One cannot protest about such things, forced sympathy is not worth having. I confess, however, that India will feel it when it becomes known, as be-

come known it must, that the U.S.S.R. alone sent no message of condolence in our hour of unparalleled sorrow.

In November 1978 Mrs. Gandhi returned to New Delhi from
London via Moscow, traveling by Aeroflot. She was received by
senior Soviet officials, including Prime Minister Kosygin, who conferred with her and gave her dinner at the airport during the scheduled three-hour stop. A year later her election manifesto stated her
government would "recognise the new revolutionary government
of Kampuchea". This was the pro-Vietnamese government of Heng
Samrin that took control of Phnom Penh in January 1979. Prime
Minister Kosygin obtained no such assurance from the Desai government, though he sought one on a six-day visit to India in March
1979. Addressing the Indian Parliament on March 9, he had said
with reference to "China's aggression in Vietnam":

> Should an armed robber or murderer attack somebody, all the rigours
> of the law are applied to him in any country. . . . But one would like
> to know what punishment deserves a criminal who has encroached on
> the life of an entire nation, and who seeks to assume the right to use
> arms against other peoples and decide their fate as he pleases? No
> peace-loving country, no person of integrity should remain indifferent
> when that sort of thing happens, when an aggressor holds human life
> and world public opinion in insolent contempt, commits an outrage
> against international law. . . . Indeed it would be unpardonable if the
> least opportunity is missed for cooperation in the struggle against
> aggression and against the policy of blackmail and *diktat*. . . . On behalf
> of the Soviet Union's Supreme Soviet, I can assure with full respon-
> sibility that any initiation by the Parliament of India serving that goal
> will find our most active support.

The language was outspoken in view of the Desai government's
policy of normalizing relations with China. In its editorial of March
10, 1979, the *Economic and Political Weekly* remarked that the
"content and tenor of Kosygin's speeches on the very first two days
of the visit have raised certain important questions about the nature
of India's relations with the Soviet Union and the extent to which
these relations circumscribe this country's freedom to pursue independent policies toward other countries." The joint communique
at the end of the visit did not mention Kampuchea, though it called
for a Chinese withdrawal from Vietnam, which India had, in fact,
called for earlier. Morarji Desai took the view that India would
neither lead an anti-China front nor be party to an anti-Soviet front.

The succeeding caretaker government asked the Soviet Union, on December 31, 1979, to "pull out from Afghanistan." Mrs. Gandhi told correspondents the same day, "We do not believe in intervention of any nation in the affairs of another nation", though on January 3, 1980, she amplified, "They [the Soviet Union] think the Western presence in Afghanistan was very strong" and that the Soviet action was not a "one-sided affair." On January 10, as prime minister-designate, she told foreign correspondents the Soviet action was "best resolved by Afghanistan itself." On January 12 the Indian statement in the United Nations General Assembly debate on the resolution calling for an immediate and unconditional withdrawal of Soviet troops largely absolved the Soviet Union of blame. While disapproving of outside interference in Afghanistan, it said, "We have no reason to doubt assurances, particularly from a friendly country like the Soviet Union, with whom we have close ties." India abstained on the resolution, while all the countries of the subcontinent, but one, voted in favor of it. The exception was Bhutan, which avoided an awkward situation with India by not participating in the vote at all.

By January 1980 the Soviet Union had support it could count on in New Delhi, whose diplomatic initiatives to "defuse" the Afghan crisis took care to recognize the Soviet Union's interests on the subcontinent, in the Indian Ocean, and in Asia—a position that set India apart from Sri Lanka, Bangladesh, Nepal, and Pakistan. India thereby, in effect, accepted the Soviet occupation of Afghanistan as justified in order to strengthen Soviet strategy in the region. Mrs. Gandhi's government's recognition on July 7, 1980, of the Heng Samrin regime in Kampuchea, also gave implicit Indian backing to Soviet policy of military support of Vietnamese hegemony over Indo-China as a counter to Chinese power in Southeast Asia.

CHAPTER EIGHTEEN

"A Dynamic Manufacturer"

The nature and conduct of Sanjay Gandhi's business transactions probably did more to injure his mother during the 1970s than any other factor, with public comment and criticism in Parliament focusing on the promotion of Sanjay's interests at the cost of policy and rules. His undefined and unaccountable political role strikingly illuminated the power structure she headed. His encroachments into affairs of state extraordinarily increased the isolation that was her natural climate, alienating her principal adviser, P. N. Haksar, and her old colleagues and confounding a large, admiring public. His business interests were sponsored by ministers, some of whom valued the perquisites of office higher than standards or integrity, and were advanced through an administration often too timid to insist on proper procedures. Indian politics has its share of syncophancy, nepotism and corruption. In more than one state, governing families have been reputed to have made fortunes in office, while there has been no dearth of politicians who have influenced the official machinery to benefit their relatives and friends. But the Sanjay phenomenon was of a new scale and dimension. It arose and flourished at the level of the Union government, at the peak of the power apparatus, and could not have done so without the approval of the prime minister herself. Mrs. Gandhi's opponents and supporters alike were baffled by her disregard of the proprieties and of vital considerations, even including defence requirements, where her younger son was concerned.

Lacking intellectual ability and competitive capacity, Sanjay had to rely on assistance and protection in order to rise to prominence. The stages of responsibility usually involved in preparing for national leadership were substituted in his case by an encapsulated "progress", bringing him, despite his doubtful reputation in business, to the fore in 1975 as the country's youth leader and in May 1980, as architect of the Congress-I victory in elections to nine State Legislative Assemblies. Both claims were exaggerated. Each national political party has its own active and committed youth organization. Sanjay's standing was confined to his mother's party and not altogether acceptable within it. And it is likely that, by the time of the assembly elections, "the new emerging forces, an alliance of lumpen youth and amoral contact men who had transformed themselves into businessmen and industrialists"[1] were attracted by a spoils system at its most inviting and opted for the party already in power at the center. Mrs. Gandhi could not have been unaware that there was promising young people in her party to choose from, some of them in politics since their student days, if leadership from among the young was to be commended. If she preferred to ignore the material available to her, it can only have been because she had set her heart on bequeathing power to her son. She treated the national controversy surrounding Sanjay's business dealings and his role in politics as quite simply a lie, the invention of her enemies.

Obviously this was a complex and in part a highly strung relationship—strained by unusual tensions, stretched by unusual elations—as any relationship must be where power is a palace preserve and the clandestine becomes a significant cog in the power machine. Sanjay shared access to vital information and intelligence. The Delhi administration, including the police, took its orders from him during the Emergency, and important Emergency officials were rehabilitated by him in Delhi and some state governments after the 1980 election victory. These included two key appointments, the lieutenant-governor and the police commissioner of Delhi, which made it easier to ensure the speedy and arbitrary dismissal of the capital's two representative bodies, the Delhi Metropolitan Council and the New Delhi Municipal Corporation, while the daily crime bulletin issued by the police was altered to withhold complete information from the press and the public.

Sanjay's conduct during the Emergency had contributed to his mother's defeat in 1977, yet he was more directly responsible for her triumphant return three years later, and Mrs. Gandhi believed she owed her political resurrection at least in part to Sanjay's advice and management. Much of her private torment and anxiety must have centered on the undisciplined young man, dangerously addicted to the shortcut, who had to be shielded from the public consequences of his actions. Inevitably, there were clashes of will and temperament. In a natural enough reaction to a strong-willed mother, both Mrs. Gandhi's sons resisted domination by her, though neither broke away from the parental roof, even after marriage, to set up a home and life of his own. In Sanjay's case the paraphernalia and panoply of power were clearly a necessary accompaniment and background for the work he needed done with the help of official channels. Guilt feelings are part of parenthood, and it is possible that Mrs. Gandhi labored under some degree of guilt toward the problem marriage that her sons felt had treated their father unfairly.

Indians understand the flesh and blood bond and are indulgent toward its frailties. A son as successor need not have presented a problem. It was Sanjay's techniques that roused hostility, above all the ruthlessness visited on helpless people who had no redress against the prime minister's son when he violated agreements, particularly during the Emergency when civil rights and habeas corpus were suspended. Fantasy ruled the day when Sanjay's past was submerged and he was hailed as heir apparent, as the symbol of youth power, enterprise and adventure, and even as the leader of a cultural revolution. The virtues attributed to him at a condolence meeting after his death, comparing him with Jesus Christ, the Buddha, and Karl Marx, testified that a myth was in the making. Judge D. C. Aggarwal had contributed to it when, on March 17, 1980, he had "discharged" Sanjay Gandhi and an associate in the "polymix case," where they had been accused of pressuring the New Delhi Municipal Corporation into buying a preparation marketed by Sanjay's company, Maruti Technical Services. The case was one among many civil and criminal cases involving Mrs. Gandhi, Sanjay Gandhi, and those associated with them, dismissed by judges after Mrs. Gandhi's return. The judgement stated: "a dynamic manufacturer like Mr. Gandhi ... can hardly be regarded as actuated by any dishonest intention to make illegitimate gain by dint of his political influence over the officers of the corporation." The facts, as revealed by the commission of inquiry appointed on May 30, 1977 under the chairmanship of Justice A. C. Gupta of the Supreme Court, to examine the affairs of Sanjay Gandhi's three concerns—Maruti Ltd., Maruti Heavy Vehicles (Pvt.) Ltd., and Maruti Technical Services (Pvt.) Ltd.—are different.

By early 1975, Maruti, the car project for the manufacture of which a letter of intent had been issued to Sanjay in 1970, had not yet produced a car, except for a few prototypes, and it never did. Yet two private companies set up by him had drawn substantial funds from the main public limited company, Maruti Ltd. The Emergency, declared on June 26, 1975, ended all debate on Maruti affairs, enabling Sanjay to step into the national limelight as the coming leader. Witnesses questioned by the Shah Commission revealed it was Sanjay who had ordered the cutting off of electrical connections to newspapers on the night of June 25th, so that many could not appear the next morning, and that he had also suggested the locking up of High Courts. The chief minister of West Bengal, Siddharth Shankar Ray, who was in Delhi to help Mrs. Gandhi prepare a draft proclaiming the Emergency, opposed these measures and remembers that Sanjay met him "in a highly excited and infuriated state of mind and told him quite rudely and offensively that he did not know how to rule the country."[2] Mr. Ray also states that the draft he prepared was not used.

The Gupta Commission examined 712 affidavits and about 2,000 files of the Union and state governments, statutory bodies, and other institutions. It held 111 public sittings between December 16, 1977 and February 16, 1979 and examined 268 witnesses. Justice Gupta submitted his report to the government on May 31, 1979. Yet the government's prevarication and indecision, and finally its fall, held up its release to the press until September. In Chapter X of a precise and heavily documented report, Justice Gupta sums up his conclusions:

> The affairs of the Maruti concerns ... appear to have brought about a decline in the integrity of public life and sullied the purity of administration. Legal and other requirements were brushed aside, and accepted norms of behaviour were forgotten on many occasions when the interest of a Maruti company was involved. This was due to, as witness after witness repeated, an atmosphere of fear then prevailing. ... And the fear was real. Threat of detention under the Maintenance of Internal Security Act or a CBI inquiry or other forms of harassment made it hazardous for the officers to insist on the rules or the dealers and depositors to insist on their rights. Persons in public life were in danger of having their political careers ruined. That it was not an idle threat is proved by instances of persons in whose case the threat was carried out. ... From the interest taken in Maruti's progress by men from the Prime Minister's Secretariat and the way even matters connected with the country's defence were subordinated to the interest of Maruti Ltd., and the prevailing sense of fear that prompted implicit obedience, one is left in no doubt as to the origin of the power

that made such a state of affairs possible. Shri Sanjay Gandhi exercised only a derivative power, its source was the authority of the Prime Minister.

A number of irregularities in the working of the Maruti companies have been noticed in the foregoing pages. The minutes books do not appear to have been kept in the prescribed manner, at least two resolutions stated to have been passed by the Board of Directors of Maruti Ltd. have not been recorded. Evidence has been adduced showing that shares of Maruti Ltd. were allotted to persons who knew nothing about the transactions, also that in February 1977 large sums of money were paid out to fictitious persons as refunds of their dealership reservation money or deposits made by them along with their alleged applications for Maruti shares. All these indicate the presence of unaccounted money. It has not been possible for the commission to examine all the vouchers, books of original entries and other records and documents. What is revealed in such examination as the commission has been able to do suggests that if a joint or co-ordinated examination of the records of the Maruti companies is done by the Departments of Revenue & Company Affairs, and their books of account are audited by a special team, many more irregularities are likely to come to light.[3]

The Gupta Commission's report is the source from which the brief and incomplete account below is taken.

The government of India had been considering the manufacture of a small low-cost car since 1959 but had taken no decision about whether it should be produced in the public or private sector, whether a new unit should be set up or existing units expanded, when Sanjay Gandhi applied for an industrial licence to produce a small car on December 11, 1968. After high school in India, he had joined Rolls Royce Motors in England as a special student apprentice, from August 1964 to July 1967. A letter from the assistant secretary, Rolls Royce Motors, to the Commission explains that, following the "normal practice for student apprentices," Sanjay "attended the local Technical College on a day-release basis (one day each week) throughout the three years he was with the company" and "received an ordinary National Certificate in Mechanical Engineering" on passing an examination in June 1967. This was a "relatively minor qualification and two years further study would have been necessary for him to obtain a significant academic qualification, which would have been a Higher National Certificate."

Four months before Sanjay applied for a licence, Fakhruddin Ali Ahmed, then minister for industrial development and company affairs and later elevated to the presidency, forwarded a project report for Maruti to the Planning Commission and the Directorate General (of) Technical Development (DGTD), bodies that do not normally look at project reports until an application for an industrial licence has been made. The Planning Commission does not in any case analyze reports from prospective licencees. On January 4, 1969 Sanjay, in a discussion with the secretary of the Ministry of Industrial Development and Company Affairs, and some DGTD officials, suggested he be given a letter of intent before his prototype car was ready, but was told that DGTD officials would have to study the prototype first.

The Maruti prototype was ready in October 1969, and the DGTD suggested improvements, modifications, and a detailed survey by Sanjay of the availability and prices of the ancillaries and parts he proposed to use. At this time the possibility of a new car unit in the public sector was still being considered by the Cabinet. On August 7, 1970, Mrs. Gandhi presided over a Cabinet meeting that decided to permit the manufacture of a car in the private sector "based on completely indigenous sources," as the minister for industrial development and internal trade clarified in both Houses of Parliament on August 10. The word "indigenous" was defined at various times by different ministers, in answer to questions in Parliament, to mean machinery, components, and materials produced in India. This was a basic requirement in terms of India's industrial policy, which included the need to conserve foreign exchange.

On September 23, 1970, the Hindustan Times reported:

> Prime Minister Indira Gandhi today commended the enterprising spirit of her son, Mr. Sanjay Gandhi, in putting forward a proposal for a small car, completely Indian. Mrs. Gandhi said she could not say whether a licence would be granted to him. She had been asking all young men to be enterprising even before her son had taken to designing a car. Her son was a delicate young man and with whatever money and energy he had, he modeled a car, not a posh one, but fairly comfortable and suitable to Indian conditions. It would suit the middle class, she added.

A week later, on September 30, a letter of intent was issued to Sanjay for the manufacture of an annual capacity of 50,000 cars at Faridabad in Haryana. It is interesting to note that the capacity achieved by established car production units during 1970–71 was 46,000, and this remained the highest figure for the next several years. The letter of intent, valid for six months, was subject to four conditions:

1) No foreign collaboration
2) No import of capital goods
3) No import of components/raw materials
4) Before the letter of intent is converted into a licence, prototype(s) will be developed and tested, and approved for roadworthiness by an authority appointed for the purpose by the government.

In October 1970, Sanjay asked for a relaxation of the condition relating to the import of raw materials. This was granted, provided raw materials normally available in the country happened to be in short supply. His letter of intent was also extended, at his request, to eighteen months (it was further extended up to December 31, 1973 and then until June 30, 1974), and he was permitted to set up his factory at Gurgaon in Haryana, (instead of Faridabad) where Chief Minister Bansi Lal had offered him facilities and his choice of land on easy purchase terms. The area chosen by Sanjay had been designated part of the rural belt by state planners. It was converted into an industrial zone to permit the construction of Sanjay's factory, and later portions of it were leased out by Sanjay, against regulations, for other purposes. Of the 291 acres selected, 157 belonged to the Defence Ministry, which controlled a 1,000-yard safety belt around an ammunition depot near an airfield. This consideration was ignored, as were the heavy losses incurred by citizens who had invested in plots in the rural belt and by villages in the area whose claims were summarily disposed of. Referring to this in the Lok Sabha on December 22, 1972, S. N. Mishra, an opposition M.P., said:

> The Chief Minister of Haryana has left nothing undone to place the Prime Minister in a situation of blackmail. He has robbed the peasants. . . . He has violated the defence rules which prohibit the setting up of such factories or any construction within a particular distance. . . . He has tried to equate public interest with private interest and also tried to say to the world that industrial estate means personal estate.

The Maruti prototype arrived for testing at the Vehicles Research and Development Establishment (VRDE) in Ahmednagar on February 10, 1974, after Sanjay failed to get the trials shifted to Delhi, under an observer chosen by the Ministry of Industrial Development. The correspondence between VRDE and Maruti Ltd. and the representations Maruti Ltd. made to the Ministry of Heavy

Industry reveal the company's persistent efforts to try to change the condition in the letter of intent requiring the prototype's testing for roadworthiness. Inspection on February 11 revealed that the car had a German engine. W. H. F. Muller, a German consultant employed by Maruti Technical Services in July 1972, had brought it into the country as part of his personal baggage:

> I had two such (NSU) engines with me in West Germany. I had purchased them long back in the sixties. . . . Shri Sanjay Gandhi wanted me to go to West Germany and bring the two engines. . . . (He) assured me that he would make arrangements for their easy passage into this country. . . . I arrived at New Delhi on 30th September 1973. . . . Shri Sanjay Gandhi advised me to get them cleared myself. . . . I had not obtained licence to import them in view of Sanjay's assurance to get these things cleared without any difficulty. . . .[4]

Asked for detailed information about the prototype, Maruti Ltd. wrote to VRDE, listing several components as "presumed to be imported" but "original supplier not available." Some parts were admitted as imported, with the rider that these would be replaced by indigenous components.

The VRDE catalogued a list of defects during the first test. The reliability test failed altogether when the car had a major breakdown of the steering rod and fell into a ditch. On July 3, 1974, S. M. Ghosh, joint secretary in the Ministry of Heavy Industry, sent Sanjay a copy of the VRDE director's letter to the ministry on the subject of the Maruti prototype's faults. Ghosh's own covering letter read:

> I shall be very grateful if you would kindly arrange to send the Chief Designer along with a team of engineers both on the manufacturing and on the design sides to Ahmednagar immediately in order that they can properly investigate into the defect and put the car back on the road after necessary rectification. I shall be grateful if you would advise me that the Chief Designer and a team of engineers have, in fact, left for Ahmednagar to remove the defects. I shall also be grateful if I could be kept apprised of the progress made in putting the car back on the road for resuming the tests.

These repeated expressions of gratitude where none were necessary, indicate an official nervousness, not surprising when any normal procedural delay in processing Maruti had met with a telephone call from Professor P. N. Dhar in the prime minister's secretariat, wanting to know the reason for delay, and R. K. Dhawan

also of the prime minister's secretariat, delivering the sharp reprimand that he would "report to the highest." Cabinet ministers*
were acquiescing in the cover-up of Maruti, and Mrs. Gandhi was
closely monitoring all developments concerning it. The record later
showed that she went through Parliamentary questions on Maruti,
and ministers replies had to be cleared with her. In late 1975 or
early 1976, she removed under cover of the Emergency, all notes
on Maruti from files in the prime minister's secretariat.

On July 4, 1974 S. M. Ghosh, ignoring VRDE's reservations,
recommended that Sanjay Gandhi's letter of intent be converted
into an industrial licence. The Maruti prototype had not met the
standards of the tests made thus far, and testing was not yet complete. Mr. Ghosh noted on the file that Maruti manufacturers had
confirmed that all major components and assemblies were of indigenous design. The licence was issued on July 25, 1974, before
the requirements of the letter of intent had been fulfilled or, as far
as the record shows, even accurately examined. It is established,
however, that it was issued in disregard of its fourth vital condition,
that is, passing the test of roadworthiness. On receipt of the licence,
Maruti Ltd. stopped the supply of fuel and oil it was required to
give to VRDE for the continuation of trials for another four months.
VRDE was instructed to return the prototype to Maruti Ltd. It did
so on June 14, 1975.

Sanjay Gandhi, as director of Maruti Technical Services, had
received a fee of Rs 300,000 for imparting technical know-how to
Maruti Ltd. Asked by an income tax officer what Sanjay had contributed to the technical side of the car project, W.H.F. Muller
replied: "Actually a set of drawings, incomplete set, in respect of
the car he had built. . . . What actually was produced was a few
prototypes hand-made."

Income Tax Officer: "It is said that some Maruti cars are running on roads. Have you any idea about this?"

Muller: "These cars were given to certain people. In all about
ten or twelve. These are all prototypes, not the same in design, etc.
They are different from one another. They were changed several
times. . . . It would be an exaggeration to say that a workable plan
or mode existed."

* F. A. Ahmed, Minister for Industrial Development; T. A. Pai, Minister for Heavy
Industry,; V. C. Shukla, Minister for Defence Production; H. R. Gokhale, Law Minister; Pranab Mukherjee, Minister for Revenue and Expenditure.

In Muller's opinion Sanjay would not "provide a feasible working prototype nor the planning required."[5]

Maruti concerns found lucrative outlets in state governments for road rollers, tractors, and other equipment supplied by them. Hardeo Joshi, chief minister of Rajasthan, told the chief engineer of the Public Works Department that, if he did not place an order for Maruti road rollers before January 3, 1976, "this is Emergency time, and anything can happen to you." The chief ministers of Uttar Pradesh, Madhya Pradesh and Himachal Pradesh pressured their officials to hurry orders from Maruti companies, and the chief minister of Punjab ordered fifteen Maruti road rollers without administrative or financial sanction.

Though the car had not appeared on the market, eighty distribution agents were appointed between 1972 and 1976, each required to deposit a sum ranging from Rs 300,000 to Rs 600,000, an exorbitant figure compared with the deposit of Rs 5,000 charged by the makers of the well-known Ambassador car. In some cases the purchase of Maruti shares was made a precondition for an agency. The Gupta Commission records the experience of several agents. Rattan Lal, a partner of Vishal Motors of Chandigarh, who had paid Rs 250,000 as deposit, did not demand its refund when the car did not appear: "Because in the meanwhile we had come to know that one or two dealers who had dared demand their deposits back were harassed, and some of them were put under detention under MISA." Om Prakash Gupta of Hapur, Uttar Pradesh, was arrested on May 16, 1974, because he asked for payment of interest as provided in the agency agreement. He was in jail for two months until the Allahabad High Court ordered his release on a habeas corpus petition. S. C. Aggarwal paid Rs 600,000 for agencies at Hissar in Haryana and Gauhati in Assam. At Sanjay's insistence he also bought a plot at Hansi in Hissar for a showroom and a garage. A car was delivered to him on June 30, 1974, for exhibition, not sale. It broke down while he was driving it to Hansi. On June 2, 1975, his firm sent a notice to Maruti Ltd., terminating the agency at Gauhati. He was threatened with arrest and later made to touch Sanjay's feet in apology. Daljit Singh, another agent, was charged Rs 20,000 for a car to exhibit. He found its brakes and clutch defective and returned it to the Maruti factory for repair. He got neither the car nor his money back. Yet Maruti's annual report for 1974–75 claimed that during the year "it was possible to start the manufacture of Maruti cars on a moderate basis" and that the car had "shown very good performance" on plain roads as well as high altitudes and was "liked and welcomed by all." Shareholders did not appear to agree. Liquidation proceedings were started against Maruti Ltd. soon after the Emergency was lifted.

The press registered its stern and shocked reaction to the Gupta Commission's findings:

> ... as with the Shah report, the cumulative effect, as classified and evaluated by a fine judicial mind, comes with an impact which is not merely horrifying, but disgusting. (*Statesman*, September 9, 1979)

> ... the finds have been ... certainly sufficient, under conditions of genuine parliamentary democracy, to keep son and mother out of public affairs for life. (*The Hindu*, September 12, 1979)

> The Roman hand of Mrs. Gandhi can be seen at every stage in the process by which land was acquired and enormous loans given to Maruti by banks whose officials were under threat or were promoted with a view to securing favoured treatment ... it would seem that, even more than the Allahabad judgement in her election case, it was Sanjay's megalomaniac plans regarding Maruti which compelled her to declare the second Emergency in June 1975 so that the Maruti scandals could be hushed up. (*Deccan Herald*, September 11, 1979)

At her Shivaji Park meeting in Bombay in September 1979, Mrs. Gandhi declared she had no time to read the "trash" published by the commissions of inquiry, and referred in her speech to the "petty judge" who had dared unseat the prime minister (on June 12, 1975). "I am unconcerned about the disclosures about Maruti," she told reporters when asked for her comment. Yet her concern for Sanjay mounted as the Janata government began to prepare a series of criminal and civil cases arising out of the report. It is certain that its submission to the government in May made the dislodging of the Janata government an urgent objective with Sanjay, who is credited with the strategy and arrangements that led to Charan Singh's defection, paving the way for a midterm election.

After Sanjay Gandhi's death, Mrs. Gandhi's government nationalized Maruti Ltd. by presidential ordinance between two sessions of Parliament, telling a press conference, on October 21, 1980, that the company had more assets than liabilities and "has to be used for the national good." Madhu Dandavate, general secretary of the Janata party, described the measure as the "nationalization of corruption," and Maruti affairs came before Parliament again in November 1980, with Opposition parties united in their objection to the public exchequer meeting the heavy liabilities incurred by Sanjay Gandhi behind the cover of nationalization.

When Sanjay Gandhi celebrated his thirty-third birthday in December 1979, he was in command of the youth wing of the Congress-I. "If Sanjay tells me, I will even put my head into an oil seed crusher." The remark, made by Hakim Singh, aged thirty-six, elected to the Lok Sabha in January 1980 from Punjab, was typical of the aggressive emotional ramparts the youth wing had erected around their leader. In its brief interlude in the wilderness, the party's youth organization had concentrated on a tempestuous campaign to obstruct court proceedings in cases against Sanjay. A crowd of supporters accompanied him on his court appearances in Delhi, Lucknow, and Dehra Dun. Court work had to be suspended on occasion when the noise outside or with the Sanjay band pouring in halted proceedings. The public prosecutor was at times not allowed to enter the court room until it was filled with the faithful. On one occasion the public prosecutor was assaulted. Books were thrown at a judge, papers torn, and furniture broken in court. The new style dominated the 1980 Parliament, where about 180 out of 351 Congress-I M.P.s were associated with the party's youth wing and loudly obstructed proceedings when they wished to express their disapproval.

On May 7, 1980, two editors commented on the distinct change in the political climate. Girilal Jain of the *Times of India* wrote:

> Mr. Gandhi is impatient with bureaucratic delays and procedures. He is a doer and not a thinker. He is generally anti-Left. His followers share some of these characteristics which are very different from those of Congressmen who prospered under Mr. Nehru.

Kuldip Nayar of the *Indian Express* wrote:

> Those who are gaining limelight are generally drop-outs from schools or colleges or the ones who were below average students. They are rootless individuals who have no respect for values or standards and who have only one aim, how to make a fast buck.

It was generally agreed that the scene was different in substance and essence from the past and that the new element in it was "activist." Romesh Thapar wrote in the *Economic & Political Weekly* of January 12, 1980:

> It would be a mistake to imagine that the ruling party represents a Congress continuity. Quite the contrary. It is a new party of Indira and

Sanjay devotees. . . . The overwhelming democratic mandate for a party described as 'authoritarian' and 'fascist' creates an extraordinary situation. . . . Indira Gandhi's earlier reliance on the bureaucratic machine (civil, military and police) to implement her vague ideas of change has been much reduced by Sanjay Gandhi's demonstration of the power of the mob . . .

Sanjay's death on June 23, 1980, when the aerobatic aircraft he was piloting without sufficient experience crashed, left a design in ruins about his mother. The Cabinet decision to hold an open judicial inquiry to investigate the reasons for the disaster was dramatically changed at the initiative of the prime minister, leaving the inquiry to departmental sources, inevitably controlled by the executive. A comprehensive public inquiry might have laid bare a labyrinth of violations, from the import of the aircraft with doubtful justification and against normal policy to its unlawful and reckless uses. Mrs. Gandhi was aware that no familiar alibi—vested interests, the opposition, or the foreign hand—could be blamed for the tragedy that had killed a young man in his prime and with him the helpless instructor who had been an unwilling companion on the flight.

Mrs. Gandhi is not a traditional Hindu, and her defeat in the 1977 election did not alone account for the change of behavior that took her to a succession of temples and shrines. Most Hindus, regardless of Westernization, plan important events by horoscopes. Her pilgrimages made it evident that hers portended ill for her family. Before she moved into the official residence as prime minister in early February 1980, priests from Varanasi conducted eight-day religious rites. During her first thirty-eight days in office, she worshipped at about a dozen shrines from Jammu in the north to Tamil Nad in the south.

The *Hindustan Times*, January 17, 1980:

> The first thing Mrs. Gandhi does after landing here by an IAF aircraft at 9.30 a.m. is to worship at the Padmanabha Swamy temple. . . . She will begin the day on Friday with prayers at the famous Guruvayoor temple.

UNI (United News of India), February 27:

> The Prime Minister, Mrs. Indira Gandhi, will arrive here tomorrow by a special plane to worship Lord Venkateswara. . . . From the airport, Mrs. Gandhi will motor straight to Tirumala where she will stay for

the night. After worshipping the Lord, she will leave for Madras the next morning.

UNI, March 4:

Prime Minister Indira Gandhi made a flying pilgrimage to the Vaishno Devi cave temple ... offering prayers under the guidance of head priest Pandit Prem Nath. ... Before entering the 120-ft.-long cave, Mrs. Gandhi and other members of her party had the customary bath. The Prime Minister and others declined to ride ponies from Sanjichat helipad and covered the 2-kilometer distance on foot.

Times of India, March 11:

Amid a hectic whirlwind tour of Gujarat yesterday, the Prime Minister, Mrs. Gandhi, spared half an hour to pray before the 'Amba Mata' at the famous temple town of Ambaji. She was deeply engrossed in prayer as she sat before the main seat of the Goddess. She lay prostrate for 'pranam' for about a minute.

PTI (Press Trust of India), March 15:

Mrs. Gandhi today prayed for the welfare of the country and its people while offering a velvet 'chaddar' on the tomb of Khwaja Moiuddin Chisti here.

PTI, April 4:

Prime Minister Indira Gandhi today rounded off her day's programme by visiting the temple of Lord Vishwanath—the presiding deity of Varanasi—and spent about an hour in the temple. Sitting before the Shiva "Linga" Mrs. Gandhi worshipped the Lord by offering flowers and "bilva patra." She also visited the temple of Annapurna and San-katmochan. During her tour of the drought affected areas she had also visited the Vidhyavashini temple.

The Statesman, April 6:

Mrs. Gandhi also visited Chitrakoot in Satna district in Madhya Pradesh and offered prayers at the historic temple of Kamla Nath. She also offered prayers at the temples of Lord Rama, Sita and Hanuman and Sati Anasuya. ... Mrs. Gandhi also visited the Janakikund, a pond in which, according to mythology, Sita had bathed. ... Before leaving Chitrakoot, she paid a visit to the holy rock where the footprints of Lord Rama are said to be inscribed. She placed flowers on the hallowed spot and bowed. Mrs. Gandhi also offered prayers at Pithambar Pith, a temple of Bagla Mukhi, the Goddess of Shakti.

The woman who, as prime minister of a religion-dominated

country, had attracted admiring comment when she told a television interviewer in Britain in 1971 that she did not believe in God, appeared to have changed fundamentally in the reliance she now placed on religious observance. The shadow of impending calamity has its own compulsions. The human being seeks courage where he can, and the ritual connected with religion is the oldest succour known to the human race. Nevertheless her dependency on astrology became the subject of national comment.

Sanjay's death brought a genuine wave of public sympathy. The loss of a child—in India, particularly a son—is a grief beyond compare, and national comment seemed to agree that no one should die at thirty-three, though there was no doubting the immense relief outside Mrs. Gandhi's party at the providential removal of the most sinister presence modern Indian politics had known. For the maturing of democracy it was regrettable that a political challenge of the sort Sanjay represented had been removed by sudden death and not overcome by the effort and organization of those opposed to him. Mrs. Gandhi's extreme and awesome stoicism in her loss conveyed as nothing else could have done that she had perhaps lived through the possibility of just such a disaster many times in her imagination. Her self-possession was widely remarked when she returned to recover Sanjay's keys and watch, both articles essential for access to his finances and documents, from his mangled body. This insured that control of these would be hers and not pass to Sanjay's widow, Maneka, and Maneka's family, with the unforeseen political implications this might involve.

Sanjay's tragedy was in reality a political climate that allowed him to use an administration, and then a party, to further his ends. But for this infatuation with power, encouraged by the unbridled authority he was permitted to exercise, he might have remained an unremarked and unremarkable young man, shaped by steadier and more ordinary processes and opportunities. The larger tragedy may well be the fever of our times, which elevates wealth, power, and speed as admirable goals, worthy in themselves.

CHAPTER NINETEEN

The Face of the Future

A prime minister's personal tragedy does not usually become a political dilemma, but Mrs. Gandhi's political career had been shaped by ever-growing personal and family considerations, and Sanjay's death left her in a political and psychological vacuum of her own making. She faced the gravest problems in her career with the weakest and most inexperienced team of ministers, most of whom had been chosen for their special equation with Sanjay. The price rise achieved new heights, tensions in the rural sector mounted, communal violence erupted, and an increasing sense of insecurity gripped the cities. An electorate that had hoped Mrs. Gandhi would be better able than a disunited coalition to cope with problems found her unequal to the task. After Sanjay's death she also faced turmoil within her party. This, unlike 1971, was not the settled weather of an exhilarating victory.

The use of her party as an instrument of dynasty should in the ordinary course have become irrelevant after Sanjay's removal from the scene, leaving his following to find its own level. The men his patronage had elevated to importance had, almost without exception, no firm political base of their own and, in the case of some new entrants from among the princes and business houses, very recent and tenuous links with the party. Sanjay's satellites found they needed a new and powerful sponsor close to Mrs. Gandhi to insure not the seats they already occupied in Parliament and state legislatures but the leverage and ultimate control they had counted on capturing. The keys of this kingdom were now out of reach, along with the expectation of a steady harvest of material advantage. The campaign to draft Sanjay's elder brother, Rajiv, as his successor shrewdly recognized Mrs. Gandhi's incapacity to repose her confidence outside her bloodline.

Mrs. Gandhi could at this stage have abandoned dynastic notions and trappings, using her own now undiluted authority to end dissensions in the party and restore it to the kind of functioning that would admit new political blood. Her reaction was quite different. She appeared to take it for granted that her elder son should now enter politics, if not as his brother's successor—which his own dislike of such a proposition made unlikely—then as his mother's aide. This development laid bare the extremity of her isolation and the extent of her estrangement from normal parliamentary government and of her own retreat behind the blood bond. As a leader she had shown little interest in, or aptitude for, the interaction and interdependence of the parts of a system that make for a balanced healthy whole. The plan to induct Rajiv into politics occasioned no surprise in public comment and none in her party. Rajiv Gandhi, uninterested in politics, reluctant to give up a career as an Indian Airlines pilot, in which he enjoyed high professional standing, found himself forced to make a difficult and unwelcome decision. It was, however, clear that he would not in any sense be a Sanjay substitute when Mrs. Gandhi moved swiftly to strip Sanjay's inner circle of the free access his key associates had had to the prime minister's house. Implicit was the warning that they no longer could count on special status or protection. The action was reminiscent of similar treatment in the past toward colleagues of her own generation who had become security risks. Yet it had its own significance. The house that Sanjay built contained elements, some disreputable and dangerous, that only he could control. The disciplining of a corps that would have presented her with problems of impatient ambition, even had Sanjay lived, seemed to free her from imminent and even ugly duress. Publicly she showed every sign of relaxation. The Youth Congress-I, too, placed under a more pliant leadership that did not seek laurels for itself, would be more amenable to her own guidance. This quiet demotion of Sanjay's following proceeded alongside memorials to him. This kept the family name before the public, while the ground was prepared for the new member, Rajiv, to fill the gap.

Not given to consensus or compromise, Mrs. Gandhi was vulnerable to the tides she had helped to create. Charisma and manipulative talent were not enough to integrate a divided polity and administration or win back a suspicious intelligentsia. Both urban and rural society were beginning to demand efficient performance from political leaders, and the blurred ideology of the Congress-I gave no indication of clear intent or direction. Mrs. Gandhi had built her reputation on radical credentials, through her break with the Old Guard of the Congress, her alliance with the CPI, and such measures, hailed as progressive, as the nationalization of fourteen banks. Sanjay Gandhi had come to the country's notice as a young man inordinately interested in money and power and not too particular how he came by either. From Sanjay's anti-Left stance, it was inferred he favored private enterprise. Yet, he did not possess the true credentials of private enterprise, as the Maruti saga had shown. It is probable that, had he remained in charge, the country could have expected, under the mantle of a bigger role for private industry, political management that would serve the interests of a group, through benefits not available to industry in general. As though this were understood, the sudden nationalization of six commercial banks in April 1980 had not created a ripple. Principally it seemed to assure the ruling clique of a controlling voice in their affairs. In a like control operation, the Planning Commission, conceived in 1950 as an independent body of experts engaged in policy perspectives, had been virtually reduced to a department of government. The draft of the Sixth Five-Year Plan, drawn up under the Janata regime, may have been the last creative exercise of its kind for some time to come.

Until his death, essential political authority vested in Sanjay, although, until he was appointed general secretary of the Congress-I shortly before he died, his position in the party was technically no higher than that of other members of Parliament. His style was evident in the administrative control established in several states by mass transfers of civil servants and their replacement. The Congress-I also launched "direct action" in the form of a blockade to prevent supplies from reaching Assam, where a statewide protest demanded the expulsion of illegal immigrants from its electoral rolls. Mrs. Gandhi assured Parliament that nothing should be done to "increase the tension or aggravate the situation in Assam." Yet, on March 19, 1980, UNI reported the ransacking by Congress-I demonstrators of the Calcutta office of the *Assam Tribune*:

> Over 300 demonstrators went into the paper's office in a procession after staging an hour-long demonstration outside the Assam House here. A group of demonstrators stormed into the office of the daily on the third floor and threw furniture out into the street. Later they set it on fire. Typewriters and other equipment were also damaged. . . . Mr. Subrata Mukherji, general secretary of the West Bengal Congress-I . . . said the only recourse to tackle the Assam movement was to

counter it by another movement. . . . [They] would be launching this movement by closing all routes of supplies to Assam to bring about an undeclared "economic blockade" against the State.

This treatment of the Assam situation, a complex one outside the scope of this study, is of interest here as an example of the direct and violent interference with the orderly and peaceful solution that Mrs. Gandhi claimed her government was seeking. Assam was declared a disturbed area and the army was moved into the state.

When the minister for Information and Broadcasting, Vasant Sathe, announced that radio and television would continue under government control, thus reversing the Janata government's decision to grant autonomy, a direction halted by the 1977 election was resumed. Two further developments also provided windows to Mrs. Gandhi's frame of mind, indicating that she was picking up with deliberation the threads where she had left them. In September 1980 she armed her government, as she had done in 1971, with arbitrary powers to arrest and detain anyone "acting in any manner prejudicial to the security of the State or to the maintenance of public order or maintenance of supplies and services essential to the community." The provisions of the National Security Ordinance (NSO) exceeded those of the Maintenance of Internal Security Act (MISA) as originally enacted in 1971, though MISA was amended during the Emergency to tighten and extend its provisions. The NSO enabled the government, in effect, to detain a citizen indefinitely without trial.* The measure, promulgated by presidential ordinance, along with several other ordinances between the monsoon and winter sessions of Parliament, showed Mrs. Gandhi's characteristic lack of confidence in the art and processes of administration and in the normal legislative process, in spite of her unassailable position in Parliament.

The second window to Mrs. Gandhi's mind was her party's sponsorship of an All-India Lawyers' Conference, October 22–23, 1980, inaugurated by her in New Delhi, holding the predominant view that the present form of government be replaced by the pres-

---

* The National Security Ordinance provides that the detainee must be given grounds for his detention, *but not if it is against the public interest to disclose these.* Detention is to last for three months at one time, or a maximum of twelve months, *but it can go on being extended by three months at a time,* so long as a government functionary thinks this is necessary.

idential system. The idea, advanced during the Emergency, had been withdrawn when the 42nd Amendment to the Constitution secured for the prime minister a position above the law. The dilution of this amendment by the Supreme Court judgement during the Janata regime apparently makes a new approach to the objective of expanded executive powers necessary.

Mrs. Gandhi may be encouraged to seek greatly enlarged executive powers once again, because a fragmented Opposition cannot obstruct her plans. Coherent opposition now comes only from the CIP-M, with governments in three states, Kerala*, West Bengal, and Tripura, and the newly formed Bharatiya Janata Party, led by Atal Behari Vajpayee, with substantial support in the Hindi heartland, and improving its position in the south. The BJP's platform of "Gandhian socialism" and its cadre structure make it the only organized non-Communist opposition in national politics at present. Mrs. Gandhi's earlier ally, the CPI, is divided into two parties, one supporting her, the other working for closer cooperation with the CPI-M. The CPI-M's battering by the Gandhi government in 1972 has taught it to walk the tightrope of Center-State relations with care, and not invite another confrontation. Unless a stronger democratic opposition emerges either among the non-Communist Opposition parties, or through a convulsion within the Congress-I, the coast is clear for Mrs. Gandhi to move toward a change of system, or expanded powers for herself within the existing system. In March–April 1982 the Rajya Sabha (Upper House) will admit new members by election through state legislatures, where her party now enjoys majorities. She will be able to get enough party members into the Upper House to create the majority her government needs to amend the constitution and usher in the changes she desires.

Any such move would have the undoubted support of the Soviet Union, as the Emergency had in 1975 to 1977, and the greater ballast provided by its presence in Afghanistan.

Mrs. Gandhi's election manifesto had promised "stability" and the control of inflation. Stability, seen as the natural consequence of government under a leader of national stature, was clearly too simplistic a conception of India in the 1980s. It did not reckon with conditions needing the government's supervision and guidance of

---

* In October, 1981, President's Rule was established in Kerala when the Communist-led coalition lost its majority with the withdrawal of its two main coalition partners.

change rather than its guardianship of the status quo. In February 1980 two villages in Bihar highlighted the terror facing the rural poor who decided to assert their democratic rights. Peasants demanding the return of expropriated land in Parasbigha, and agitating for the minimum wage in Pipra, met with slaughter and carnage by the landlords' hired assassins who apparently had the local government's protection. Crime figures showed the continuing decline of law and order in the cities, while according to the Home Ministry's Annual Report published in April 1981, 1980 registered the highest figures of communal violence since 1976.

There was no relief from the rise in prices. J. D. Singh commented in the Times of India, June 6, 1981, on official statistics released the day before:

> Since the present government assumed office in January 1980, the wholesale index has risen by 24 percent. The increase in retail prices has been much sharper, thus causing distress to millions of families in the country.

A project to collect black (unaccounted) money by the sale of government bonds on attractive ten-year tax-free terms, after which the money would be accepted as legitimately earned, met with a limited response. The government collected only about one third of its target figure of 10,000 million rupees, perhaps because the major portion of unaccounted money was already profitably invested, and certainly because the public doubted that anonymity would be respected. A parallel economy of this dimension could not have existed without political backers and manipulators who were its main beneficiaries, and it was believed that the bonds project was conceived as a means of converting political collections into legitimate legal tender.

The government was faced with convulsions in two states. In Assam the popular movement demanding the expulsion of illegal immigrants was able to halt its most vital industry, oil production and transportation with calls for civil disobedience. In Gujarat caste, and the government's faulty implementation of the reservation policy laid down in the Constitution, became a live issue when doctors held demonstrations against reservations at the postgraduate level of medical education for backward castes and tribes.

Against this disturbed domestic background the induction of Rajiv Gandhi, inexperienced and hesitant, as Mrs. Gandhi's assumed successor, showed her curious apathy to political and economic realities. Rajiv was elected Member of Parliament from Amethi, his late brother's constituency, in June 1981. He had, prior to this, while still holding his job as an Indian Airlines pilot, assembled aides who, it rapidly became known, were the new "durbar", dispensing influence, patronage and privilege, though discretion replaced the arrogance, aggressiveness and vulgar display of authority flaunted by Sanjay's men. No more is heard of this coterie, or of Sanjay's young widow, Maneka.

The government took a categorical turn away from the Janata regime's concept of non-alignment as equidistance from the super powers, when it identified itself with the Soviet Union's global and regional perceptions. When the Foreign Ministers of non-aligned countries met in New Delhi, February 9–12, 1981, India's desire not to offend the Soviet Union isolated it from the majority view at the conference, in spite of the appearance of unity achieved by a consensus declaration. The conference revealed the gap that now exists between the Soviet Union and most of the non-aligned, one that will make India's role as a leader of the nonaligned movement both problematic and suspect.

A new society, Friends of the Soviet Union, inaugurated by Mrs. Gandhi on May 27, 1981, Jawaharlal Nehru's death anniversary, established her own party's direct links with the Soviet Union, and served as a rebuke to the CPI, no longer cooperating with her as it had done 1969–77. Present on the occasion was S. A. Dange, expelled Chairman of the CPI, and now Secretary General of the new All India Communist Party, solidly behind Mrs. Gandhi.

With an amazing new lease of power, after a near total eclipse, what had Mrs. Gandhi achieved? The withdrawal of court cases against her had wiped awkward past history off the record, insofar as it blemished her, her associates and her son, Sanjay, who had attained rare heights in manipulating the administration for his private purposes. Colleagues and officials who had been significant instruments in the misuse of power were reinstated. This whole development had the implicit sanction of the highest legislature in the land. On May 7, 1981, the Lok Sabha—with the main opposition absent in protest—adopted a resolution revoking its predecessor's expulsion of Mrs. Gandhi on December 19, 1978. She was thereby absolved of her guilt of breach of privilege and contempt of Parliament. Her crowning achievement, however, was the entry of Rajiv into politics. The calamitous setback to her dream of family rule by Sanjay's death had been smoothly and swiftly overcome with the replacing of one son by another, accompanied by the loud acclamation of her party. As a Member of Parliament, Rajiv is poised to succeed his mother, should she continue in power until the appropriate time.

This virtuoso performance, with its unerring ability to exploit the most pervasive strands in Indian culture, had not, by mid-1981, redeemed the ruling party's pledge to provide "a government that works." Unemployment, prices, law and order remained deteriorating problems. The Janata government's programs for an assault on poverty had been dismantled or eroded, and no alternative had appeared. The question is, can the triumph of the family principle survive the neglect of bare necessities?

Though Mrs. Gandhi still believes in her family's right to rule, the country—with the possible exception of sections of her party—does not. The Janata experiment ended in confusion but its lessons were important. It was a reaffirmation of the case for liberty, and it halted an inexorable tide. None of its quarreling constituents would have compromised on the principle of individual freedom or the checks and balances that distinguish the democratic form of government. In favoring decentralization, it accepted the reality that only local institutions, given the support they need, can stimulate effort and self-confidence. A strong and stable central government, a necessity for India, is the end result of the satisfaction of legitimate local needs and aspirations and cannot survive as the independent creation of a despot. Indeed, the centralization of power, above all if it vests in an individual or a family, and the strongarm techniques implicit in centralization are discredited answers for societies in need of change. With the dismantling of authoritarian rule, the Janata government's two and a half years in power also registered the highest growth the country had known. During this period, too, the country became a signatory to two international convenants to safeguard human rights.

The Janata experiment was the first attempt at a national consensus since Nehru, despite his big majorities, sought and attained one in the nation. Its composition was evidence of the new elites that democracy had brought to power and of the rapid social transformation that had taken place, until recently without violence, especially in the changing patterns of land ownership since independence. Continuance in democracy will require an understanding of the new forces that have arisen during the past decade, and changes in the system's structure to cope with them. Enlightened opinion, ranging over the Opposition, believes there must be more not less democracy to resolve the current tensions, and that the exercise of human rights is the only guarantee of a greater voice to the deprived layers of society. The Emergency was a salutory experience in this regard. Those accustomed to taking their civil liberties for granted and suddenly deprived of them were compelled to become aware of the majority whose human rights remained largely on paper, and for whom both justice and compassion still need translation into daily life. It will need a leadership of example, with a rigorous commitment to democracy, to restore India's political system to health and to assert the priorities that will narrow the gap between the privileged and the great majority. Mrs. Gandhi's record shows that, though she asserts these commitments, she has led her Congress away from the party's early vision and inspiration, rendering it incapable, in its present form, of serving democratic ideals.

Founded in 1855 by an Englishman, A. O. Hume, the Indian National Congress began as a "loyal Opposition to Her Majesty's Government," elite in composition and moderate in its objectives. Under Mahatma Gandhi's leadership from 1920, it launched a countrywide struggle for freedom that mobilized the working class and the peasantry and cut across caste and class. In 1947 the Congress made the successful transition from liberation movement to ruling party, providing the continuity, stability, and psychological security the country needed as it faced the traumas of partition and the challenges of independence. Jawaharlal Nehru could, in addition, invite and sustain the broad consensus vital to the tasks of development. The first departure from this tradition of containment was Mrs. Gandhi's break with the party in 1969. Her rival Congress acquiesced to a cult of personality and family, served as her stepping stone to arbitrary rule, and became her means of promoting her son as her successor. The Emergency alienated many in it who favored or tolerated Mrs. Gandhi's special status but were not willing to accept Sanjay as her political heir, and the Congress split again in 1978. Yet in 1980 the hereditary principle had triumphed and the Congress-Indira was frankly a family concern.

This outcome, feudal and despotic in character, is wholly at variance with the Congress party's evolution. As a democratic, egalitarian organization, its strength came from different levels of state and local leadership that had played an active role in the political education of the Indian people. The Congress had been a political tradition as much as a political party, the middle road committed to democratic government and growth in freedom. Mrs. Gandhi's preference for a one-leader, one-party state and finally her imposition of an emergency startlingly altered this course, completing her party's divorce from the historic Congress. As the exclusive preserve of a family, her party had reached the end of the road. With an organization based on this inspiration at the helm of affairs, the threat to India's unity and progress does not come from internal or external challenges so much as from the possibility that these real or imagined dangers will be used as an argument to rebuild an authoritarian structure of power.

The question may be asked how 351 members of Parliament in a democracy can be regarded as part of a leadership's personal estate and expected to do its bidding. This is not the paradox it seems. It is the result of a system whose politics of patronage have come home to roost. With government the monolithic source of crucial production and distribution, a high degree of centralization has provided the means to set an unparalleled trend of political interference. Where routine business depends on obeisance to power, and public recognition on an intimate identification with the power structure, the politician has come to exercise more than normal influence within his ambit. His enormous powers of patronage give him control over important levers of economic and social development. Mrs. Gandhi broke with the undivided Congress in 1969, defining the break as her fight against the political bosses—the "vested interests"—who held progress to ransom. Yet, in place of the small group she broke with and whose functions had been kept within the limits imposed by the democratic and decentralized functioning of the party, a proliferation of bosses now reign in the countryside. The local political boss, particularly if he belongs to the current ruling party, treats his territory as a fiefdom, anchoring his hold in those who depend on his bounty, at times in alliance with an established local mafia, as in the coal region of Bihar. He commands local levels of the police and the bureaucracy as of natural right, and uses them to keep his own interests—on the land or in industry—secure. He is the means whereby political parties control bloc votes and ensure their delivery at the polling booth. Mrs. Gandhi's, and earlier her son's, command of a following resembling, in fact, proclaiming, itself as a bodyguard of militant personal loyalty has climaxed and legitimized this process at the national level. A situation that is by no means confined to the party in power obviously has much more to offer the party in power.

Mrs. Gandhi's appears to have been as much a search for a secure personal identity as it has represented the road to personal power. Her style, more than most, has been shaped by the traits and inhibitions of her personality—its solitariness, its reserve, its suspicion of the outsider. She thought of her childhood in terms of two kinds of people, those identified with the struggle for freedom, and all the rest, and life remained for her a stark and narrow weave, unlike the many-textured fabric of her father's personality and growth. The vital human difference between them made for very different political values and expression. Nehru's temperament was the fireside at which many warmed their hands, took strength, and went on their way to personhood, more confident for the encounter with him. Indira's was the flame—lone, dependent on shelter for its glow and survival, leaving its surroundings dark. Nehru nurtured the institutions that would safeguard a democratic future. Indira's confrontations with democratic institutions shook established norms and finally found expression in the Emergency of 1975–77. Nehru, effortlessly a leader of men, had the self-confidence of which equal relationships, personal and political, are born. Indira clung to "family" as anchor, making it a platform for superiority. Though her style represented a clear departure from that of her predecessors, it resembled that of a number of Third World leaders who saw themselves as the savior of their people. She has, however, been the only one to get her son accepted by her party as her successor—a feat that she may accomplish a second time.

In May 1964, when Nehru died, dynasty was by no means a goal with her. But ideas like this do not spring full-blown from a void. Indira frankly believed she was uniquely qualified to lead the country, and in some respects better qualified than her father, whose civilized attributes could, she believed, be a disadvantage in politics. Yet it was the Congress party, not Indira, that planted the seed of dynasty when, in January 1966, it backed her to succeed Lal Bahadur Shastri, convinced that as prime minister she would be its best vote-getter in the approaching general election of 1967. The seed found fertile soil in an imagination nourished on patriotism, with a belief that her family had played an exclusive role in the fight for freedom and with an exaggerated view of her own. After seventeen years of Nehru government, and over a decade of

Indira's, it was not surprising that her relatives too spoke, not always jokingly, of belonging to the royal family. These and other beneficiaries of the family cult have been glad to fan the feudal flame and keep it alive. Yet the idea of family succession as a birthright, tragic and retrograde for a republic, will, if it succeeds, provide an ironic ending to a heroic experiment in democracy, unique in Asia.

Indian Political Parties

Communist Party of India (CPI) formed in 1924, follows the Moscow line. Split in 1964 as a consequence of the worldwide split in the Communist movement. Became an ally of Mrs. Gandhi during her break with the Congress in 1969, and thereafter its members entered the Congress to become Ministers and advisers in Mrs. Gandhi's government. Cooperation lasted until the Emergency was lifted, when one section of the CPI opposed support to Mrs. Gandhi.

Communist Party of India-Marxist (CPI-M) formed in 1964 after the split in the CPI. Opposed Mrs. Gandhi's policies and, along with the Jan Sangh, became a special target for punishment during the Emergency. Indian Communists are now under pressure from the USSR to end their differences and unite to back Mrs. Gandhi.

Congress for Democracy formed in 1977, as a breakaway from the Congress, under Jagjivan Ram. Became a constituent of the Janata Party in 1977.

D.M.K. (Dravida Munnetra Kazagham) founded approx. 1949, in Tamilnad, represents the rise of non-Brahmin interests in the South.

Forward Bloc a doctrinaire group of the Left. Includes Revolutionary Socialist Party (RSP) and Marxist Coordination Committee.

Hindu Mahasabha founded in 1916, represented a militant Hinduism.

Indian National Congress popularly known as the Congress, was founded in 1885, led the national movement for freedom under Mahatma Gandhi, and took power at independence in 1947. It split in 1969, and the portion backing Mrs. Gandhi was briefly known as the New Congress. After the midterm general election of 1971, when Mrs. Gandhi's party won a two-thirds majority, it came to be known once again as the Congress. The Old Congress, relegated to the sidelines by Mrs. Gandhi's victory, became a constituent of the Janata Party in 1977. The Congress was split once again in 1978, when Mrs. Gandhi formed the Congress-Indira (Congress-I) Party.

Jan Sangh conservative nationalist party, founded in 1951, espousing Hinduism and Hindi as the dominant culture and language of India. Became a constituent of the Janata Party in 1977. After the breakup of the Janata Party, the Jan Sangh became the backbone of the new national party, the Bharatiya Janata party, formed in 1980.

Janata Party formed in 1977, consisting of five constituents: the Jan Sangh, the Old Congress, the Socialist Party, the BLD, and the Congress for Democracy.

Muslim League founded 1906, later led by Mohammed Ali Jinnah to become spearhead of demand for a separate Muslim nation, Pakistan. The remnant forms a Muslim lobby.

National Conference a regional party of Jammu & Kashmir State, headed by Sheikh Abdullah

Socialist Party first known as the Congress Socialist Party, founded in 1934 as a radical group within the Congress. Became a separate entity in 1948, to splinter and regroup under different names.

Praja Socialist Party (PSP)—united factions of the Socialist Party after the general election of 1952.

Samyukta Socialist Party (SSP)—broke with the PSP to become a separate party under Ram Manohar Lohia in 1956.

Swatantra Party conservative party, formed in 1959. Merged with six national and regional parties to form the Bharatiya Lok Dal (BLD) in 1974. The BLD became a constituent of the Janata Party in 1977.

Constitutional Structure of India

The Indian Union is a federation of states and union territories with an independent judiciary. In matters of legislation there are three divisions: (1) the Union List; (2) the States List, and (3) the Concurrent list. Residual power is vested in the Center.

The aims of the Constitution are listed as follows:

To secure to all its citizens:
JUSTICE, Social, Economic, and Political;
LIBERTY of Thought, Expression, Belief, Faith, and Worship;
EQUALITY of Status and of Opportunity.
And to promote among them all:
FRATERNITY, assuring the Dignity of the Individual and the Unity of the Nation.

The Fundamental Rights of Citizens are as follows:

(1) Equality before Law;
(2) Equality of Opportunity;
(3) Prohibition if discrimination on grounds of religion, race, caste, sex, or birth;
(4) Right to Freeedom, including Freedom of Speech, Assembly, Profession, etc.;
(5) Protection of Life and Personal Liberty;
(6) Right against Exploitation;
(7) Freedom to Profess, Practice, and Propagate any Religion;
(8) Cultural and Educational Rights of minorities;
(9) Right to Property (this is not now recognized as a fundamental right);
(10) Right to Constitutional Remedies for the enforcement of the fundamental rights.

The head of state is the President. He is not the chief executive but the constitutional and ceremonial head of the country. He is elected for a term of five years and is eligible for reelection. His election is through an electoral college consisting of members of both houses of Parliament and State Legislative Assemblies.

The Vice-President is elected by members of both houses of Parliament for a period of five years. He discharges functions of the President if the latter is unable to do so because of illness or absence from the country. He does not automatically become President in case of death in office of the President. He is Chairman of the Upper House of Parliament, the Rajya Sabha.

The Prime Minister is the leader of the majority party elected to the Lok Sabha (House of the People). He chooses his Council of Ministers (officially appointed by the President) and is the Chief Executive of government. The Cabinet functions under the principle of collective responsibility to Parliament.

The Central Legislature (Parliament) consists of the Rajya Sabha (Council of States) and the Lok Sabha (House of the People). The Rajya Sabha numbers half the membership of the Lok Sabha. Of these, twelve are nominated by the President, on the advice of the Prime Minister, from well-known national personalities. Others represent the States and Union Territories. Representatives are elected by members of Legislative Assemblies of the States. The Rajya Sabha is a permanent body with one-third of its members retiring every second year.

The Lok Sabha is elected once every five years (unless dissolved earlier) by national adult franchise. The seats allotted to each State are in ratio to its population. The Prime Minister and his Council of Ministers, which form the Cabinet, must be members of one of the two houses of Parliament.

Every State has a Governor appointed for five years by the President on the advice of the Prime Minister. The Governor is the ceremonial head of the State. The State Legislature also consists of two houses—the Legislative Assembly, elected by adult franchise once every five years, and the Legislative Council, elected by members of the Legislative Assembly, members of municipalities, district boards, and other local authorities, and graduates of State educational institutions. Like the Rajya Sabha, the Legislative Council is a permanent body with one-third of its members retiring every second year.

Union territories are administered by the Center.

Notes

1. India's Third Prime Minister is Chosen

1. *Times of India*, February 8, 1959.
2. Indira Gandhi, *My Truth* (New Delhi: Vision Books Pvt. Ltd., 1981) pp. 107–108.
3. Interviewed by Kuldip Nayar of the United News of India (UNI).
4. Gandhi, *My Truth*, pp. 107–08.

2. The Person

1. Speech to Federation of Indian Chambers of Commerce and Industry (FICCI), New Delhi, March 12, 1966.
2. Speech to Planning Commission, New Delhi, July 12, 1966.
3. Speech to Planning Commission, New Delhi, July 12, 1966.
4. Speech to Administrative Staff College, Hyderabad, June 24, 1966.
5. Speech in the Lok Sabha, August 1969.
6. In an article commemorating Motilal Nehru's birth centenary.
7. August 12, 1967.
8. April 13, 1969.
9. Rajinder Puri, *India: The Wasted Years* (New Delhi: Chetana Publications, 1975).
10. Vijaya Lakshmi Pandit, *Prison Days* (Calcutta: Signet Press, third edition, May 1946).
11. Promilla Kalhan, *Kamala Nehru: An Intimate Biography* (New Delhi: Vikas, 1973.)
12. Letter to the author, June 7, 1979, from Dehra Dun.
13. Letter to Vijaya Lakshmi Pandit, September 12, 1934, from Naini Central Prison, Allahabad.
14. From "Farewell to Anand Bhawan," *Hindustan Times*, November 8, 1970. For an account of the author's childhood at Anand Bhawan, read *Prison and Chocolate Cake* (New York: Alfred Knopf, 1954).

3. Emergence—1967–1969

1. Indira Gandhi, *My Truth* (New Delhi: Vision Books Pvt. Ltd., 1981), pp. 107–08.
2. Kuldip Nayar, *Between the Lines* (New Delhi: Allied Publishers, 1969).
3. Kuldip Nayar, *India After Nehru* (New Delhi: Vikas Publishing House, 1975).
3. March 19, 1968.
4. *My Truth*, New Delhi, 1981, pp. 107–08.
5. Trevor Drieberg, *Indira Gandhi: A Profile in Courage* (New Delhi: Vikas Publishing House, 1972).
6. Rajinder Puri, *India: The Wasted Years* (New Delhi: Chetana, 1975).

4. The Congress Breaks—1969

1. Press Information Bureau release, Government of India.
2. Trevor Drieberg, *Indira Gandhi; A Profile in Courage* (New Delhi: Vikas Publishing House, 1972).
3. *Hindustan Times*, January 26, 1959.
4. Rajinder Puri, *India: The Wasted Years* (New Delhi: Chetana, 1975).
5. *Sunday Standard*, article by Nayantara Sahgal, November 23, 1969.
6. *Sunday Standard*, article by Nayantara Sahgal, December 21, 1969.

5. The New Congress Reveals Its Style—1970

1. Kuldip Nayar, *India After Nehru* (New Delhi: Vikas Publishing House, 1975).
2. News conference, December 29, 1979.

6. The Midterm Election

1. Balraj Madhok, *Murder of Democracy* (New Delhi: S. Chand and Co. Pvt. Ltd., Ram Nagar, 1973).

7. "The New Dawn"

1. N. A. Palkhivala, *Our Constitution Defaced and Defiled* (New Delhi: Macmillan, 1974).

2. For a full account of the Magarwala case, see Rajinder Puri, *India: The Wasted Years* (New Delhi: Chetana, 1975).
3. Amnesty International Report published in the *Economic and Political Weekly*, Vol. IX, No. 38, September 24, 1974.

9. Rhetoric and Reality

1. E. N. Mangat Rai, *Patterns of Administrative Development in Independent India* (University of London: The Athlone Press, 1976).

10. Jayaprakash Narayan

1. Ajit Bhattacharjea, *Jayaprakash Narayan: A Political Biography* (New Delhi: Vikas Publishing House, 1975).
2. Lakshmi Narain Lal, *Jayaprakash: Rebel Extraordinary* (New Delhi: Indian Book Company, 1975).
3. Article by Jayaprakash Narayan entitled "Incentives to Goodness" in *Freedom First*, a journal of the Democratic Research Services, September, 1952, its ideas amplified in a speech to the First Asian Socialist Conference in Rangoon, Burma, January, 1953.

11 The Bihar Movement—1974

1. JP's statement reproduced from *JP on Bihar: A Citizen Action Pamphlet* (299 Shantashram, Nana Chowk, Bombay: Govindrao Deshpande).
2. Ajit Bhattacharjea, *Jayaprakash Narayan: A political Biography* (New Delhi: Vikas Publishing House, 1975).
3. Nayantara Sahgal, *Everyman's Weekly*, April, 1975.
4. J. D. Sethi, *Tribune*, November 15, 1974.
5. G. S. Bhargava, *Everyman's Weekly*, December 1, 1974.
6. *Indian Express*, article by Nayantara Sahgal, November, 1974.

12 January to June 1975

1. R. V. P. Sinha's remarks made to newspaperman after L. N. Mishra's death, reported in *Indian Express*, January, 1975.
2. J. D. Sethi in *Everyman's Weekly*, February 23, 1975.
3. Nayantara Sahgal, "The Return of Satyagraha," *Indian Express*, March 6, 1975.
4. Interview reproduced in *Indian Express*, May 1975.

5. *Political Role of the Army in Developing Countries*, printed by Tarun Sengupta, New Age Printing Press, Rani Jhansi Road, New Delhi-110055, and published by him for the Communist Party of India, Ajoy Bhavan, Kotla Marg, New Delhi-110001, 1974.
6. Ibid, page 13.
7. Ibid, page 20.
8. Ibid, page 22.
9. *Indian Express*, March 24, 1975.

13. The Flowering of a Style

1. Anthony Lukas, "India is as Indira Does," *New York Times Magazine*, April 4, 1976.
2. Sheikh Abdulla's speech reported by Press Trust of India (PTI) on October 19, 1975.
3. From the statement of Ram Jethamalani, Chairman of the Bar Council of India, before a House of Congress subcommittee on international relations in September 1976. Jethmalani had sought and received political asylum in the United States.
4. Letter circulated via the underground protest movement in India.
5. Letter circulated via the underground protest movement in India.

16. The Janata Government Assists Mrs. Gandhi's Return

1. In a letter to the author dated July 26/27, 1977.
2. Home Minister Charan Singh speaking in the Lok Sabha.
3. Shah Commission of Inquiry, Interim Report I, printed by the Manager, Government of India Press, Ring Road, New Delhi-110064, and published by the Controller of Publications, Delhi-110054, 1978, Chapter I, Page 1.
4. Ibid, Interim Report II, Chapter XV, Page 141.
5. Shah Commission of Inquiry, Interim Report II, Chapter XV, Page 141.
6. *Economic & Political Weekly*, June 14–21, 1980.
7. This account is taken from Arun Shourie's article, "Sloath, Lunacy or Conspiracy," *Indian Express*, June 28, 1979, based on departmental records of thE CBI, the IB and the Finance Ministry.

17. The President Confers a Bonus

1. Raj Krishna, "Performance of the Economy-III." *Times of India*, January 12, 1979.

18. *"A Dynamic Manufacturer"*

1. *Economic & Political Weekly,* September 6, 1980.
2. Shah Commission of Inquiry, Interim Report I, Chapter V, page 24.
3. Report of the Commission of Inquiry on Maruti Affairs, printed by the manager, Government of India Press, Ring Road, New Delhi-110064, and published by the Controller of Publications, Delhi-110006, 1979, Chapter X, page 141.
4. Ibid, W. H. F. Muller's affidavit affirmed on December 16, 1977, page 15.
5. Statements made by W. H. F. Muller under Section 131 of the Income Tax Act, 1961, on January 23 and February 3, 1978. Copies of these statements were brought on the record of the Commission of Inquiry on Maruti Affairs, page 77 of the report.

Index